wittgenstein

blackwell great minds

edited by Steven Nadler

The Blackwell Great Minds series gives readers a strong sense of the fundamental views of the great western thinkers and captures the relevance of these figures to the way we think and live today.

wittgenstein

Hans Sluga

WILEY-BLACKWELL

A John Wiley & Sons, Ltd., Publication

This edition first published 2011
© 2011 Hans Sluga

Blackwell Publishing was acquired by John Wiley & Sons in February 2007.
Blackwell's publishing program has been merged with Wiley's global Scientific,
Technical, and Medical business to form Wiley-Blackwell.

Registered Office
John Wiley & Sons Ltd, The Atrium, Southern Gate, Chichester, West Sussex, PO19
8SQ, United Kingdom

Editorial Offices
350 Main Street, Malden, MA 02148-5020, USA
9600 Garsington Road, Oxford, OX4 2DQ, UK
The Atrium, Southern Gate, Chichester, West Sussex, PO19 8SQ, UK

For details of our global editorial offices, for customer services, and for information
about how to apply for permission to reuse the copyright material in this book please
see our website at www.wiley.com/wiley-blackwell.

The right of Hans Sluga to be identified as the author of this work has been asserted
in accordance with the UK Copyright, Designs and Patents Act 1988. ·

Wiley also publishes its books in a variety of electronic formats. Some content that
appears in print may not be available in electronic books.

Designations used by companies to distinguish their products are often claimed as
trademarks. All brand names and product names used in this book are trade names,
service marks, trademarks or registered trademarks of their respective owners. The
publisher is not associated with any product or vendor mentioned in this book. This
publication is designed to provide accurate and authoritative information in regard to
the subject matter covered. It is sold on the understanding that the publisher is not
engaged in rendering professional services. If professional advice or other expert
assistance is required, the services of a competent professional should be sought.

Library of Congress Cataloging-in-Publication Data
Sluga, Hans D.
Wittgenstein / Hans Sluga.
  p. cm. – (Blackwell great minds ; 13)
Includes bibliographical references and index.
ISBN 978-1-4051-1847-7 (hardcover : alk. paper) – ISBN 978-1-4051-1848-4
(pbk. : alk. paper)
1. Wittgenstein, Ludwig, 1889–1951. I. Title.
B3376.W564S58 2011
192–dc22

                              2011009297

A catalogue record for this book is available from the British Library.

This book is published in the following electronic formats:
ePDFs ISBN: 9781444343281; Wiley Online Library ISBN: 9781444343311;
ePub ISBN: 9781444343298; Mobi ISBN 9781444343304

Set in 9 on 12 pt TrumpMedieval by Toppan Best-set Premedia Limited
Printed in Malaysia by Ho Printing (M) Sdn Bhd

1   2011

contents

preface

Ludwig Wittgenstein is, without doubt, a decisive figure in twentieth-century philosophy. In the radicalness of his questioning, in his determination to reshape the philosophical landscape, and in the power of his thinking and language he can be compared only to Martin Heidegger, who was his exact contemporary and came from an adjoining region of Europe. Why the two most original philosophical thinkers of the last century stemmed from related backgrounds can be understood only when we realize that all great philosophizing originates from a context of (social, political, cultural) endangerment. Plato and Aristotle shared such a context and so did Descartes and Hobbes, and so did, finally, our two twentieth-century thinkers.

Wittgenstein and Heidegger lived through a particularly turbulent age in which European world domination came to an end in a series of painful contractions; they were born as Europe's cultural crisis (the crisis of modernity) was becoming acute, and grew up in an area particularly exposed to its disruptions. These developments affected the two philosophers, however, in somewhat different ways. In a previous book I have sought to characterize Heidegger's philosophizing in the historical and political context of his time. Here I am looking at Wittgenstein's philosophical thought with an eye to our political realities. The circumstances of Wittgenstein's life are, certainly, of the greatest interest in this respect. The philosopher belonged to a talented and successful family that occupied a pivotal place in the Austro-Jewish culture of late imperial Vienna – at a moment of last flourishing and incipient disintegration. Many of Austria's cultural elite were associated with the Wittgenstein family and with the philosopher himself (Johannes Brahms, Gustav Mahler, Sigmund Freud, Gustav Klimt, Adolf Loos, Karl Kraus). When he took up philosophy, Wittgenstein also came to know some of the most creative philosophical thinkers of the age, men like Gottlob Frege, Bertrand Russell, G.E. Moore, Moritz Schlick, and Rudolf Carnap. In England, where he spent large parts of his adult life, he became in addition acquainted with leading intellectuals like John Maynard Keynes, Lytton Strachey, and Alan Turing. This glittering background stands, however, in sharp relief to Wittgenstein's foreboding sense of the darkness of his time and to his feeling of alienation from European and American civilization. While his work incorporates all the impulses he had received from this civilization he sought at the same time to overcome it in his thinking. An heir to the rich heritage of modern European philosophy and culture, he saw himself nonetheless as a man alone at the crossroads.

My primary goal in this book is to make Wittgenstein's thought transparent for readers who have as yet little or no familiarity with it. I begin with an account of Wittgenstein's life in order to illuminate the historical, political, and personal conditions from which his philosophical work emerged. The chapters that follow seek to identify some of the key concepts and ideas in Wittgenstein's work. Given the scope of that work, I will have to omit much detail. My exposition will also more or less bypass what the experts have said about Wittgenstein's thought. I will seek to present Wittgenstein's thought, instead, predominantly in my own words. Knowledgeable readers will come to understand very quickly that the selection of topics and the emphases I have chosen in this book are very much my own. Philosophical texts are, after all, like the puzzle pictures that interested Wittgenstein so much. They can always be seen in more than one way. I will argue in Chapter 8 that because of the cultural and political changes that Wittgenstein and his contemporaries lived through, and in consequence of the no less dramatic changes in the way we live now, our deepest and most pressing problems must concern the conditions and the possibility of our human social and political existence. In examining Wittgenstein's ideas and concepts I am therefore particularly interested in asking how they relate to the historical and political context in which they arose and how they might be used in understanding that context. In the last chapter I will try to summarize these observations by asking how Wittgenstein's thought may help us to face the peculiar problems of our contemporary social and political existence.

Wittgenstein is best known for two of his writings. The first is the dazzling and precocious *Tractatus Logico-Philosophicus* – a work he composed while serving as a soldier in World War I. Written in short, numbered propositions that range from technical discussions of logic to reflections on the meaning of life, the book represents a challenge even to readers trained in philosophy. After completion of that work, Wittgenstein abandoned the active pursuit of philosophy for almost 10 years. When he returned to the subject, he began to revise his earlier assumptions and this new work eventually crystallized into his *Philosophical Investigations*, composed between 1936 and 1947 but published only in 1951 after Wittgenstein's death. Since then, a large body of other writings has come to light such as the *Blue and Brown Books* of the early 1930s as well as Wittgenstein's philosophical notes from the last years of his life, published now under the title *On Certainty*. Other volumes range from philosophical *Notebooks* written during World War I through the *Philosophical Remarks*, the *Philosophical Grammar*, the *Remarks on the Foundations of Mathematics*, and *Zettel* containing material from the 1930s, to extensive writings on the philosophy of psychology from the 1940s.

The development of philosophy in the twentieth century would, certainly, have taken another course without that work. Wittgenstein influenced, in the first instance, two generations of philosophers. In the 1920s he was of particular importance to thinkers like Bertrand Russell and F.P. Ramsey in England and to the philosophers of the Vienna Circle for whom the *Tractatus* became a handbook of logical positivism. Interpreters working in this tradition see Wittgenstein still primarily as a logician and as a theorizer about language, and as someone who seeks to resolve philosophical problems systematically through such investigations. After World War II, Wittgenstein and his *Philosophical Investigations* inspired a new generation of English and American philosophers who, in contrast to this first group, resisted large-scale and formal theorizing and who sought to solve philosophical problems, instead, piecemeal by attending to common sense and ordinary language. A third wave of thinkers has drawn more recently on the skeptical strands in Wittgenstein's thinking. Yet others have sought to understand him as first and foremost engaged in questions concerning the human mind. Some have gone so far as to call him primarily an ethical thinker.

For all his influence, Wittgenstein remains an unsettling presence in philosophy. His way of thinking and writing have proved too personal to be fully incorporated into the academic practice of philosophy. Wittgenstein himself maintained, moreover, a peculiar ambivalence not only to his own work but to philosophy as a whole. This attitude manifests itself already in the *Tractatus*, which concludes with the words that anyone who has understood his book will set its propositions aside as senseless. This dismissive gesture is repeated in Wittgenstein's later writings when he declares it to be his goal to free himself from philosophical puzzlement and not to construct any kind of theory.

Wittgenstein's philosophical writings are by no means easy to read and their study calls for much patience and persistence. Their author makes few concessions to his readers. While he writes an admirably lucid and simple prose, only rarely using technical terms, the course of his thinking is often difficult to follow. He seldom prepares the reader for what is ahead and he never provides introductions or summaries. His writings are characterized almost everywhere by their lack of descriptive titles and chapter headings. They consist typically of sequences of numbered propositions and paragraphs in which a variety of topics is examined in an intricately interwoven fashion. Those who are willing to take on the burden of seriously studying these texts will, however, discover in them an intense preoccupation with some of the most pressing issues of modern philosophy. The world and its structure, language and meaning, the character of the human self, the function of rules, the nature of necessity, mathematical truth, the diversity of world-views, questions of ethics and the meaning of life are among the many themes that concern him. Wittgenstein writes about these matters, moreover, in an almost hypnotic manner that returns to the same issues again and again in ever-new formulations, thus forcing the reader to become increasingly sensitized to the complexity of the problems under discussion.

In discussing Wittgenstein's thought I will often cite his words. In doing so my primary purpose is to provide supporting evidence for my particular reading of his texts. But I also hope to give the reader a sense of Wittgenstein's tone of voice and the beauty of his prose. Though Wittgenstein did much of his philosophical work in England, he almost always wrote in German. Practically all his work has been published in translation. Though these translations are adequate for most purposes, I have found it preferable to revise them at many points or even to replace them with my own.

In writing this book I have drawn on the help of many others. Rupert Read, David Stern, Andrew Norris, and Michael Hymers deserve particular credit for having read much or all of my manuscript and their comments have proved immensely helpful in finishing my work. I am also grateful to the participants in a seminar on Wittgenstein which I conducted at the Chinese University of Hong Kong in the spring of 2010.

abbreviations

The three most frequently cited Wittgenstein texts:

TLP   *Tractatus Logico-Philosophicus*, translated by C.K. Ogden (London: Routledge, 1922);
       Tractatus Logico-Philosophicus, translated by D.F. Pears and B.F. McGuinness (London: Routledge, 1961)
       References are to the numbered propositions of the text, unless otherwise indicated.

BB   *The Blue and Brown Books* (New York: Harper & Row, 1960)

PI   *Philosophical Investigations*, translated by G.E.M. Anscombe (Oxford: Blackwell 1958). References are to the numbered sections of the text unless otherwise indicated.

Other Wittgenstein texts cited:

CV   *Culture and Value*, edited by G.H. von Wright, translated by Peter Winch (Oxford: Blackwell, 1980)

GT   *Geheime Tagebücher. 1914–1916*, edited by W. Baum (Vienna: Turia & Kant, 1991)

LC   *Lectures and Conversations on Aesthetics, Psychology and Religious Belief*, edited by Cyrill Barrett (Berkeley: University of California Press, 1972)

LE   "Lecture on Ethics," in *Philosophical Occasions* by James Klagge and Alfred Nordmann (Indianapolis: Hackett Publishing, 1993)

NB   *Notebooks, 1914–1916*, edited by G.H. von Wright and G.E.M. Anscombe, translated by G.E.M. Anscombe, second ed. (Chicago: University of Chicago Press, 1979)

OC   *On Certainty*, edited by G.E.M. Anscombe and G.H. von Wright, translated by Denis Paul and G.E.M. Anscombe (Oxford: Blackwell, 1969). References are to numbered sections.

PR   *Philosophical Remarks*, translated by Raymond Hargreaves and Roger White (University of Chicago Press, Chicago 1975)

RC   *Remarks on Colour,* edited by G.E.M. Anscombe, translated by Linda McAlister and Margaret Schättle (University of California Press, Berkeley, 1978). References are to numbered sections.

RF   "Remarks on Frazer's *Golden Bough,*" in *Philosophical Occasions* by James Klagge and Alfred Nordmann (Indianapolis: Hackett Publishing, 1993)

RFM *Remarks on the Foundations of Mathematics,* translated by G.E.M Anscombe, revised edition (MIT Press, Cambridge, MA: 1983)

Z   *Zettel,* edited by G.E.M. Anscombe and G.H. von Wright, translated by G.E.M. Anscombe (Berkeley: University of California Press, 1967). References are to numbered sections.

the situated thinker

The movement of thought in my philosophizing should be discernible in the history of my mind, its moral concepts, and in the understanding of my situation.

Ludwig Wittgenstein, *Denkbewegungen*

Some while ago a friend at Cambridge took me to the ancient graveyard of St Giles where Ludwig Wittgenstein lies buried. The place was deserted except for some birds in the untended bushes. After a little searching we found the grave in the wild grass. A plain slab in the ground records Wittgenstein's name and the years of his birth and death (1889–1951) – nothing else. A nearby tree had shed leaves on the stone. Someone had scattered flowers on it, a couple of coins, and, surprisingly, the stub of a pencil. It all struck me as right. All the complexities of Wittgenstein's life and thought, so it appeared to me at the time, had been folded here into complete simplicity.

What reason is there now to drag the philosopher from the anonymous peace he has sought in that Cambridge graveyard? After all, he "purposely lived in obscurity, discouraging all attempts to make him into a celebrity or public figure,"[1] so why should we now dwell on Wittgenstein's life, if our concern is really to bring his thought to bear on our own pressing problems? It is true that the man himself and the circumstances of his life have provoked the curiosity of biographers, cultural historians, and literary authors. But what do we have to know about the man and his life in order to understand his thought? Every thought is, admittedly, someone's thought. But every utterance also stands apart from its author and may have uses and meanings that the author never intended. A written text, in particular, is capable of leading a fertile life apart from its author, and to tie it too closely to its author may diminish its vitality and importance. Still, some biographical facts prove useful when we try to decipher Wittgenstein's writings.

wittgenstein, First Edition. Hans Sluga.
© 2011 Hans Sluga. Published 2011 by Blackwell Publishing Ltd.

A Man at the Crossroads

Perhaps the most important thing to know about Wittgenstein is that he lived his life at a number of crossroads – some personal, some cultural and historical in character. It is this, above all, which makes his work crucial to us since his crossroads are also very much ours.

One of these crossroads is that of secular and religious culture. Wittgenstein's family had thrown off its Jewish past and become Christianized at some time in the mid-nineteenth century.[2] His great-grandfather had taken the first step by changing the family name from the Jewish-sounding "Mayer" to the German (and aristocratic) "Wittgenstein." His grandfather, who moved the family from Saxony to Vienna, had become a Protestant and reputedly also an anti-Semite. The philosopher was, in turn, baptized a Catholic but grew up in a largely secular household. During World War I he became inspired, however, by a non-dogmatic version of Christianity which he discovered with the help of Tolstoy, and this outlook was to mold his ethical thinking from now on to the end of his life. "I am not a religious man," he would say later on to his friend Drury, "but I cannot help seeing every problem from a religious point of view."[3] Much of this view was focused on the Christian and, specifically, the Catholic tradition. To Drury he said accordingly also: "The symbolisms of Catholicism are wonderful beyond words." But then he said, characteristically, that "any attempt to make it into a philosophical system is offensive."[4] By contrast he looked at his Jewish background with deep ambivalence. "Judaism is most problematic [hochproblematisch]," he wrote in his diary in 1930,[5] and "even the greatest of Jewish thinkers is no more than talented."[6] When he said to a friend in 1949, "My thoughts are one hundred percent Hebraic,"[7] he meant, in any case, to include the Christian in the Hebraic as maintaining, in contrast to the "Greek" view of things, that good and evil cannot in the end be reconciled. If we are to classify him at all, we would certainly have to call Wittgenstein a religious thinker within the Christian tradition. But that characterization is not easy to reconcile with the content of Wittgenstein's actual philosophical work, where religious issues are never directly apparent. That aspect of Wittgenstein's thought has therefore been understandably ignored by most interpreters. Still, we cannot doubt that Wittgenstein considered questions of ethics and religion with utter seriousness and that this attitude expressed an abiding distrust of modern secular culture. While this may not affect Wittgenstein's particular views on language or the mind, it will certainly bear on the question of what his work can mean for political thinking.

A second crossroad for Wittgenstein, related to the first, was that of scientific/technological and philosophical culture. His father, Karl Wittgenstein, had made himself a rich man in the Austrian steel industry and he expected his sons to follow him in this career. Ludwig, the youngest, who showed some mechanical aptitude, was sent to the technical high school in Linz. After completing his high school education, Wittgenstein enrolled in the Technical

University of Berlin and later on in the University of Manchester to study engineering. But in Manchester he developed an unexpected fascination with the foundations of mathematics, which made him turn to philosophy in 1911 (just as his father lay dying). The move was not altogether surprising given Wittgenstein's early immersion in the culture of *fin de siècle* Vienna.[8] We are told that he had, in fact, early on read Arthur Schopenhauer, who was widely admired in late nineteenth-century Vienna. Traces of Schopenhauer's thought can certainly be found throughout Wittgenstein's philosophical work. His earliest writings also reveal, moreover, familiarity with such figures as the physicist Rudolf Boltzmann, the philosopher of science Ernst Mach, his student, the philosopher of language Fritz Mauthner, the philosopher of sexuality Otto Weininger, the cultural critic and satirist Karl Kraus, and the modernist architect Adolf Loos.

Robert Musil and Hermann Broch – two of Wittgenstein's contemporaries with a similar outlook and development – depict Vienna in their writings as a world steeped in the pessimism of Schopenhauer that curiously combined deep nostalgia for the old with a curiosity for the new and modern.[9] The same duality is manifest in Wittgenstein's work, which combines an interest in the study of language, mathematics, and the mind characteristic of the new currents in Viennese thinking with an exceedingly somber view of life. His doubts about secular culture and about the promises of our scientific and technological civilization combine ultimately into a devastating assessment of where we are today. To his friend Drury he could summarize his – and our – situation by saying in 1936, "The dark ages are coming again."[10]

From Vienna to Cambridge

It is not enough, however, to think of Wittgenstein in terms of his Viennese background. He is just as intimately linked to England and the Cambridge of the first half of the twentieth century, and we can speak here therefore of yet another crossroad in Wittgenstein's life.

When he was at Manchester as a student in engineering, Wittgenstein's attention had been drawn to Russell's *Principles of Mathematics* of 1903, a book that had sought to deduce the entire body of mathematics from an enlarged logic. Wittgenstein found himself particularly intrigued by Russell's account of the post-Aristotelian logic of the German mathematician, logician, and philosopher Gottlob Frege. On the strength of this he decided to visit Frege in Jena, who advised him, in turn, to go to Cambridge and work with Russell.[11]

Russell was at the height of his philosophical career at the time. He had just finished his monumental treatment of logic in *Principia Mathematica* (written in collaboration with A.N. Whitehead) and was keen to apply himself to new things. He wanted to use his logic, in particular, to deal with some of the fundamental problems of metaphysics and epistemology. Once settled in Cambridge, Wittgenstein quickly became Russell's student, collaborator, and critic in pursuing this project. Accordingly, Russell could write to his mistress,: "Wittgenstein has been a great event in my life . . . He is *the* young man one hopes for."[12] Russell's influence is evident in Wittgenstein's *Tractatus*, where its author pays homage to both "Frege's magnificent work and . . . the writings of my friend Mr. Bertrand Russell" (TLP, p. 3). But even in that work, written only a few years after his encounter with Russell, Wittgenstein was already moving decisively beyond the ideas of his mentor. In later life his admiration for Russell turned cold, when he called Russell's thought in a somewhat vengeful mood "immeasurably shallow and trivial" (Z, 456). Russell, in turn, became convinced that the later Wittgenstein had abandoned serious thinking in philosophy.[13]

In retrospect we can see that the philosophical movement we now know by the name of "Analytic Philosophy" began its life in the interactions between Frege, Russell, and the young Wittgenstein. United in the project of building a new logic that could solve (or resolve) important philosophical problems, each of them contributed a distinctive set of ideas to this evolving philosophical movement. Frege introduced essentially Kantian assumptions about different kinds of truth and the foundational organization of human knowledge into the analytic debate; Russell added ontological concerns with the nature and structure of reality to it; Wittgenstein, finally, contributed a positivistic conception of science and philosophy, a preoccupation with language, a wariness toward theoretical constructions, and a yearning for a simple, unmediated existence to this mixture – ideas that all derived from his Viennese background. "Analytic philosophy" was thus constructed from a mélange of ideas drawn from various strands of the European tradition.

Historically, the rise of analytic tradition marks, however, first and foremost a point of transition away from the cultural dominance of German and Continental European philosophy to Anglo-American thought. The common distinction between "Continental" and "Analytic" philosophy reflects the upheavals of the twentieth century in which Anglo-American civilization became increasingly more powerful. The distinction is, however, not as sharp as it is often made out to be. In his life and work Wittgenstein sought to bridge that divide again and again, and it is in this sense also that we can call him a man at the crossroads.

The Two Sides of the *Tractatus*

Wittgenstein's collaboration with Russell in the period between 1911 and 1914 was intimate, stormy, and immensely productive. World War I, however, was to bring this period to an unanticipated close since Wittgenstein, as an enemy alien, was now forced to return to Austria. There he considered it his duty to enroll as a soldier. But he remained, at the same time, determined to continue with his philosophical work. Two days after he had been assigned to his regiment, therefore, he began to keep a philosophical diary that he continued throughout the war. It opens with the anxious question, "Will I be able to work now?" (GT, p. 13),[14] but it turned out that he could do so even under the most daunting conditions. In December 1914 he noted, for instance, the "heaviest thunder of canons from all sides – gun fire, conflagrations, etc.," adding laconically: "Worked much and with success." (GT, pp. 48–49)

Quite naturally, the diary begins where his discussions with Russell had left off. But as the war dragged on, new themes appear in it that are far removed from this initial agenda. Where concerns with logic had preoccupied Wittgenstein in the first period of the war, we find him suddenly writing in June 1916: "What do I know about God and the purpose of life?" (NB, p. 72). And soon after: "The I, the I is what is deeply mysterious" (p. 80). Deeply traumatized by the war and increasingly pessimistic about its outcome, Wittgenstein addressed himself now to questions of ethics and aesthetics, to the distinction between the good and the bad conscience, the nature of happiness and the problem of suicide and sin. To his friend Paul Engelmann he wrote at the time: "My relationship with my fellow men has strangely changed. What was all right when we met is now all wrong, and I am in complete despair."[15]

The book Wittgenstein extracted from his wartime notebooks, the famed *Tractatus Logico-Philosophicus*, reflects the entire course of his thinking from his initial reflections on logic to his later ethical and mystical musings. In large part it can be read as an attempt to reconcile Russell's metaphysical atomism with Frege's epistemological apriorism. When the work was published, Russell could thus rightly praise it as an important contribution to the theory of logic.[16] But the book is equally moved by moral and metaphysical considerations – which Russell largely ignored, to Wittgenstein's irritation. Angrily, he wrote to his former teacher: "Now I'm afraid you haven't really got hold of my main contention . . . The main point is the theory of what can be said in propositions – i.e. by language – (and, which comes to the same, what can be thought) and what cannot be said in propositions, but only shown [*gezeigt*]; which, I believe is the cardinal problem of philosophy."[17] In the same letter Wittgenstein complained that Frege had also failed to understand his book. Mournfully, he conceded: "It is very hard not to be understood by a single soul."

The *Tractatus* has, indeed, proved to be a baffling piece of work. Composed in an exceedingly severe and compressed style, and organized by means of an elaborate numbering system borrowed from *Principia Mathematica*, the book meant to show that traditional philosophy rests on a radical misunderstanding of "the logic of our language." Much of the work is concerned with spelling out Wittgenstein's conception of the logical structure of language and the world and these sections of the book have understandably drawn most of the attention of philosophers within the analytic tradition. But for Wittgenstein himself the decisive part of the book lay in his conclusions concerning the limits of language, which are reached only in the last pages of the work. He argues there that all sentences which are not pictures of concatenations of objects or logical composites of such pictures are, strictly speaking, senseless. Among these are all the propositions of ethics and aesthetics, all propositions dealing with the meaning of life, as well as all the propositions of logic, indeed all philosophical propositions, and finally all the propositions of the *Tractatus* itself. While these sentences are strictly senseless, Wittgenstein sought to show that they nevertheless aim at saying something important. But what they try to express in words can really only be shown. This claim has led to some confusion. Did he mean to say that there are truths that defy verbal expression? Or that these sentences are quite literally nonsensical? Wittgenstein concluded, in any case, that anyone who understood the *Tractatus* would finally have to discard these propositions, that he would have to throw away the ladder after he had climbed up on it. Someone who has reached that state would then have no more temptation to say something philosophical. He would see the world rightly and so would recognize that the only strictly meaningful propositions are those of natural science. Natural science could, of course, never touch upon what is really important in human life, the ethical and the mystical. But those matters would have to be faced in silence. For "whereof one cannot speak, thereof one must be silent," as the last proposition of the *Tractatus* declared.

These philosophical views were to find their most surprising expression eventually in a house that Wittgenstein built in Vienna in the late 1920s together with his friend Paul Engelmann.[18] Engelmann, who had studied with Adolf Loos, had met Wittgenstein during World War I and he had subsequently undertaken various architectural projects for the Wittgenstein family. Thus, when Ludwig's eldest sister Margarete decided to build a new mansion for herself in Vienna, she commissioned Engelmann for the job. Wittgenstein, who was at a loose end at the time, got quickly drawn into the project and the building ended up as much his work as Engelmann's. Conceived in the spirit of Loos, the house shuns all decoration and all reminders of the architectural styles of the past. Aesthetic values are, instead, to be realized in pure architectonic forms. In pursuit of this ideal, Wittgenstein dedicated himself to the design of the smallest details: the exact height of the ceilings, the metal and glass doors, the glass-enclosed elevator showing the inner mechanics, the door handles, the vents of the under-floor heating system, the radiators, even the feet on which those radiators stood. Austerely minimalistic (there were bare light bulbs hanging from the ceilings instead of the traditional chandeliers), the house is indubitably a specimen of cultural modernism.[19] It is also, however, a direct expression of the ideas of the *Tractatus*. One of Ludwig's younger sisters, indeed, called it, appositely, "logic turned into a house, not a human habitation."

The Return to Vienna

Given the conclusions of the *Tractatus*, it was obvious for Wittgenstein that he should not seek to pursue an academic career in philosophy. After his release from an Italian prisoner-of-war camp, he considered briefly joining a monastery but quickly decided that he lacked the necessary faith. Finally, he chose to undergo training as a schoolteacher, and in 1920 began to teach primary school in the mountains of lower Austria.[20]

Wittgenstein's six-year experience as a schoolteacher was to prove not an altogether happy one. His own unsettled state of mind, his demanding intellect, and his impatience made him less than an ideal instructor of the village children. The experience was, nevertheless, to prove an essential source of philosophical insight for him in later life. While the *Tractatus* had looked at language exclusively as a medium of representation, as a means of formulating scientific theories, and as something to be analyzed in purely logical terms, the later Wittgenstein was to interest himself above all in the informal language of everyday life whose multiple, communicative functions could not be accounted for in terms of strict, logical rules. Where the *Tractatus* had taken language as a fixed and given structure, the later Wittgenstein spoke of it rather as a dynamic and pluralistic system; and he focused specifically on the various ways in which language is learned and on the whole process of enculturation of which the acquisition of language is a part.

This shift of perspective took Wittgenstein eventually back to the work of Fritz Mauthner, whose *Beiträge zu einer Kritik der Sprache* he had known since the time of the *Tractatus*. Then he had sided with Russell against Mauthner's anti-formalist and skeptical views. The later Wittgenstein would, however, agree with Mauthner's assertion that language cannot be understood on the model of the logical calculus; that it must be considered, instead, as a tool designed for the satisfaction of a multiplicity of human needs. He would also sympathize with Mauthner's wariness toward scientific theorizing, his skepticism toward empirical psychology, his anti-Cartesian view of the human self, and, perhaps most of all, with his deep-seated skepticism.[21] While being trained for the teaching profession, Wittgenstein had also read the work of the educational psychologist Karl Bühler. Though he dismissed Bühler later on as a charlatan, he is likely to have been alerted by him to the issues of Gestalt psychology, a topic that surfaces repeatedly in Wittgenstein's later work. We also know of Wittgenstein's continuing fascination with Otto Weininger's *Sex and Character* in those years. It is unclear, however, what he drew from Weininger's peculiar mixture of transcendental philosophy and gender-theoretical, anti-feminist, and self-laceratingly anti-Semitic speculations. To his friend Drury, Wittgenstein was to speak later of Weininger as a "remarkable genius" who had recognized the importance of Freud's ideas before anyone else had taken much notice.[22] Freud himself also became a subject of interest to Wittgenstein when his sister Margarete decided to be psychoanalyzed. Though he remained skeptical of Freud's theoretical claims, he was sufficiently intrigued by the analytic practice to speak of his own work later on as therapeutic in character. At times he even called himself "a disciple" and "a follower of Freud" (LC, p. 41).

Among the books Wittgenstein read in this period (mostly at the suggestion of his sister Margarete) was Oswald Spengler's *The Decline of the West* of

1918. This brilliant, speculative, and exasperating book was not meant to provide merely an analysis of the military, economic, and political disasters of the just-finished war – as its title may suggest – but intended to set out "a sketch of a morphology of world history," as the subtitle said. It asked: is there a systematic structure to historical processes? Is there a historical logic? Can we specify the structure of cultures? Opposed to the idea of history as a linear and cumulative process, Spengler claimed that individual cultures are differentiated from each other by specific unifying ideas. These characterize everything that goes on in the culture, from its music and its religious practice to its science and mathematics. The forms of different cultures are, moreover, incommensurable. One culture cannot be understood in terms of another. We can grasp the unifying idea of a culture not by theorizing about it but only through the attempt to achieve *Übersicht*, a perspicuous representation of it. Spengler sought to interpret the current state of European culture in these terms. Each culture with its unifying idea possesses, according to him, a life of its own that leads from simple beginnings through an age of maturity to a terminal phase which Spengler called "civilization." In Spengler's words: "Every culture has its own civilization . . . Civilization is the inevitable *destiny* of a culture."[23] He was certain, moreover, that Western culture had now entered this terminal phase.

These readings were to bear fruit in the philosophical work that Wittgenstein was going to do in the 1930s and 1940s. They helped him, in particular, to overcome his old, narrowly logic-oriented conception of language and meaning. Where he had previously thought of psychology as a waste of time, his later work would focus extensively on issues in the philosophy of psychology. Where he had previously thought of the world in terms of a single, unified logical structure, he would end by reflecting on the ways the world presents itself to us in our different and, indeed, incommensurable world-views. Above all, those readings would lead him to a new conception of his work as a philosopher.

The Vienna Circle

While Wittgenstein was busy on his sister's house, a group of philosophers and scientists had been meeting regularly at the University of Vienna to map out a new "scientific world-view." They were eventually to call themselves 'The Vienna Circle," and in the manifesto they published in 1929 they were to name Frege, Russell, and Wittgenstein (among others) as forerunners of their movement. When the members of the Circle discovered that the author of the *Tractatus* was actually living in Vienna, they naturally invited him to their meetings. Wittgenstein, however, declined to join them and instead agreed only to meet a delegation of two or three of them to discuss questions about the *Tractatus*.

He later downplayed the significance of his contact with the Vienna Circle, but the association was to have at least three significant consequences for him. It drew his attention, first of all, back to the *Tractatus* and to philosophy. While he was by no means ready to abandon the views expressed in that work, his discussions with Moritz Schlick, Friedrich Waismann, and (at times) Rudolf Carnap alerted him to its obscurities and shortcomings. This realization was eventually to bring Wittgenstein back to an active engagement with philosophy and it would lead, in due course, to the total destruction of the system of the *Tractatus* and the emergence of an entirely new set of philosophical ideas. The second effect that Wittgenstein's contacts with the Vienna Circle had on him was to expose him to naturalistic and empiricist views in philosophy and this drew him away from the concern with pure, formal logic that was so characteristic of the *Tractatus*. The notes that Waismann kept of their conversations reveal that Wittgenstein may actually have invented one of the Circle's crucial doctrines: the principle that the meaning of a sentence is fixed by the method of its verification. Later on, he would, however, transform this principle into the more comprehensive claim that the meaning of a sentence is its use.

Wittgenstein's contact with the Vienna Circle was significant, thirdly, because it reignited his early interest in the philosophy of mathematics, which had taken a secondary place in the *Tractatus*. In late 1928 some members of the Circle took him to a talk by the Dutch mathematician L.E.J. Brouwer from which he emerged galvanized, according to all reports.[24] In that lecture Brouwer had laid out a program for a constructivist conception of mathematics. There is no reason to think that Wittgenstein ever subscribed to Brouwer's "neo-intuitionism" for, unlike Brouwer, he never rejected the use of the principle of the excluded middle in mathematics. But Brouwer must nevertheless have struck a responsive chord in him – possibly because of his attack on formalism and the assumption of the reliability of logic and language, and because he insisted that mathematics was a human construction. Wittgenstein may also have been intrigued by Brouwer's appeal to Schopenhauer's philosophy. Brouwer's talk contributed, in any case, to Wittgenstein's decision to return to philosophy. It may also have renewed his interest in the philosophy of mathematics, for in the decade and a half that followed, Wittgenstein addressed himself intensively to that topic.

Back to Cambridge

Meanwhile, Wittgenstein's former associates at Cambridge had been trying to bring him back to England. With the help of John Maynard Keynes they finally secured a grant that would make this possible. When Wittgenstein returned in 1929, he did so with the firm goal of trying to tie up the loose ends of the *Tractatus* that he thought he had now identified. But things turned out differently from what he had expected. Once he had begun to rethink some of the assumptions of the *Tractatus*, he found himself forced to dismantle more and more of its structure. Within a few months the whole, elaborate edifice of the *Tractatus* had collapsed. The realization of this proved liberating and opened a floodgate of new ideas. In no other period in Wittgenstein's life did ideas flow so easily and in no other period did he write with such abandon. His most decisive step in this period was to give up the belief that meaningful sentences must have a precise (though hidden) logical structure, and the accompanying belief that this structure corresponds to the logical structure of the depicted facts. He concluded now that these assumptions were based on a piece of unwarranted metaphysics of exactly the kind he had set out to combat. Where he had once, before the *Tractatus*, considered it possible to ground metaphysics on logic, he was now certain that metaphysics can only lead the philosopher into complete darkness.

In Cambridge, Wittgenstein found himself all of a sudden back in an academic community. Having obtained a belated PhD for the *Tractatus*, he could now take up a regular teaching position. When G.E. Moore attended Wittgenstein's lectures in the period between 1930 and 1933, he was impressed by "the intensity of conviction with which he said everything which he did say, . . . [and] the extreme interest which he excited in his hearers."[25] His classes attracted a small but regular following of gifted students, among them Norman Malcolm, Rush Rhees, and Elizabeth Anscombe, and the mathematicians Alan Turing and Georg Kreisel. Their lecture notes and later reminiscences give us a vivid picture of Wittgenstein's presence and work in this period.[26] O.K. Bouwsma, who came into contact with Wittgenstein in the 1940s, wrote later on:

> Wittgenstein is the nearest to a prophet I have ever known. He is a man who is like a tower, who stands high and unattached, leaning on no one. He has his own feet. He fears no man . . . But other men fear him . . . They fear his judgment. And so I feared Wittgenstein, felt responsible to him . . . His words I cherished like jewels . . . It is an awful thing to work under the gaze and questioning of such piercing eyes, and such discernment, knowing rubbish and gold![27]

Of the greatest significance for understanding the direction of Wittgenstein's thinking after the *Tractatus* are two texts which he dictated to his students from 1933 to 1935. They have come to be known as the *Blue* and the *Brown Book*, respectively. The two works delineate a body of thought that foreshadows the best-known and most finished piece of writing of Wittgenstein's later years, the *Philosophical Investigations*, composed between 1936 and 1947. In a number of important respects they represent, nonetheless, a distinctive phase in Wittgenstein's philosophical development. Because Wittgenstein scholars have become increasingly aware of this, it is common now to distinguish three phases in Wittgenstein's philosophical thinking:

the early, Tractarian Wittgenstein (roughly 1914 to 1930);
the middle Wittgenstein (1930–1936);
the late Wittgenstein (1936–1951).

These divisions are somewhat arbitrary, however, and do not reflect the continuities in Wittgenstein's thinking and its overall dynamic character. One can equally make a case for there being only one Wittgenstein or, alternatively, for distinguishing more phases in his thought. It is quite plausible, for instance, to argue that the ideas of the *Tractatus* differ from those that Wittgenstein pursued earlier on in conjunction with Russell. The so-called middle period may, in turn, be divided into two separate phases: that of the disintegration of the *Tractatus* system and the tentative exploration of various new ideas (1930–1933) and that of *The Blue and Brown Books* (1933–1935). One can also make a case for arguing that Wittgenstein's work after 1948 goes in an importantly new direction beyond the ideas of the *Philosophical Investigations*. So, according to taste, we may also speak of six periods in his work. Alternatively, we may want to emphasize the dynamic and fluid character of Wittgenstein's thinking, as his friend Waismann did when he wrote in 1934: "He has the wonderful gift of always seeing things as if for the first time . . . He always follows the inspiration of the moment and tears down what he has previously sketched out."[28]

Sketches of Landscapes

Wittgenstein's thinking was not always as much in flux as when Waismann wrote these words. By 1936 much of the turbulence produced by the disintegration of the *Tractatus* had run its course and Wittgenstein's thought could settle into a steadier flow. But much had changed in the meantime. Where he had previously sought to resolve philosophical problems with the help of the logic devised by Frege and Russell (and modified by himself), he was now setting out to examine philosophical matters by looking at the working of everyday language. Unwittingly, he became in this way the initiator of a new style of philosophizing, the "ordinary language philosophy" that flourished in the English-speaking world in the 1950s and particularly so at Oxford. By 1936 Wittgenstein had also arrived at a new way of writing. Gone was the tightly numerical arrangement of the propositions of the *Tractatus*. Instead, he was now composing his text as a series of loosely organized, successively numbered remarks. These were sifted from notebooks in which he meticulously worked over his ideas in ever-new formulations and variations. In contrast to the dogmatism of the *Tractatus* he pursued a much more reflective form of writing that sought to do justice to the complexity he saw now in the philosophical problems. The premature confidence of the earlier work that he had resolved those problems once and for all was gone. Where the *Tractatus* had celebrated the art of short, apodictic assertion, the later writings are full of questions, interjections, suggestions, observations, illustrative stories, and imaginative metaphors. Most notably, Wittgenstein wrote now in a conversational tone, developing his ideas in dialogical interchanges between imagined speakers. The linear exposition of the *Tractatus* had given way to "sketches of landscapes" made in the course of "long and involved journeyings" (PI, p. v). Those, he wrote in the preface of the *Philosophical Investigations*, had forced him to "travel over a wide field of thought criss-cross in every direction . . . The same points or almost the same points were always being approached afresh from different directions, and new sketches made" (ibid.).

The major outcome of this new work was the *Philosophical Investigations* on which Wittgenstein labored persistently between 1936 and 1947. Over time Wittgenstein entertained various conceptions of the nature and content of the work. The earliest part of it consisted of sections 1 to 188. They contained an account of his new view of language, a critique of the *Tractatus*, a statement on how he saw philosophy, and a discussion of rules and rule-following. At some point he meant to continue the work with reflections on the notions of truth and proof in mathematics but then replaced those with thoughts about consciousness and the mind and the concepts of feeling and thinking. What has been called Part II of the *Investigations* represents material added after 1945. Though Wittgenstein felt almost ready to publish this material, it never quite reached its final shape in his hands, and so the work appeared only after his death.

The Last Years

When World War II began, Wittgenstein felt once again called to service. He was now too old for the military, but he volunteered to work as a hospital porter and later on as a technical assistant in a medical laboratory. The new disruption signaled in effect the end of his academic career in which he had never felt quite at home. In 1947 he gave his last lectures at Cambridge and then resigned his professorship.

Those last years were not merely a period of consolidation. Perception and knowledge became now new topics of interest to him. In the *Philosophical Investigations* he had repeatedly drawn attention to the fact that language must be learned. This learning, he had said, is fundamentally a process of inculcation and drill. In learning a language the child is being initiated in a form of life. In the last stage of his thinking Wittgenstein took up the notion of a form of life as identifying the entire complex of natural and cultural conditions that make language – and, indeed, any understanding of the world – possible. In notes written between 1949 and 1951 (now published under the title *On Certainty*) he insisted that particular beliefs must always be seen as part of a system of beliefs which together constitute a world-view. All confirmation and disconfirmation of a belief is internal to that system. Far from advocating a careless relativism, his view represented rather a form of naturalism which assumes that forms of life, world-views, and language games are ultimately constrained by the nature of the world. The world teaches us that certain games cannot be played.

Wittgenstein's final notes give vivid evidence of his continued philosophical creativity; they also illustrate the continuity of his fundamental philosophical concerns throughout all the changes his thinking. They reveal once more how skeptical he was about any kind of philosophical theorizing and how he understood his own work as an attempt to undermine the need for such theorizing. The considerations of *On Certainty* were, in fact, directed against both philosophical skepticism and philosophical refutations of skepticism. Against the philosophical skeptics Wittgenstein insisted that there is real knowledge. But this knowledge is always dispersed and not necessarily reliable; it consists of things we have heard and read, of what has been drilled into us, and of our own contributions to this inheritance. We have in general no reason to reject this inherited body of knowledge; we do not generally doubt it, and we are, in fact, never in a position to doubt everything at once. But the certainty we have of the truth of our convictions is only a function of our inability to doubt everything. The fact that we consider some our beliefs to be certain, Wittgenstein argued, indicates only that those beliefs play an indispensable and normative role in our language game; they are the riverbed through which the thought of our language game flows. But this does not mean that they express absolute philosophical truths. All philosophical argumentation must come to an end, but its end is not self-evident truth, it is rather the certainty of our natural human practices.

The Alienated Thinker

Wittgenstein's thinking is characterized throughout by an ambivalent and even paradoxical attitude toward philosophy. For he entertained, on the one hand, a profound skepticism with regard to philosophy – hence his quick and often harsh dismissals of the claims of traditional philosophy – but he tempered that attitude with a genuine appreciation of the depth of the philosophical problems. In the *Tractatus* he had maintained, for instance, that the whole of philosophy is full of fundamental confusions, and that "most of the propositions and questions to be found in philosophical works are not false but nonsensical" (TLP, 3.324 and 4.003). But this critique had eventually been modified by his appreciation of the truth contained in these confusions and mistakes. "In a certain sense one cannot take too much care in handling philosophical mistakes," he wrote later, "they contain so much truth" (Z, 460). In consequence, he was critical not only of traditional philosophy, but also of those who in his opinion failed to appreciate the depth of the philosophical problems. This dual belief resulted in a peculiarly ambivalent attitude toward philosophy – an ambivalence that is, perhaps, best captured in the following statement: "How does it come about that philosophy is so complicated a structure? It surely ought to be completely simple, if it is the ultimate thing, independent of all experience, that you make it out to be. – Philosophy unties knots in our thinking; hence its result must be simple, but philosophizing has to be as complicated as the knots it unties" (Z, 452).

Though Wittgenstein dismissed traditional philosophy, he did so always for philosophical reasons. He was certain, in any case, that something important could be rescued from the traditional enterprise of philosophy. In the *Blue Book* he spoke of his own work accordingly as an heir, "one of the heirs of the subject that used to be called philosophy" (BB, p. 28). The characterization suggests that traditional philosophy is now dead, but at the same time also that it has left an inheritance to be disposed of; it suggests, furthermore, that there are a number of heirs to the philosophical heritage and that Wittgenstein's work should be thought of as one (but only one) of them.

Wittgenstein's wary attitude toward philosophy may remind us of Schopenhauer's (in)famous denunciation of "University philosophy." According to Schopenhauer, genuine philosophy is bound in the end to transcend all metaphysical theorizing and its true endpoint is found in mystical surrender and silence. What Wittgenstein rejected in traditional philosophy was, above all, its theory-constructing impulse, which lies behind all the great systems of philosophy. Of his critique of philosophical doctrines he writes: "Where does our investigation get its importance from, since it seems only to destroy everything interesting, that is, all that is great and important? (As it were all the buildings, leaving behind only bits of stone and rubble.)." And to this challenge he answered: "What we are destroying is nothing but houses of cards and we are clearing up the ground of language on which they stand" (PI, 118). As an alternative to the traditional aim of philosophy to construct a great theoretical system, he proposed the idea of philosophy as critical inquiry. Already in the *Tractatus* he had insisted that "philosophy is not a body of doctrine but an activity" (TLP, 4.112). To this he added in the *Philosophical Investigations* that "it was true to say that our considerations could not be scientific ones . . . And we may not advance any kind of theory" (PI, 109).

Wittgenstein was convinced that the theory-constructing impulse in philosophy was deeply anchored in our civilization. In 1930 he wrote: "Our civilization is characterized by the word 'progress' . . . Typically it constructs. It is occupied with building an ever more complicated structure and even clarity is sought only as a means to this end, not as an end in itself. For me on the contrary clarity, perspicuity are valuable in themselves" (CV, p. 7). And he insisted that, by contrast, the spirit of the great stream of European and American civilization was "alien and uncongenial" to him, that he had no sympathy for it and did not even fully understand its goals, "if it has any" (CV, p. 6). These protestations have made some of Wittgenstein's critics uncomfortable. For one thing, Wittgenstein appears to assume in them a sharp division between philosophy and science. Thus he rejects any conception of philosophy that would make it into a quasi-scientific enterprise. He writes, accordingly, in the *Blue Book*: "Philosophers constantly see the method of

the situated thinker

science before their eye, and are irresistibly tempted to ask and answer questions in the way science does. This tendency is the real source of metaphysics and leads the philosopher into complete darkness" (BB, p. 18). It is also clear that he feels generally antipathetic to science or, at least, that he feels distanced from it. "I am not aiming at the same target as the scientists," he writes, "and my way of thinking is different from theirs" (CV, p. 7). And: "We cannot speak in science of a *great*, essential problem" (CV, p. 10). And finally: "I may find scientific questions interesting, but they never really grip me" (CV, p. 79). To those who are steeped in the values of science such remarks will naturally sound offensive, if not obscurantist.

If Wittgenstein's goal is not the formulation of any philosophical theory, then what does he see as the outcome of his undertakings? This he describes variously as showing what cannot be manifestly expressed in language or as describing the evident features of our practices. In either case he holds that "the work of the philosopher consists in assembling reminders for a particular purpose" (PI, 128). That purpose is at times described as therapeutic in character and the therapies are understood by him, in turn, as multiple and diverse. "There is no such thing as *one* philosophical method , but there are methods, like different therapies" (PI, 133). The ultimate goal of these therapies is to bring about the disappearance of the problem of life. "We feel that even when all *possible* scientific questions have been answered, the problem of life remains completely untouched . . . The solution of the problem of life is seen in the vanishing of the problem" (TLP, 6.521–6.522). Elsewhere, he describes philosophy as "a battle against the bewitchment of our intelligence by means of language," and declares "the real discovery" to be "the one that gives philosophy peace" (PI, 109, 133).

Wittgenstein's Standing

Despite Wittgenstein's indubitable influence on twentieth-century thought, his standing within academic philosophy has been and will always remain uncertain. His resistance to systematic philosophical theorizing, the unique style of his writing both in the *Tractatus* and in his later works, his frequently expressed anti-philosophical sentiments, his profound cultural pessimism, and the highly personal tone of his thought all make it difficult to fit him into the framework of academic philosophy. That judgments about Wittgenstein should differ so much is surely not surprising in a thinker whose views are always unique and sometimes radically idiosyncratic. We might compare him in this respect to Nietzsche in that both thinkers have been acclaimed as new starting points in philosophy and both have been dismissed as not really being philosophers at all. Besides those who speak of Wittgenstein as "a philosopher of genius" or say that in his writings one enters "a new world"[29] we can thus easily find others who maintain with equal seriousness that his importance for philosophy has been highly overrated.

Even as a strictly philosophical thinker Wittgenstein is not easily classified. We can read the *Tractatus* simply as a contribution to logical theory in the way Russell and generations of analytic philosophers have done. But we can do so only at the price of ignoring Wittgenstein's insistence on the broader ethical purpose of his work. We can similarly read the *Philosophical Investigations* straightforwardly as a contribution to the theoretical study of language but only at the price of ignoring Wittgenstein's characterization of the work as therapeutic in intent. There is much to be said for concluding that Wittgenstein was most deeply motivated by ethical and religious considerations. But an exclusive focus on this side of Wittgenstein's thought has its problems. It makes it look as if large parts of the *Tractatus* and the *Philosophical Investigations* were somehow inessential to his thought. A third line of reading emphasizes his wariness toward philosophy. Was Wittgenstein, perhaps, after all just a skeptic? That account also runs into difficulties. Why does he explore questions of truth and meaning, of logic and language at such length, if he only means in the end to reject such explorations as senseless?

Yet a fourth group of interpreters has argued that it is best to ignore Wittgenstein's programmatic remarks about philosophy (whether ethical, therapeutic, or skeptical in nature) and to concentrate, instead, on his treatment of concrete philosophical problems. Some of these interpreters have even maintained that it is then possible to discover a coherent and important system of philosophy in his writings. That conclusion can be reached, however, only by doing substantial violence to Wittgenstein's texts. What remains true is that Wittgenstein covers an exceptionally wide range of philosophical and quasi-philosophical matters and that he manages to speak about them with an unusual freshness, in a precise and stylish language, often with the help of surprising images and metaphors. This has suggested to yet a fifth group of readers that what is of greatest interest in Wittgenstein's work is the manner in which he engages with philosophical questions. On this view, Wittgenstein teaches us above all some valuable methodological lessons.

Wittgenstein's influence on twentieth-century philosophy is due not only to his written work or to the particular claims he seems to be making. Of equal importance has been his practice of philosophy and his teaching of this practice. It produced, in the first instance, a generation of followers and students who preserved, transmitted, and interpreted his work. They have also transmitted to us how he went about doing philosophy. In their memoirs and in their own practice of philosophy they have communicated to us something of the intensity and the moral seriousness with which Wittgenstein pursued philosophy. Unhurried and yet relentless, he teased and harried the problems that concerned him, hunting them down into their most hidden caves and corners. No turn of the question was too small for him, no trail too insignificant to pursue. "Where others pass by," he said, "I stand still" (CV, p. 66). Profoundly concerned with the very words into which we cast our philosophical predicaments, he never loses sight of the great issues that lie behind them. In his writings he suggests, asks, admonishes, calls for experiments in thought, action, and imagination. He demands from his readers a constant active engagement in thinking. It is, perhaps, in these characteristics that he reveals to us his true significance as a thinker. We need not agree with the conclusions that he is led to, we need not be preoccupied with the particular questions that concern him, but he can still serve as a model of what it means to be a philosopher.

Wittgenstein remained philosophically active till the end of his life. True to the course he had chosen for himself (or, rather, on which he found himself), he persisted in his thinking even when he felt that it was not taking him anywhere. In the last month of his life he wrote ironically of himself: "I do philosophy now like an old woman who is always mislaying something and having to look for it again: now her spectacles, now her keys" (OC, 532). But that did not stop him from going on. The last entry in his philosophical notebook is dated only days before his death of prostate cancer on April 29, 1951. Since he had always wanted to live to the end the life of a thinker, he could truthfully tell his friends on his deathbed that, despite all his suffering and unhappiness, he had after all lived "a wonderful life."[30]

notes

1 Norman Malcolm's Ludwig Wittgenstein: A Memoir (London: Oxford University Press 1958), p. 59. Paradoxically, Malcolm's Memoir has done much to pull Wittgenstein out of obscurity.
2 Wittgenstein's family background is described in Brian McGuinness, Wittgenstein: A Life, vol. 1, Young Ludwig 1889–1921 (Berkeley: University of California Press, 1988). There exist now a number of biographical studies. The most detailed biography is Ray Monk's highly readable Ludwig Wittgenstein: The Duty of Genius (New York: The Free Press, 1990).
3 M. O'C. Drury, "Some Notes on Conversations with Wittgenstein," in Rush Rhees, ed., Ludwig Wittgenstein: Personal Recollections (Totowa, NJ: Rowman and Littlefield 1981), p. 94.
4 Drury, "Conversations with Wittgenstein," p. 117.
5 Ludwig Wittgenstein, Denkbewegungen, Tagebücher 1930–1932/1936–1937, edited by Ilse Somavila (Innsbruck: Haymon 1997), part 1, p. 68.
6 Wittgenstein, CV, p. 18.
7 Wittgenstein, CV, p. 175.
8 The best characterization of that milieu is to be found in Carl E. Schorske's Fin-de-Siecle Vienna: Politics and Culture (New York: Alfred A. Knopf, 1980). Alan Janik and Stephen Toulmin's widely read book, Wittgenstein's Vienna (New York: Simon and Schuster, 1973), is more anecdotal, less reliable, and more superficial in its analyses.
9 Of particular interest in this connection are Musil's The Man Without Qualities, translated by Sophie Wilkins (New York: Alfred A. Knopf, 1994), and Broch's Hofmannsthal und seine Zeit (Munich: Piper, 1964).
10 Drury, "Conversations with Wittgenstein," p. 152.
11 Ronald W. Clark, The Life of Bertrand Russell (New York: Alfred A. Knopf, 1976), chapters 7 and 8, gives us a vivid description of their encounter.

12 Quoted from Monk, *Ludwig Wittgenstein*, p. 41.

13 Bertrand Russell, *My Philosophical Development* (London: Allen and Unwin, 1959), pp. 216–217.

14 It is useful to read Wittgenstein's *Geheime Tagebücher* together with his *Notebooks, 1914–1916*.

15 Paul Engelmann, *Letters from Ludwig Wittgenstein with a Memoir* (Oxford: Blackwell, 1967), p. 25.

16 Even some recent interpreters have characterized the book without further qualification as "a work in philosophical logic." See H.O. Mounce, *Wittgenstein's Tractatus: An Introduction* (Chicago: University of Chicago Press, 1981), p. 1.

17 Ludwig Wittgenstein, *Letters to Russell, Keynes, and Moore*, edited by G.H. v. Wright (Ithaca, NY: Cornell University Press, 1974), p. 71.

18 Paul Wijdeveld, *Ludwig Wittgenstein, Architect* (Cambridge, MA: MIT Press, 1994).

19 Peter Galison has discussed the confluence of the philosophical ideas of Wittgenstein and the Vienna Circle and the stylistic conceptions of the Bauhaus in his essay "Aufbau/Bauhaus: Logical Positivism and Architectural Modernism," in *Critical Inquiry*, 16 (1990), pp. 709–752.

20 The significance of this episode of Wittgenstein's life for his subsequent philosophizing has as yet been insufficiently explored. An important start is made in Konrad Wünsche, *Der Volksschullehrer Ludwig Wittgenstein* (Frankfurt: Suhrkamp 1985).

21 For a discussion of Mauthner's significance for Wittgenstein see Hans Sluga, "Wittgenstein and Pyrrhonism," in *Pyrrhonian Skepticism*, edited by Walter Sinnott-Arnstrong (Oxford: Oxford University Press, 2004).

22 Drury, Conversations with Wittgenstein," p. 106.

23 Oswald Spengler, *The Decline of the West*, translated by C.F. Atkinson (New York, 1926), p. 31.

24 L.E.J. Brouwer, "Mathematik, Wissenschaft und Sprache," *Monatshefte für Mathematik*, 36 (1929), pp. 153–164.

25 G.E. Moore, "Wittgenstein's Lectures in 1930–33," in *Philosophical Occasions, 1912–1951*, edited by James Klagge and Alfred Nordmann (Indianopolis: Hackett, 1993), pp. 50–51.

26 Ludwig Wittgenstein, *Lectures, Cambridge 1930–1932*, edited by Desmond Lee (Chicago: University of Chicago Press, 1980); *Lectures, Cambridge 1932–1935*, edited by Alice Ambrose (Chicago: University of Chicago Press, 1979); *Lectures on the Foundations of Mathematics*, edited by Cora Diamond (Ithaca, NY: Cornell University Press, 1976).

27 O.K. Bouwsma, *Wittgenstein. Conversations 1949–1951* (Indianapolis: Hackett, 1986), pp. xv–xvi.

28 Cited from *Wittgenstein and the Vienna Circle*, recorded by Friedrich Waismann, edited by Brian McGuinness, translated by Joachim Schulte (Oxford: Blackwell, 1979,) editor's preface, p. 26.

29 Peter Strawson, "Review of Wittgenstein's Philosophical Investigations," in G. Pitcher, ed., *Wittgenstein* (London: Macmillan, 1968), p. 22; David Pears, *The False Prison* (Oxford: Clarendon Press, 1987), vol. 1, p. 3.

30 N. Malcolm, *Ludwig Wittgenstein: A Memoir*, 2nd edition (Oxford: Oxford University Press, 1984), p. 81.

further reading

Malcolm, Norman. *Ludwig Wittgenstein: A Memoir*. London: Oxford University Press, 1958.

Monk, Ray. *Ludwig Wittgenstein: The Duty of Genius*. New York: The Free Press, 1990.

the world and its structure

A s a student at Oxford I once sought to convince my supervisor, Gilbert Ryle, that the *Tractatus* was Wittgenstein's greatest achievement. Ryle dismissed all such speculation with a single word. "Interesting!" he growled dismissively, and that was that. I would not now repeat that earlier claim. Certainly, from the perspective I have adopted in this book, the *Tractatus* can hardly be considered Wittgenstein's most important work. Still, there are plenty of philosophers (from Russell onward) who would have agreed with my careless youthful judgment. I still believe, however, that the *Tractatus* is a singular philosophical achievement. Written when Wittgenstein was a 29-year-old soldier, it lays out an entirely original, comprehensive picture of the world in a mere 70 printed pages. If the book were a piece of music, one might call it a *bravura* aria. In this and the next chapter I want to describe two fundamental ideas of the *Tractatus* that bear most directly on the broader issues I am after. The first is Wittgenstein's pluralistic view of the world (his "logical atomism"); the second is his conception of the limits of language.

"The world is everything that is the case"

The *Tractatus* begins with a sentence that is at once straightforward and deeply puzzling. It seems an obvious fact and almost a triviality. The puzzle is what point Wittgenstein might be seeking to make with this first sentence. Not many modern thinkers have found it useful or even possible to begin a philosophical treatise with this sort of all-encompassing statement. In our age of high specialization we have come to be suspicious of such large-scale generalizations.

One exception is Schopenhauer, who opens his main work, *The World as Will and Representation*, with the proposition: "The world is my representation."[1] Wittgenstein may well have modeled his first sentence on that proposition. In their scope and cadence they are certainly much alike. And there is something else the two propositions have in common. While they are initially

wittgenstein, First Edition. Hans Sluga.
© 2011 Hans Sluga. Published 2011 by Blackwell Publishing Ltd.

asserted with apparently apodictic certainty, they are eventually suspended at the end of each of the two books. Thus, Schopenhauer replaces his initial statement with the declaration that "to those in whom the will has turned and denied itself, this very real world of ours with all its suns and galaxies, is – nothing."[2] The world of representation dissolves here into nothingness and mystical silence. And in a similar spirit, Wittgenstein writes at the end of the *Tractatus:* "My propositions are elucidatory in this way: he who understands me finally recognizes them as senseless" (TLP, 6.54). And, like Schopenhauer, he concludes his book with a call to silence: "Whereof one cannot speak, thereof one must be silent" (TLP, 7).

Once we have come to appreciate these similarities, we will also notice some revealing differences. Most striking is that Schopenhauer's first sentence speaks of a world that exists only for a thinking subject; Wittgenstein's first sentence characterizes the world, on the other hand, as in no way subject dependent. It is true, of course, that he corrects himself later on in the *Tractatus* by adding that "the world is *my* world" (TLP, 5.62) and that "I am my world" (TLP, 5.64). But there remains nonetheless a significant difference between the two standpoints. While Schopenhauer means to endorse a form of idealism, Wittgenstein maintains that idealism (or solipsism, as he says in the *Tractatus*) "strictly carried out coincides with pure realism" since the I in question "shrinks to an extensionless point and there remains the reality co-ordinated with it" (TLP, 5.64).[3] Schopenhauer's formula implies, at the same time, a distantiation from the claims of empirical science. He holds that we do "not know a sun and an earth, but only an eye that sees a sun, a hand that feels an earth."[4] The Wittgenstein of the *Tractatus*, on the other hand, endorses objective, empirical science. For him, "the totality of true propositions is the total natural science" (TLP, 4.11) and the archetypal science is, for him, without doubt, physics and even more specifically, classical mechanics (TLP, 6.341). Later on, he will add that it is characteristic of physics that it does not use the word "I" (PI, 410).

This disagreement makes evident that there exists a fundamental difference between Schopenhauer's and Wittgenstein's metaphysical views. Schopenhauer writes in *The World as Will and Representation* that "the thing-in-itself, as such, is free from all forms of knowledge." We can access the thing-in-itself, however, in another way by attending to the non-cognitive, inner side of our being. We discover then that the inner nature of the world is "will." For Schopenhauer, the ultimate reality identified by that name "lies outside time and space, and accordingly knows no plurality, and consequently is one."[5] The young Wittgenstein may well have been attracted to this metaphysical "monism." We find traces of it as late as 1916 when he writes in his notebook: "I can also speak of a will that is common to the whole world. But this will is in a higher sense *my* will. As my representation is the world, in the same way my will is the world-will" (NB, p. 85). But this kind of speculation has completely disappeared from the *Tractatus*, which seems to commit itself in its first pages instead to a pluralistic metaphysical realism.

The Substance of the World

In the first two propositions of section 2 the *Tractatus* maps out, so it appears, a pluralistic account of the overall structure of the world. We read: "What is the case, the fact, is the existence of states of affairs. A state of affairs is a joining of objects (items, things)" (TLP, 2–2.01). This, together with some of the surrounding propositions, suggests a four-layered structure of the world, facts, states of affairs, and objects such that:

The world = the totality of facts (TLP, 1.1)
A fact = the existence of states of affairs (TLP, 2)
A state of affairs = a combination of objects (TLP, 2.01)

The facts that make up the world are absolutely discrete. "One thing can be the case or not the case and everything remains the same." This implies a narrow concept of fact. If we were to take, for instance, "A is a red cube" and "A is red" to be facts they would, of course, not be independent of each other. For Wittgenstein states of affairs must also be independent of one another (TLP, 2.061). This doctrine of mutual independence of facts and of states of affairs is fundamental to the pluralistic picture of the world that Wittgenstein propounds at this point. It was also to prove one of the weak points of the *Tractatus*, as Wittgenstein came to understand later on.

States of affairs have, however, a peculiar position in this scheme. While the world "**is** (everything that is the case)" while a fact "**is** (the existence of states of affairs)," and while the object "**is** . . . (the existent)," the ontological status of states of affairs is somewhat obscure. If they exist, they are facts. But what are they, if they do not exist? We might call them, then, possible facts. But what is the ontological status of such possibilities? Russell at some point argued for the subsistence of non-existing things. Wittgenstein, however, never felt that temptation. We must turn to what he says about language to see what he means by a state of affairs, for it is only "a proposition that presents the existence and non-existence of states of affairs" (TLP, 4.1). A non-existent state of affairs exists, in other words, only in language, nowhere else. Language allows us to make pictures of possibilities. Non-existent states of affairs are thus not on the same ontological level as facts and objects. They are merely fictional in nature.

Wittgenstein emphasizes right from the start that the world is for him a totality of facts, "not of objects" (TLP, 1.1). Fact is thus the primary notion for him, not object. We can conceive of objects only as occurring in states of affairs (and thus in terms of their occurrence in facts). "Every thing is, as it were, in a space of possible states of affairs. I can think of this space as empty, but not of the thing without the space" (TLP, 2.013). Nonetheless, objects occupy a privileged place in the structure of the world in so far as they constitute "the substance of the world" (TLP, 2.021). These objects are, however, nothing like the things of which we commonly speak (the sun, the moon, the table, the book); they are rather ultimate components of reality. As substance of the world, "they cannot be compound" (TLP, 2.021). They are "simple"; we cannot even speak of them as having properties. "The substance of the world *can* only determine a form and not any material properties." They are differentiated from each other only by being different. They are independent of what is the case. "The object is the fixed, the existent; the configuration is the changing, the variable" (TLP, 2.0271). These objects may be infinite in number (TLP, 4.2211). But there is no determination of their number since it is strictly senseless to speak of "the number of all objects" (TLP, 4.1272). Objects, so conceived, are, however, fundamental to the structure of the world in that "objects contain the possibility of all states of affairs" (TLP, 2.014) and the totality of existent states of affairs is the world.

Intriguing as all this sounds, one must add that there remains a great deal of obscurity in the details of Wittgenstein's picture of the world. What are we to make, for instance, of his two claims that (a) material properties are "first formed by the configurations of objects," and (b) that "the configuration of objects forms the state of affairs" (TLP, 2.0231 and 2.0272)? Nothing in the text helps us to understand them either singly or in combination. And it is far from obvious that Wittgenstein himself would have been able to resolve our difficulties.

Logical Atomism

The first question one might want to ask about the *Tractatus* is from where does Wittgenstein take his account of the structure of the world? It is certainly not a product of observation or empirical research. The answer is to be found in a series of propositions that begins at 2.1 with the observation that "we make to ourselves pictures of facts." Logical pictures, he goes on to say, represent the logical form of what they depict. The logical picture of the facts is the thought which expresses itself perceptibly in the sentence. Two points stick out from this. The first is that the structure of the world can be found (and can only be found) through a process of logical analysis, and the second, that logical analysis will involve an analysis of language. These are quite extraordinary claims when one thinks about it. According to the first claim, the philosopher and the logician in their private study are most qualified to determine the structure of the world; they are most qualified to tell us what there is and how it all hangs together, not the physicist or any other natural scientist. This belief in the revelatory power of logic goes back to the beginnings of Western thought; but with the invention of a new logic by Frege, Russell, and Wittgenstein it has gained a surprising new life. Russell, in particular, was convinced that logical analysis could establish the truth of metaphysical pluralism. He therefore called his doctrine, appropriately, *"logical atomism."*[6]

The first pages of Wittgenstein's *Tractatus* reveal how deeply important Russell's logical atomism was for him; it was with this help from Russell that he overcame his attraction to Schopenhauer's metaphysical idealism and monism. Wittgenstein adopted, in particular, Russell's notion of logical analysis and their precedent has spawned a whole school of contemporary thought known as "analytic philosophy." But it should be noted that the concept of analysis used in this context has undergone profound change over time, and that many so-called analytic philosophers do not practice logical analysis in the sense of Russell and the early Wittgenstein.[7] Even the later Wittgenstein suggested that analysis might be conceived more broadly as a process in which one (philosophically confusing) form of expression is replaced by another (philosophically clearer) one (PI, 90). He now rejected the idea that there might be a final, complete analysis of anything. And he threw doubt on the belief that analysis would necessarily promote understanding, that the "analyzed" form of a sentence shows what is really meant by the unanalyzed sentence. He opposed now the thought "if you have only the unanalyzed form you miss the analysis; but if you know the analyzed form that gives you everything" with the question whether it might not be the case that "an aspect of the matter is lost on you in the *latter* case as well as the former?" (PI, 63).

In one respect, however, his conception of analysis remained the same from the *Tractatus* to the *Philosophical Investigations*. And that was his conviction that "we are not analyzing a phenomenon (e.g. thought) but a concept (e.g. that of thinking), and therefore the use of a word" (PI, 383). That his form of analysis was to be linguistic had already been made clear in the *Tractatus* where he had written: "In a proposition a thought can be so expressed that to the objects of the thought correspond the elements in the propositional sign. These elements I call 'simple signs' and the proposition completely analyzed" (TLP, 3.2–3.201). The idea that logical analysis would be an analysis of linguistic signs had been alien to Russell. He had been busy analyzing entities of various kinds, not verbal expressions. The idea of *linguistic* analysis was introduced into the analytic tradition by Wittgenstein. It derived from his early interest in language and his familiarity with the work of Fritz Mauthner. From Mauthner Wittgenstein also took an interest in everyday language and in the uses of language, an interest that would become strikingly evident in the later work. But even in the *Tractatus* there are indications of such interest. In contrast to Frege and Russell, who thought of their logical notation as a substitute for the imperfect notations of ordinary language, Wittgenstein argued that "all propositions of our ordinary language are actually, just they are, logically completely in order" (TLP, 5.5563). But that logical order was hidden below the surface grammar since (ordinary) "language disguises the thought" (TLP, 4.002). In order to determine the deep, logical structure of such propositions we must look at their application, their use. And in this respect he certainly differed from Mauthner and found himself in agreement with Russell. For Mauthner had argued that ordinary language had no logical order. While Wittgenstein was willing to say with Mauthner that all philosophy had to concern itself with language and could thus be called a "critique of language," as Mauthner had suggested in the title of his main work, this critique could not be conducted in Mauthner's sense. And then he added: "Russell's merit is to have shown that the apparent logical form of the proposition need not be its real form" (TLP, 4.0031).

There is, however, another and more radical disagreement with Russell that emerges toward the end of the *Tractatus*. And this concerned doubt about the entire enterprise of Russell's metaphysical theorizing. In stark disagreement with Russell, the *Tractatus* concludes, indeed, with the assertion that anyone who wants to say something metaphysical has "failed to give meaning to certain signs in his propositions" (TLP, 6.53). And among those propositions will, of course, also be the ones that spell out the doctrine of logical atomism. This final, surprising comment generates, naturally, a deep tension between the beginning and the end of Wittgenstein's own book that interpreters have found difficult to deal with. I will say more on this topic in the next chapter.

Right now, the important point is only that the initial pages of the book cannot be taken to be as straightforward as they may look at first sight. There was, of course, a period in Wittgenstein's life (roughly from 1911 to 1916) when he subscribed without qualification to the metaphysics of logical atomism. At that time he had been able to agree with Russell in holding that "philosophy consists of logic and metaphysics: logic is its base."[8] But by the time he composed the *Tractatus* that earlier certainty was gone. For the rest of this chapter I will concern myself with the logical atomism that Wittgenstein was interested in up to 1916, as it makes its appearance in the early pages of the *Tractatus*.

"The proposition only asserts something, in so far as it is a picture"

Russell had come to his own version of logical atomism by opposing himself to the logical monism advanced by F.H. Bradley. According to Bradley all our words and propositions speak ultimately of one single thing, the totality of which Bradley calls alternatively, "The Absolute" and "The One." Russell and his friend G.E. Moore were initially enthralled with Bradley's philosophy but they revolted against it around the year 1899. In his breakthrough essay "On the Nature of Judgment" Moore argued for the eccentric view that our reality is, in fact, made up of judgments since judgments are inevitably complex reality and must contain a multitude of entities. Following this argument, Russell insisted in 1903 his book *The Principles of Mathematics* that "every word occurring in a sentence must have some meaning" and that "words all have meaning in the simple sense that they are symbols which stand for something other than themselves."[9] What a word stands for Russell called a "term" and he went on to say that "a man, a moment, a number, a class, a relation, a chimaera or anything else that can be mentioned is sure to be a term."[10] Every such term exists and is, moreover, "immutable and indestructible."[11] When combined, terms form propositions which, like Moore's judgments, are to be conceived as complexes existing in the world, not as linguistic or mental items. If we are to make sense of this strange doctrine, it may help to replace Moore's and Russell's terminology of "judgment" and "proposition" with the more familiar-sounding "state of affair" or "fact." It then becomes clear that Moore and Russell were anticipating Wittgenstein's doctrine that the world is the totality of fact, that facts consist in the existence of states of affairs, and that states of affairs are combinations of objects which, in turn, form the substance of the world. Wittgenstein's logical atomism was, in other words, an adaptation of Moore's and Russell's earlier version of that doctrine.

After 1903, Russell came to realize that his initial super-realism leads to logical paradoxes. Did it not imply, for instance, that expressions of the form "all men," "some women," "no child," and "the largest prime" all stand for something? In order to preserve his super-realist intuitions he was willing to commit himself at first to an intricate and highly counterintuitive theory of "denoting complexes." But learning from Frege's analysis of universal and existential proposition he came to dispense with such complexes altogether in his 1905 essay "On Denoting." Another problem for super-realism arose for him from the realization that there are well-formed expressions that cannot consistently be assumed to stand for anything. Thus, the assumption that the term "the class of all those classes that do not contain themselves" stands for a class leads to a straightforward contradiction. These doubts led Russell eventually to adopt a new form of logical atomism. According to that view, we must first subject our sentences to logical analysis before we can say what things they are speaking about. Russell thus came to insist on the importance of distinguishing between the surface and the deep grammar of our sentences. He no longer maintained that every word in a sentence stands for something, but instead argued that only "logically proper" names stand for something. Accordingly, in 1918 he was to write that "Socrates, Piccadilly, Rumania, Twelfth Night or anything else you like to think of, to which you give a proper name, they are all apparently complex entities . . . For my part, I do not believe in complex entities of this kind."[12] But he remained certain even at this point that there are many separate things. "I do not regard the apparent multiplicity of the world as consisting merely in phases and unreal divisions of a single indivisible Reality."[13]

When Wittgenstein arrived in Cambridge in 1911, Russell had just completed work on *Principia Mathematica* and had turned his attention back to issues relating to his logical atomism. Russell had now worked himself round to the idea that the simples had to be "sense-data," their immediate properties, and perhaps also certain "logical objects" referred to by terms like "not," "and," "all," and "some." The world consisted now of these items and their combination in facts; everything else was a "logical fiction." In order to motivate this Russell had concluded that the structure of a completely ana-lyzed sentence mirrors the structure of reality.

Wittgenstein initially bought into this form of logical atomism. It provided him the outline of an atomistic metaphysics and also an answer to the ques-tion how that metaphysical reality can be known. The *Tractatus* begins accordingly with an outline of the metaphysical structure of the world and then proceeds to explain our knowledge of this structure. "We make to our-selves pictures of facts," Wittgenstein writes. And "the picture is a model of reality" (TLP, 2.1, 2.12). And again:

> One name stands for one thing, and another for another thing, and they are connected together. And so the whole, like a living picture, presents the atomic fact. The possibility of propositions is based upon the principle of the representation of objects by signs . . . The proposition is a picture of a state of affairs, only in so far as it is logically articulated. (TLP, 4.0311–4.032)

The doctrine that the structure of the logically analyzed sentence mirrors the structure of reality has by now become so strongly identified with the *Tractatus* that it is usually called Wittgenstein's "picture theory of meaning," even though Russell had arrived at it well before Wittgenstein.[14] Wittgenstein's contribution to logical atomism was, however, not that "theory" but its clari-fication and substantial modification.

He first of all introduced the idea that a proposition could be treated as a picture of the state of affairs or the fact that it is about. But he recognized at once that he was using here a somewhat technical conception of a picture. He certainly did not mean that propositions are pictures in the sense in which paintings or drawings or photographs are. They are not visual, only "logical pictures" of facts. In order for one thing to be a picture of another in any sense of the term, he insists, "there must be something identical" in the picture and what is depicted (TLP, 2.161). This means, more precisely, that "in the propo-sition there must be exactly as many distinguishable parts as there are in the state of affairs, which it represents. They must both possess the same logical (mathematical) multiplicity" (TLP, 4.04). The proposition is a logical picture in the sense that the distinguishable parts are represented by conventional names rather than by images. The basic idea is certainly not difficult to under-stand. If we envisage a fact involving a relation between two things such as a cat and a mat, then the sentence "The cat is on the mat" can be taken to be a logical picture of that fact. In the sentence the relation of the two things is depicted by a relation between the names of these two things. The names "cat" and "mat" do not, of course, look like the objects they stand for and the proposition is therefore only a logical, not a visual picture.

Wittgenstein also realized, however, that this doctrine could quickly run into difficulties, if accepted without further qualification. One of these became apparent to him from the version of the picture conception of meaning that Russell was entertaining at the time of his collaboration with Wittgenstein.

Russell had held at the time that a logically complex sentence like "The cat is on the mat or the dog is growling" must be said to depict a logically complex ("disjunctive") fact different from the atomic facts depicted by the component sentences "The cat is on the mat" and "The dog is growling." He had also maintained at the same time that logical particles like "and," "or," "if-then" stand for objects ("logical objects") just like the words "cat" and "dog." Wittgenstein had never been sympathetic to this view and Russell had eventually abandoned it, though probably only after Wittgenstein had left Cambridge.[15] Unaware of this change of mind, Wittgenstein had still believed himself at odds with Russell when he emphasized in the *Tractatus* that only (true) elementary propositions can be said to picture facts, that there are no negative, conjunctive, conditional, or general facts and that there are no such things as logical objects.

This view was plausible enough but it also immediately generated some new difficulties. A proposition might look elementary but might, for all that, be really logically complex. Russell himself had, after all, distinguished between the surface and the deep grammar of propositions. On this point Wittgenstein certainly agreed with him. "Language disguises thought," he wrote in the *Tractatus*, "so much so that from the external form of the clothes one cannot infer the form of the thought they clothe" (TLP, 4.002). And: "It is Russell's merit to have shown that the apparent logical form of the proposition need not be its real form" (TLP, 4.0031). Only by means of logical analysis could the logical form of the proposition be discovered. But Russell had failed to understand the seriousness of this insight. For how was one to determine whether the logical analysis was complete and the true logical form of a proposition had been identified? It might be, for instance, that in an as yet incompletely analyzed proposition there appears a sign that looked like the name of an object, but further logical analysis might replace that sign by some logically complex expression and thus the apparent object would disappear. What then was logical atomism really committed to?

There is a further consequence of the picture conception of meaning to which we must pay attention. It is that the deep structure of all languages will be the same. While surface grammars may vary distinctly, the propositions of every possible language must have the same deep structure if they are to describe the same facts, since that deep structure has to be isomorphic with the structure of the depicted fact. We might even say that from the perspective of deep structure there exists only one language, according to the *Tractatus* ("Like the two youths, their two horses and their lilies in the fairy tale. They are all in a sense the same," TLP, 4.014). This explains also why Wittgenstein speaks at times of "the language" in the singular, "*the* language which alone I understand" (TLP, 5.62). I emphasize this because here we find one of the points at which Wittgenstein's later views diverge radically from those of the *Tractatus*. By the mid-1930s he has abandoned his earlier "monistic" view of language in favor of the idea that there are many languages (or language games, as he prefers to say). He no longer assumes now that language has an embedded deep structure and this, of course, closes off the possibility of determining the structure of reality from that of language.

Also important is Wittgenstein's realization in the *Tractatus* that the picture conception of meaning cannot be properly stated since such a statement would involve a comparison between a fact and a proposition. But we can never look at this supposed relation in an independent manner, from outside. The fact is available to us only through our thinking or speaking about it and that means by having a picture of it. What then remains of the picture conception? Is it a presupposition for our language having meaning at all? One which we must accept unquestioned? Is it something that shows itself but cannot be argued for or explained? Is it to be discarded just like the doctrine of logical atomism may have to be? We are finding ourselves back, in other words, in the deepest quandaries of the *Tractatus*.

A Very Short History of Logical Atomism

Nothing is more natural, in a way, than the view that there are many things. Sensory experience presents us, after all, with a kaleidoscope of impressions; it acquaints us with diverse objects, plants, animals, and people, with different kinds of things such as rocks and rivers and clouds, with qualities, states, events, relations, etc. Monism, on the other hand, is by nature a purely theoretical standpoint. It is forced to dismiss the evidence of the senses and typically insists on a sharp distinction between appearance and reality. For Parmenides, the first of the great monist philosophers, those who trust the senses are "deaf and blind at once, altogether dazed," and what they come to believe is entirely untrustworthy. Logic, on the other hand, reveals to us that Being is indivisible, continuous, unchanging, and uniform, "like the bulk of a well-rounded sphere."[16] Logical atomism, in turn, seeks to challenge the monist position not by affirming the reliability of sensory experience but by advancing logical considerations of its own. A short look at the various arguments put forward in favor of logical atomism is helpful in that they will all be eventually re-examined in Wittgenstein's work.

Against the Parmenidean form of monism Leucippus and Democritus proposed what we know as the earliest form of logical atomism. They argued "that motion is impossible without a void, that the void is not-being and that no part of being is not being," and they held at the same time that being is not one but divided into an infinite number of elements that are invisible only because of their smallness. These atoms "move in the void, and by their coming together they affect coming-into-being, by their separation perishing."[17] The intuitive assumption here is that in order to understand change we must assume that there exist unchangeable elements which can enter into various combinations. We may call this the change narrative in favor of logical atomism.

In the *Theaetetus* Plato sketches an atomistic doctrine that is motivated by quite different but equally formal concerns. Socrates describes a dream in that dialogue according to which there are "primary elements, as it were, of which we and everything else are composed."[18] Those elements can only be named, for if we were to say anything of them we would be adding something to them. By contrast to the elements, the things composed of them can be characterized or described by means of reference to the elements. The *Theaetetus* never tells us what the primary elements of Socrates' dream are meant to be. They are certainly not the material atoms of Democritus and Leucippus. We may conjecture that Plato is thinking of them as ideas or forms but we must note that he does not mention the theory of ideas at all in the *Theaetetus*. When we ask what motivates the atomistic hypothesis in the *Theaetetus*, we can identify two different lines of reasoning. The first is an analysis narrative according to which the assumption that there exist complexes commits us to the idea that there are also simples. In addition, Plato advances what we may call a representation narrative, which proceeds from the observation that our language has an atomistic structure. Propositions are composed of words as their simple elements and written words are composed of letters. This, the Socrates of the *Theaetetus* gives us to understand, justifies the conclusion that the things we talk about must also consist of complexes and simples.

The change, the analysis, and the representation narrative are all taken up in Leibniz's version of logical atomism. This is not surprising since Leibniz's system of philosophy is syncretistic in character in that it seeks to accommodate all previous philosophical theorizing. We thus read in his *Monadology*, in accordance with the analysis narrative: "There must be simple substances, since there are composites; for the composite is only a collection or aggregatum of simple substances."[19] Leibniz also takes up the Platonic representation narrative. In his "Dialogue on the Connection between Things and Words" he writes that "characters must show, when they are used in demonstrations, some kind of connection, grouping, and order which are also found in the objects."[20] The Leibnizian "monads" differ, however, from both Leucippus and Democritus' atoms and from Plato's primary elements. In contrast to Leucippus and Democritus, they are mind-like rather than material in nature and, in contrast to Plato's primary elements, they are individual substances. They share, however, with the atoms of the ancients the property that they do not naturally come into or go out of existence. On one significant point Leibniz is, however, more explicit than his forebears. He assures us that monads must be conceived as entirely independent of each other. The existence or non-existence of one monad determines in no way the existence or non-existence of any other monad.

Wittgenstein never speaks of the atomism of Democritus and Leucippus, though he was surely familiar with it. In the *Philosophical Investigations* he does, however, compare his own and Russell's logical atomism to that of the *Theaetetus* (PI, 46). Through Russell he must, moreover, have known also of Leibniz's system of monads.

Wittgenstein's Motivations

According to the Greek atomists, change can be explained only if we assume that there is an unchanging substratum to the world, a multiplicity of individual atoms that can enter into various changing configurations. But this narrative had played no role in Russell's version of logical atomism and it is marginal also to the *Tractatus*. Wittgenstein refers to it only once, at 2.027f.: "The fixed, the existent, and the object are one. The object is fixed, the existent; the configuration is the changing, the variable."

One reason for this neglect is that both Russell and Wittgenstein describe the world in essentially non-temporal, structural terms. We find, in fact, few references in the *Tractatus* to the concept of time, none to that of history, and only one deprecating reference to evolution. As far as history is concerned, Wittgenstein had written in his *Notebooks*: "What has history to do with me? Mine is the first and only world!" (NB, p. 82). And in the *Tractatus* he had said of evolution: "The Darwinian theory has no more to do with philosophy than any other hypothesis of natural science" (TLP, 4.1122). That turns out to be nothing at all since "philosophy is not one of the natural sciences. (The word 'philosophy' must mean something which stands above or below, but not beside the natural sciences.)" (TLP, 4.111). The world of the *Tractatus* is not one of processes, forces, or streams of energy; it is rather a world of objects and their configurations. I emphasize this point because it reflects directly on some of the things the *Tractatus* says about language. We should certainly not be surprised to discover that the book describes language in purely non-temporal, structural terms. Wittgenstein appears at this point not to be interested in the fact that language has many other uses than that of making true or false assertions. He is also not concerned with the communicative function of language. He does not ask how language is acquired and how it changes over time and what is revealed by the fact that there are different languages with different structures. All these matters he will raise only later on.

It comes naturally to him then to explain his atomism in structural terms. In words reminiscent of Leibniz's *Monadology*, Wittgenstein writes in his *Notebooks*:

> It seems that the idea of the SIMPLE is already to be found contained in that of the complex and in the idea of analysis, and in such a way that we come to this idea quite apart from any examples of simple objects, or of propositions which mention them, and we realize the existence of the simple object – *a priori* – as a logical necessity. (NB, p. 60)

We may wonder, of course, whether the process of analysis really requires the assumption of such simples. Wittgenstein, indeed, also asks himself in the *Notebooks*: "At any rate, then, there is a process of analysis. And can it now be asked whether this process comes to an end? And if so, what will the end

the world and its structure | 31

be?" (NB, p. 46). Given that the analysis starts from something complex, could it not go on indefinitely without ever reaching the ground of ultimate simples? Wittgenstein concludes that this possibility conflicts with our sense "that the world must be what it is, it must be definite." To deny that there are ultimate elements of analysis would imply that the world could be indefinite in the way our knowledge may be uncertain and indefinite. But, "the world has a fixed structure" (NB, p. 62). And this is obviously a rock-bottom conviction for him.

That the process of logical analysis must terminate in ultimate simples holds, according to Wittgenstein, whether or not that process is finite. Even if the analysis were to go on infinitely, we would still be justified in saying that it will terminate in simple objects. But we would in that case, of course, be unable to enumerate those objects and we might not even be able to determine their general characteristics. All we might be able to say is that there must be simple objects and that they will be identified when our logical analysis is complete. Assume that we have carried the analysis to a certain point, what can be deduced from the fact that we are unable to extend it further? Could the failure not be ours? Are we perhaps only entitled to say that there are objects which are simple *for us*? Is our notion of simplicity, perhaps, relative? Wittgenstein certainly considers that possibility: "The simple thing for us IS: the simplest thing we are acquainted with. – The simplest thing which our analysis can attain" (NB, p. 47). But in the end he returns to the idea that there must be absolutely simple objects. That brings us back to the question whether we can ever identify them. Are there objective markers for when we have reached the ultimate level of analysis? What would they be?

Wittgenstein writes in agreement with both Plato and Russell that objects can only be named. But what is to count as a name? We commonly assume that we can name all kinds of things such as tables, watches, books, or colored surfaces. Wittgenstein writes in his *Notebooks*: "It is quite clear that I can in fact correlate a name with this watch just as it lies here ticking in front of me, and that this name will have reference outside any proposition in the very sense I have always given that word, and I feel that that name in a proposition will correspond to all the requirements of 'the names of simple objects'" (NB, p. 60). Should we then say that everything we ordinarily take to be a name stands for an object? "From this it would now seem as if in a certain sense all names were *genuine names*. Or, as I might also say, as if all objects were in a certain sense simple objects" (NB, p. 61). That would return us to something like the super-realism of the early Moore and Russell. Another possibility is that names can stand for the most varied forms and that only the syntactical application of the sign determines whether we are naming a simple object. But, "what is the syntactical application of names of simple objects?" (NB, p. 59).

Given these considerations, it becomes clear why Wittgenstein does not seek to characterize the objects of the *Tractatus* in other than formal terms. His critical reflections on the analysis and representation narratives in the

Notebooks certainly makes it impossible for him to agree with Russell's version of logical atomism, according to which the simple objects are directly accessible to us and are, in fact, sense-data and their perceptible properties. It is true that Wittgenstein toys with that possibility in the *Notebooks*: "As examples of the simple I always think of points in the visual field (just as parts of the visual field always come before my mind as typical composite objects)" (NB, p. 45). And it is also true that a faint echo of this thought is still to be found in the *Tractatus* when he writes: "Space, time, and colour (colouredness) are forms of objects" (TLP, 2.0251). There is, however, little to suggest that he actually subscribed to Russell's view of the simples. In the *Notebooks* he considered that view only among other possibilities. Thus, he also entertained the thought that "the division of the body into *material points*, as we have it in physics, is nothing more than analysis into *simple components*" (NB, p. 67). But, in the end, he set all such speculations aside and opted for a purely formal characterization of the simple objects as the necessary end-points of analysis. He wrote accordingly:

> It would be vain to try to express the pseudo-sentence "are there simple things?" in symbolic notation. And yet it is clear that I have before me a concept of a thing, of simple correlation, when I think about this matter. But how am I imagining the simple? Here all I can say is always "'x' has reference." Here is a great riddle. (NB, p. 45)

And from this he concludes: "There doesn't after all seem to be any setting up of a kind of logical inventory as I formerly imagined" (NB, p. 66).

Such formulations have driven some interpreters to argue that for the Wittgenstein of the *Tractatus* the names of simple objects are nothing but placeholders, "dummy variables," whose only function is to indicate that the world has a certain multiplicity. These interpreters rely, in particular, on the assertion that when we abstract from their external properties, "objects of the same logical form are . . . differentiated only in that they are different" (TLP, 2.0233). Wittgenstein himself seems to have wavered between this possibility and an alternative view (expressed in his conversations in 1929 with the Vienna Circle) that the task of determining the nature of these objects had to be left to the empirical sciences.

The Critique of Logical Atomism

In his writings from the mid-1930s Wittgenstein began to explore the possibility that the notion of simplicity on which the doctrine of logical atomism rested might, in fact, be language-relative: that in one language one class of signs might count as simple names and in another language another class. By the time he wrote the *Philosophical Investigations*, he had, however given up on the whole idea of simple objects. He had become skeptical, in particular, of the idea that lies behind the doctrine of simple objects according to which thought or language is "the unique correlate, picture of the world" (PI, 96). This idea, we read in the *Investigations*, surrounds thought with a halo. The assumption that logic presents us with an order "which must be common to both world and thought" is nothing but an illusion generated by treating words like "world" and "thought" as "*super*-concepts." "But, if the words 'language,' 'experience,' 'world,' have a use, it must be as humble a one as that of the words 'table,' 'lamp,' 'door'" (PI, 97). In the *Philosophical Investigations* Wittgenstein directs, in fact, three sharp criticisms against the three supporting narratives of logical atomism.

The meaning of names. Wittgenstein aims his first arrow at the representation narrative. The *Tractatus*, he writes, had treated naming "as a *queer* connection of a word with an object" (PI, 38). According to it "a name ought really to signify a simple" (PI, 39). But this can be true only of a distinctive class of expressions which we may call "real" names. What we ordinarily take to be a "name" can never qualify as such. That much follows directly from the fundamental principles of the *Tractatus*. For assume that an ordinary, complex object had a name and that this object was the meaning of the name. On this assumption that name would lose its meaning when the object ceases to exist. But that is evidently not the case for ordinary "names." Such "names" must, therefore, really be implicit descriptions. Once we analyze our propositions ordinary names will disappear and if the analysis is complete we will have only names naming simples left over. On the view of the *Tractatus*: "It will be reasonable to call these words the real names." But the *Philosophical Investigations* reject this entire line of reasoning and they advocate instead the view that "the meaning of a word is its use in the language" (PI, 43). This allows Wittgenstein to conclude that a name for an object that has ceased to exist will still have a meaning as long as the name retains a use in the language. There is no need to distinguish real names from ordinary ones and no need to postulate simple, non-perishable objects as the correlates of real names.

The concept of simplicity. Wittgenstein's second arrow is directed against the concept of simplicity employed in the analysis narrative. He writes in the *Investigations*: "We use the word 'composite' (and therefore the word 'simple') in an enormous number of different and differently related ways" (PI, 47). We can ask, for instance, whether the ivory color of a square on a chessboard is simple or whether it consists of pure white and pure yellow. And we can ask more generally whether white is simple or consists of the colors of the rainbow. "Is this length of 2 cm. simple, or does it consist of two parts, each 1 cm. long? But why not of one bit 3 cm. long and one bit 1 cm. long measured in the opposite direction?" We must remember "that we are sometimes even inclined to conceive the smaller as the result of a composition of greater parts, and the greater as the result of a division of the smaller" (PI, 48). In sharp contrast to the *Tractatus* doctrine that "the object is simple," Wittgenstein asserts now that there is no such thing as absolute simplicity or absolute complexity. When we call something either simple or composite we do so always in relation to a certain standard or measure. "If I tell someone without further explanation: 'What I see before me now is composite,' he will have the right to ask: 'What do you mean by "composite"?' For there are all sorts of things that that can mean!" (PI, 47).

Indestructibility. Wittgenstein's third arrow is fired against the change narrative. The *Tractatus* had argued that there is something which must be indestructible and simple since everything composite can go out of existence by decomposition. In the *Philosophical Investigations* he objects that this is only a particular image that floats in our minds:

> For certainly experience does not show us these elements. We see *component parts* of something composite (of a chair, for instance). We say that the back is part of the chair, but is in turn itself composed of several kinds of wood; while a leg is a simple component part. We also see a whole which changes (is destroyed) while its components remain unchanged. These are the materials from which we construct that picture of reality. (PI, 59)

When we mention composite objects we are not really trying to say something about their simple parts. When I call for the broom, I am not calling for the stick and the brush attached to it. When I say something about a red object, I am not implicitly talking about "red itself" as something that cannot be destroyed.

The *Philosophical Investigations* do not try to lay out an alternative picture of the world to the one that I sketched in the *Tractatus*. Instead Wittgenstein limits himself now to showing that the logical atomist conception of reality is based on dubious assumptions about how language works. Despite the cogency of his critique, logical atomism has, however, by no means lost its charm for philosophers. It is, in fact, still in fashion – though not generally under its old name. Among its recent incarnations are various forms of "possible worlds" semantics and "possible worlds" metaphysics – both of which have roots in the *Tractatus*. We have seen that, according to the *Tractatus*, the world is the totality of facts; that each of these facts can in principle be described by a sentence; and that the world as a whole can thus be completely described by the totality of true sentences. "Possible worlds" semantics concludes that we can equally describe a possible world by means of a totality of possibly true sentences. "Possible worlds" metaphysics goes one step further in asserting that possible worlds exist in some sense and that there is thus not only a metaphysics of the actual world but also of possible worlds. Both "possible worlds" semantics and "possible worlds" metaphysics are committed to the idea that every possible world consists of objects to which certain properties are assigned in each of these worlds. The objects themselves conceived across worlds are, in other words, colorless and simple. The persistence of these forms of logical atomism points to the deep attraction of this kind of doctrine. How are we, after all, to think about the world, if we are not willing to subscribe to some form of monism? All forms of pluralism seem to lead back to the postulate that there are things and combinations of things in the world and that these things either have or lack certain properties and that they stand or do not stand in certain relations. Those assumptions are the simple, intuitive basis on which all forms of logical atomism are built.

The later Wittgenstein did not give in to those intuitions. In the *Philosophical Investigations* "the world" is mentioned only as the place where certain language games are played or not played (PI, 205). Late in life, Wittgenstein turned to the examination of "world-views" and "world pictures." A world picture, he wrote in his last notebooks, is above all "the substratum of all my enquiring and asserting," and the "matter-of-course foundation" of my research (OC, 162, 167). It provides a "system" of thought, of verification, of belief, of conviction, and even of doubt; it is within such a system that our daily thinking moves. We may say that he had moved, by this time, from a metaphysics of the world to a pragmatics of world pictures.

But the question remains whether we can do any kind of philosophy without some picture or other of the nature of our reality. The later Wittgenstein certainly made no more grand assertions about the world as a whole. But we might point out that he said all kinds of things about what there is in the world: physical bodies, actions, language games, etc. Does this not imply some kind of metaphysics? We can also, possibly, deduce a more comprehensive picture of reality from the way he describes the functioning of language in his later writings. This account of language certainly suggests an abandonment of the view that the world has a fixed structure; instead, there is the idea that what we see as the logical order of the world is actually created in our language games. The world appears from this perspective as a field of overlapping similarities that shade off in all kinds of directions, and it is on this wide-open field that we impose the more or less precise grid of our language. The image is attractive, but can we make sense of it? Do the requirements of human language not return us again and again to the idea that there are individual entities corresponding to our words and complexes to our sentences; that the world has, after all, a determinate structure whether we know of it or not?

Coda

Russell considered logical atomism important as a counter-position to Bradley's monism to which he had once adhered. It proved to him that reality consisted of many things rather than one. Wittgenstein's early adherence to logical atomism immunized him, similarly, against all varieties of monism: those advanced by Parmenides and Bradley but also the ones held by Spinoza and Schopenhauer. While Schopenhauer continued to interest him in other respects, Wittgenstein would never again be tempted to adopt Schopenhauer's metaphysical system after he had passed through the kitchen of Russell's logical atomism.

That atomism was, of course, pluralistic only in a very specific and narrow sense. It maintained that the world consisted of many individual objects and properties while it maintained at the same time that the world had a single logical structure. The later Wittgenstein became pluralistic in another and deeper sense. After his break with the *Tractatus* (and only after that) his understanding of language, thought, and world-views turned thoroughly pluralistic. In the end he reached the conclusion that logic has also a pluralistic character. In his final notes, he described it as the riverbed through which our thoughts move. "And the bank of that river consists partly of hard rock, subject to no alteration or only to an imperceptible one, partly of sand, which now in one place now in another gets washed away, or deposited" (OC, 99). It was true therefore that "there is also something like *another* arithmetic. I believe that this admission must underlie any understanding of logic" (OC, 375). But in order to understand that logic "you must look at the practice of language, then you will see it" (OC, 501), and that linguistic practice is certainly, according to the later Wittgenstein, multifold and variable and thoroughly human.

notes

1   Arthur Schopenhauer, *The World as Will and Representation*, translated by E.F.J. Payne (New York: Dover Publications, 1969), vol. 1, p. 3.

2   Schopenhauer, *World as Will and Representation*, p. 412.

3   For Wittgenstein's association of idealism with solipsism see *Notebooks*, p. 85, where he also writes that "idealism leads to realism if it is strictly thought out."

4   Schopenhauer, *World as Will and Representation*, p. 3.

5   Schopenhauer, *World as Will and Representation*, p. 128.

6   Bertrand Russell, "The Philosophy of Logical Atomism," in *Logic and Knowledge: Essays 1901–1950*, edited by Robert Charles Marsch (London: Allen & Unwin, 1956).

7   On this topic see P.M.S. Hacker's illuminating discussion in *Wittgenstein's Place in Twentieth-Century Analytic Philosophy* (Oxford: Blackwell, 1996). See also my essay, "What Has History to Do With Me? Wittgenstein and Analytic Philosophy," *Inquiry*, March 1998.

8   "Notes on Logic" (1913) in NB, p. 106.

9   Bertrand Russell, *The Principles of Mathematics*, 2nd edition (London: Allen & Unwin, 1956), pp. 42 and 47.

10 Russell, *Principles of Mathematics*, p. 43.

11 Russell, *Principles of Mathematics*, p. 44.

12 Russell, "Philosophy of Logical Atomism," p. 190.

13 Russell, "Philosophy of Logical Atomism," p. 178.

14 One needs to add that Wittgenstein would not have accepted the characterization of this view of meaning as a "theory" since he writes in the *Tractatus* that "philosophy is not a theory but an activity" (TLP, 4.112).

15 Russell's change of mind is recorded in "The Philosophy of Logical Atomism," where he writes, for instance: "I do not suppose there is in the world a single disjunctive fact corresponding to 'p or q'" (p. 209).

16 Parmenides, *Poem*, Fragment 8, cited in G.S. Kirk and J.E. Raven, *The Presocratic Philosophers* (Cambridge: Cambridge University Press, 1964), p. 276.

17 Aristotle, *On Generation and Corruption*, A 8, 325a; cited in Kirk and Raven, *Presocratic Philosophers*, pp. 404–405.

18 Plato, *Theaetetus*, 201e.

19 Gottfried Leibniz, "Monadology," in *Selections*, edited by Philip P. Wiener (New York: Scribner's, 1951), section 2.

20 Gottfried Leibniz, "Dialogue on the Connection Between Things and Words," in *Selections*, p. 10.

further reading

Griffin, James. *Wittgenstein's Logical Atomism*. Oxford: Clarendon Press, 1964.

Mounce, H.O. *Wittgenstein's Tractatus: An Introduction*. Chicago: University of Chicago Press, 1981.

the limits of language

According to its preface, the *Tractatus* means to "draw a limit to thinking, or rather – not to thinking, but to the expression of thoughts" in order to show in this way that philosophical problems arise from "a misunderstanding of the logic of our language." Wittgenstein is convinced that those problems cannot be properly posed given the limits of language and "what lies on the other side of the limit will be simply nonsense" (TLP, p. 27). But, having announced this radical theme, he leaves the curious reader to work himself through half of the book before he addresses the matter any further. First he outlines the structure of the world (TLP, 1–2.063), then more extensively that of language (TLP, 2.1–4.0641), and only at 4.1 does he return to question of the limits of language and the limitations of philosophy. "The purpose of philosophy" (i.e., the right kind of philosophy, not the mistaken one he combats) "is the logical clarification of thoughts," he declares at 4.112. This may not as yet sound controversial, but the bombshell comes in the next sentence: "Philosophy is not a body of doctrine but an activity" (TLP, 4.112). So, what are we to make of the close to 300 dogmatic assertions that have preceded this remark, assertions about facts, states of affairs, and objects, about picturing and meaning, thoughts, propositions, and names? It appears now that "philosophy does not result in 'philosophical propositions,' but rather in the clarification of propositions" and that philosophical work consists therefore essentially of "elucidations" (ibid.). Does Wittgenstein then deny that his assertions in the first half of the *Tractatus* are "philosophical propositions"? Are they intended to be merely "elucidations"?

We may be puzzled even further when we discover that after this discussion of the limits of language and philosophy, Wittgenstein returns at 4.2 to making more apodictic assertions about logic. It is only in section 6 of the *Tractatus* that he comes back once more to the theme of the limits of language. And then he does so with a breathtaking final, rhetorical flourish: "My propositions are elucidatory in this way: he who understands me finally recognizes

wittgenstein, First Edition. Hans Sluga.
© 2011 Hans Sluga. Published 2011 by Blackwell Publishing Ltd.

them as senseless, when he has climbed out through them, on them, over them. (He must so to speak throw away the ladder, after he has climbed up on it.) He must surmount these propositions; then he sees the world rightly" (TLP, 6.54).

How to Read the *Tractatus*

Philosophers attracted to metaphysical speculation and to logical atomism, in particular, have tended to ignore or dismiss this concluding broadside. Bertrand Russell, who had himself a vested interest in the issue, wrote ironically: "What causes hesitation is the fact that, after all, Mr. Wittgenstein manages to say a good deal about what cannot be said" (TLP, p. 22). It is, indeed, not easy to reconcile the skeptical conclusion of the *Tractatus* with its dogmatic beginning. Had Wittgenstein not said in his preface that "the *truth* of the thoughts communicated here seems to me unassailable and definitive"? (TLP, p. 29). How can Wittgenstein's assertions be at once unassailably true and senseless? His interpreters have rightly been befuddled by this question.

Three different readings of the *Tractatus* have in consequence emerged. The first, "metaphysical," reading holds that Wittgenstein means, after all, to develop a full-blooded theory of logical atomism and that his retraction of it in the last parts of the book should simply be ignored. The second, "transcendental," reading concludes in accordance with Wittgenstein's final remarks that the first sentences of the book are, indeed, strictly senseless but it claims that these remarks point nevertheless at something true. Those who interpret Wittgenstein along this line draw attention to his assertion that "there is indeed the inexpressible. This *shows* itself" (TLP, 6.522), and in the accompanying statement: "What *can* be shown, *cannot* be said" (TLP, 4.1212). Could it be that metaphysics belongs in this category? Thus Wittgenstein asserts that the "truth" of solipsism – clearly a metaphysical doctrine – shows itself. "In fact what solipsism *means*, is quite correct," he writes, "only it cannot be said, but it must show itself" (TLP, 5.62). So, is logical atomism – and, indeed, the entire metaphysics of the *Tractatus* – true after all even though the attempt to express it in words must fail? This solution, unfortunately, simply circumvents the radical conclusion which the *Tractatus* ultimately reaches; it does nothing to defuse it. The third, "resolute," (i.e., radically positivist) reading of the book argues that there is nothing true either said or shown in the first sentences of the *Tractatus*, that they are meant to exemplify, rather, typical metaphysical nonsense of the kind Wittgenstein wants to dismantle. But this reading cannot easily account for the assertive tone of the initial passages of the work. It is forced to admit, moreover, that not all the propositions of the *Tractatus* are strictly senseless (TLP, 6.53). If they were, then proposition 6.53 would itself also have to be senseless. There are, in any case, many assertions in the *Tractatus* (for instance, about the structure of propositions) that sound as if Wittgenstein actually took them to be pointing at something that is the case. Finally, the resolute reading must explain why Wittgenstein reasserts the doctrine of logical atomism once more around 1930 with the proviso that his statements were meant "to have the value only of elucidations" and "circumscriptions."[1]

There might be still another possibility. The interpreters may be wrong in assuming that the *Tractatus* means to give us a single, coherent "system" of thought, a comprehensive conception of "the world" from a totalizing perspective. Every such reading is forced to downplay Wittgenstein's energetic assertion that philosophy is not a theory but an activity. When we put Wittgenstein's writings from the time before the *Tractatus* side by side with his book we discover, in fact, that the finished text follows roughly the course of his thinking from 1911 to 1918. In the earliest notes he appears fully committed to the metaphysics of logical atomism. But already by June 1915 he has come to have serious doubts about details of that program. Russell's version of the picture conception of meaning comes under scrutiny; Russell's belief that we can actually determine the logical form of atomic propositions comes to be questioned; Russell's conception of simple objects as "sense-data" and their properties is dismantled. In the last of the preparatory notebooks in 1916, Wittgenstein's thoughts have turned to reflections on God and the world, happiness, sin, and suicide, ethics, aesthetics, and the meaning of life. In a letter to his friend Engelmann from April 1917 there appears for the first time also the idea of the limits of language and the importance of the unsayable.

Should we then read the *Tractatus* as recording a course of thinking rather than the characterization of a single, systematic philosophical viewpoint? Is the book in essence a "Pilgrim's Progress"? As such it would correspond to the organization of Schopenhauer's *World as Will and Representation*, which moves in a parallel fashion from empirical to metaphysical knowledge of the world, then from aesthetic to ethical experience, and finally to philosophical silence as differentiated steps on the road to liberation from suffering. Such a biographical interpretation will, however, still need to determine what the successive stages of Wittgenstein's thinking are, how we are to look at each step from the perspective of the later ones.

Recognizing Metaphysics as Senseless

Logical atomism turns out to be problematic in the *Tractatus* because the concepts in which it is cast prove to be pseudo-concepts. "The world" may look grammatically like a name and the first proposition of the *Tractatus* may look like an ordinary subject–predicate sentence. But the linguistic surface form is misleading in both respects. "The world" does not, in effect, name an object with determinate properties. All we can legitimately do is to enumerate the propositions that describe the facts in their totality, for "The specification of all true elementary propositions describes the world completely" (TLP,

4.26). In addition the concepts of *object, thing, entity, complex, fact, function, number* are all are "pseudo-concepts" whose use leads to "senseless pseudo-propositions" (TLP, 4.1272). It follows that utterances like "Objects form the substance of the world" and "A fact is the existence of a combination of objects," and finally "The world is the totality of facts" will all be pseudo-propositions. One cannot even meaningfully say "There are objects" or speak of the totality or "the number of all objects." The first sentence of the *Tractatus* and the ones that follow are thus all philosophical monstrosities.

Wittgenstein's concern with pseudo-concepts can be traced back to Frege's characterization of the distinction between concepts and objects. In words that would have sounded attractive to the early Wittgenstein, Frege had argued in his 1892 essay on the topic that "one cannot require that everything shall be defined, any more than one can require that a chemist shall decompose every substance. What is simple cannot be decomposed, and what is logically simple cannot have a proper definition." Adding that what is logically simple is never given at the outset and can only be reached through scientific work, he notes: "On the introduction of a name for something simple, a definition is not possible; there is nothing for it but to lead the reader or hearer, by means of hints, to understand the words as is intended."[2] Frege was, however, no logical atomist in Russell's or Wittgenstein's sense. He certainly never postulated simple objects as the substance of the world. The simples he had in mind in the passage just quoted were, rather, the notions of object and concept themselves. The distinction between those two, he went on to write in his essay, was, in fact, "of the highest importance."[3] It involved, we might say, a difference in "logical form." "A concept (as I understand the word) is predicative. [It is, in fact, the meaning of a grammatical predicate.] On the other hand, the name of an object, a proper name, is quite incapable of being used as a grammatical predicate."[4] Frege took this to imply, in particular, that "what is being said concerning a concept does not suit an object."[5] If concepts and objects are of different logical form – if they belong, as we might put it, to different "categories" – then there will (on Frege's account) be no predicate that can be meaningfully applied to both. And this implies, of course, that the distinction between them is indefinable and, indeed, indescribable and in this sense, logically simple.

Assume, as is natural, that "x is an object" can be meaningfully predicated of objects. But then, by assumption, it cannot be predicated of concepts. Whenever we meaningfully predicate "x is an object" of something it will be trivially true that it is an object. This also means we can't use that predicate to discriminate between objects and concepts. The same thing holds of the predicate "x is a concept." In this case it is natural to suppose that the predicate can meaningfully be applied to concepts. But then it cannot meaningfully be predicated of objects. And so that predicate can also not be used to characterize the distinction between concepts and objects. And any other attempt to describe this distinction will run into the same difficulty. Language proves here systematically inadequate for the task of drawing a distinction that is nonetheless of the highest importance. "By a kind of necessity of language my expressions, taken literally, sometimes miss my thought; I mention an object, when what is intended is a concept. I was relying upon a reader who would be ready to meet me half-way – who does not begrudge a pinch of salt."[6]

Russell had found these ideas paradoxical and entirely unacceptable when he reviewed Frege's work in his *Principles of Mathematics*. He had held, instead, that every term can be the subject of every possible predicate. He denied, in other words, that there was any distinction of logical form between concepts and objects. But this, he discovered, soon leads to contradictions. To avoid these, Russell saw himself forced to rework Frege's distinction between objects and concepts into a theory of types according to which every entity belongs to a specific logical type and a concept can be predicated only of an entity of the next lower type. One consequence of this doctrine is that the theory cannot be stated in terms compatible with that theory. This was something that Wittgenstein had first mentioned to Russell in 1913 when he wrote that "every theory of types must be rendered superfluous by a proper theory of symbolism," and to Moore a year later that "a THEORY of *types* is impossible" (NB, pp. 122, 109). The same observation is implicit in Wittgenstein's words in the *Tractatus* (TLP, 3.332).

Despite his insistence that Frege and Russell failed to understand this point, Wittgenstein was in reality only reformulating and radicalizing their ideas. What he writes about formal concepts in the *Tractatus* – which he also calls pseudo-concepts – is, in fact, fully in line with the ideas of his two predecessors. This is evident from 4.12721, where we read: "The formal concept is already given with an object, which falls under it. One cannot, therefore, introduce both the objects which fall under a formal concept *and* the formal concept itself, as primitive ideas."

The error of metaphysics (which inevitably employs the notions of object and concept) is then that it uses formal concepts as if they were proper ones. Another way of putting this point is that metaphysics fails to appreciate the nature of categorical distinctions and tries to make comprehensive statements about items that belong to different logical categories – if only to say that they are of different categories. But categorical distinctions can show themselves only in the differential functioning of our words. They cannot become subject to substantive theoretical assertions. In trying to speak about the world in its totality, metaphysics is forced to ignore and bypass the boundaries of categorical distinctions. That mistake is particularly evident in the first sentences of the *Tractatus*: "The world is everything that is the case. The world is the totality of facts, not of things. The world is determined by the facts, and by these being *all* the facts." The prominence of the words "everything," "totality," and "all" reveals that the metaphysical picture of the world these sentences seek to describe is in conflict with the logic of our language.

Logic as Mirror of the World

For Russell and the pre-*Tractatus* Wittgenstein metaphysics and logic were intimately connected. Their atomism was based, after all, on entirely logical considerations and so was the monism that they sought to oppose. It is not surprising then that Wittgenstein would consider logic the basis of metaphysics. But as metaphysics was becoming more doubtful to him, the link between logic and metaphysics was also becoming more problematic. The abandonment of metaphysics could hardly mean the abandonment of logic. One indication of this loosening bond between metaphysics and logic is found in the assertion that there are no distinctive numbers in logic and that "therefore there is no philosophical monism, dualism, etc." (TLP, 4.128). Presumably, then, there is also no such thing as a philosophical pluralism of the sort that logical atomism is meant to be.

While Wittgenstein was abandoning the idea that metaphysics could be derived from logic, he certainly did not believe that logic needed in turn metaphysical foundations. Instead, he said repeatedly that "logic must take care of itself" (TLP, 5.473). That statement marks, in fact, the beginning of Wittgenstein's wartime notebook and is called there "an extremely profound and important insight" (NB, p. 2). In this passage Wittgenstein goes on to link that insight to the observation that "the whole theory of things, properties, etc., is superfluous" for logic (ibid.). And he complains that Frege and Russell are mistaken in treating their logics as theories of objects and functions, value ranges and classes. Further consequences of his insight are that "every possible sentence is well-formed," that "every well-formed sentence must make sense," and that "it must therefore in a certain sense be impossible for us to go wrong in logic" (ibid.). Finally, it follows for him that "the task of philosophy" must be other than Russell and he himself had once thought. Then they had worried, for instance, over the question whether there are facts "of the subject–predicate form," but if logic takes care of itself then "everything that needs to be shown is shown by the existence of subject predicate SENTENCES" (NB, p. 3). In other words: Russell's and Wittgenstein's concern with the ontology of facts was pointless. The passage concludes with a restatement of the crucial assertion: "Logic takes care of itself; all we have to do is to look and see how it does it" (NB, p. 10).

But to see this proved extremely difficult. There are, however, a number of propositions in the *Tractatus* that can help us to get closer to the meaning of this epigram. First and foremost is the claim that "logic is not a theory" and that it is "transcendental" (TLP, 6.13). Wittgenstein has undoubtedly borrowed the term "transcendental" here from Kant's philosophy. Like Kant he seeks to distinguish between the empirical and the non-empirical; like Kant he rejects any attempt to treat logic as an empirical science and logical truths as high-level generalizations of an empirical kind. Frege – who had in turn been influenced on this point by Kant – was also evidently in Wittgenstein's mind. But Wittgenstein goes further than Kant and Frege. Where Kant had thought it possible to construct a transcendental philosophy as a supplement and foundation for empirical science, Wittgenstein identifies the transcendental with the unsayable. And where Frege had spoken of logical truths as substantive, Wittgenstein considered them to be saying nothing. The transcendental lies for Wittgenstein, therefore, outside the boundary of what we can theorize about but also outside the boundary of the substantively true.

The prime target of Wittgenstein's criticism is, however, Russell. Russell's theory of types had spoken of concepts and classes as stratified into separate types and had then proceeded to construct a logical notation to reflect such type distinctions. The *Tractatus* objects that "in logical syntax the meaning of a sign ought never to play a role" (TLP, 3.33). While he does not dispute the need for type distinctions, Wittgenstein believes that these must be embodied in the form of the expressions themselves and that they must not require explanation in terms of concepts, functions, and classes. The signs of a properly constructed language must, in other words, rule out the very possibility of type confusions. Wittgenstein illustrates the point with the observation that "no proposition can say anything about itself because the propositional sign cannot be contained in itself" and he claims that this is, in effect, what the whole so-called "theory" of types actually comes to (TLP, 3.332).

He is also critical of what he takes to be Frege's and Russell's undue reliance on the notion that logic is based on self-evidence. It is language itself which must prevent logical mistakes. Logic is a priori not because its truths are self-evident but because "we *cannot* think illogically" (TLP, 5.4731). Frege's and Russell's error is to assume that the laws of logic have substantive content and that they state certain very general facts. Logical laws are for Wittgenstein, by contrast, mere "tautologies." The term, borrowed from Fritz Mauthner, refers literally to something of the form "a = a," where the same object is mentioned twice, and by extension to such propositions as "a = b" and "b = a" which are equivalent because they say, in effect, the same thing twice over. On Wittgenstein's view all logical truths are essentially of this kind. As early as 1913, he had written to Russell: "All propositions of logic are generalizations of tautologies" (NB, p. 128). They are therefore not pictures of reality. They present no possible state of affairs, for they allow "every possible state of affairs." In the tautology "the conditions of agreement with the world – the depicting relations – cancel one another, so that it stands in no depicting relation to reality" (TLP, 4.462). Tautologies are, in fact, "the limiting cases of the combinations of symbols," they are empty by-products of our symbolic notation. Wittgenstein succeeds in making this plausible in the *Tractatus* for the truths of propositional logic, but he has considerable difficulty in maintaining his thesis for the logic of universal and existential propositions. Set theory resists even more such a reductive treatment. Wittgenstein solves that problem by drastically declaring the theory of classes "altogether superfluous" (TLP, 6.031). And where Frege and Russell had sought to show that arithmetic – or mathematics in general – consists of logical truths and would thus have to be tautologies, on Wittgenstein's view mathematics is only "a logical method" and its equations are "pseudo-propositions" rather than tautologies (TLP, 6.2).

The principle that logic must take care of itself lies behind all these assertions. Its final and most challenging implication is that there can be no theorizing about logic, no theory of truth, and more generally, no theory concerning the logical syntax and semantics of our language. This is a challenging and controversial claim. Even Russell, who is otherwise complimentary of Wittgenstein's achievement of "work of extraordinary difficulty and importance," finds this to be doubtful. In his introduction to the *Tractatus* he grants Wittgenstein that every language has a structure "concerning which, *in the language*, nothing can be said." But he goes on to argue that "there may be another language dealing with the structure of the first language, and having itself a new structure, and that to this hierarchy of language there may be no limit" (TLP, p. 23). Russell never elaborated this suggestion. That was left to Alfred Tarski. But he is clear about why Wittgenstein would not in any case accept his proposal since he believed himself to be concerned with the totality of languages – with "*the* language which I understand" (TLP, 5.62) – and not simply with one level or layer of this totality. Russell concludes: "The only retort would be to deny that there is any such totality" (TLP, p. 23).

The Self, the Subject, the I

Wittgenstein's attitude toward metaphysics remained uniformly hostile, even after he had abandoned the particular objections to it that he had voiced in the *Tractatus*. Later on he told his students that the problem with metaphysics was the fact that philosophers are blinded by the method of science and are constantly tempted to imitate it: "This tendency is the real source of metaphysics and leads the philosopher into complete darkness" (BB, p. 18). Still later, he objected that metaphysical propositions employ words of ordinary language in an inappropriate manner. "When philosophers use a word . . . and try to grasp the *essence* of the thing, one must always ask oneself: is the word ever used in this way in the language game which is its original home?" And he saw it now as his task to bring words "back from their metaphysical to their everyday use" (PI, 116).

Wittgenstein's attitude toward logic also underwent change. He remained resistant to the thought that logic might be a science but no longer spoke of it as a transcendental mirror of the world. He questioned, instead, the assumption that logic is "something sublime" (PI, 89) and dismissed the idea of the "crystalline purity of logic" as a mere postulate (PI, 107). According to that later view "the philosophy of logic speaks of sentences and words in exactly the sense in which we speak of them in ordinary life" (PI, 108). This clearly implied a much broader, less formal, and more flexible notion of logic than the one he had relied on in the *Tractatus*. As a consequence there could now be for him even alternative kinds of logic and alternative forms of arithmetic (OC, 375).

All these considerations bear, of course, on the understanding of our social and political situation. Conceptions of social and political life are frequently justified by appeal to some metaphysical view or other. If Wittgenstein is right, such appeals do not carry real weight. They are merely restatements of the social and political attitudes they are said to undergird and are often used as rhetorical tools in social and political struggles. Wittgenstein's views on logic also have relevance to the way we must think about social and political matters. While the *Tractatus* still maintained the classical view that there is *one* logic with an absolute, unconditioned validity that privileges science, his later philosophy of logic undermined both the assumed privilege of scientific discourse and the belief in a single, unconditioned form of human rationality.

Of potentially equal significance is Wittgenstein's examination of the human self, "the subject" or "I" – a topic that has, of course, been of the greatest interest to philosophers for both metaphysical and ethical reasons. Distancing himself from positive conceptions of the self such as those advanced by Descartes, Kant, and Russell and aligning himself, instead, with deconstructive views of the self held by Schopenhauer and Ernst Mach, he asserts unconditionally that "the thinking, representing subject does not exist" (TLP, 5.631). His claim is that such a self would have to have incompatible properties. On the one hand, it would have to be a simple substance since "a composite soul would no longer be a soul" (TLP, 5.5421). On the other, it would also have to be complex in order to be able to represent or think anything at all (the presupposition here being that only a complex can represent another complex).

What Wittgenstein writes on this topic connects to his broader concern with the possibility of a philosophical psychology. In his first years at Cambridge, he had actually engaged in some psychological experimentation. But in the *Tractatus* he had set empirical psychology aside as being of no more interest to philosophy than any other natural science (TLP, 4.1121). At the same time, he had turned against any form of philosophical psychology. He had been particularly scathing about the theory of knowledge – an area of traditional philosophy that he dismissed as being merely "the philosophy of psychology." The barb was directed most of all at Russell who had been at work on a book on epistemology when Wittgenstein first appeared in Cambridge. Wittgenstein's criticism of it was so withering that Russell finally abandoned it in despair. Wittgenstein had been particularly agitated over Russell's postulation of a self or I as necessary for understanding perception and thought. On Russell's account there had to be an I that *has* sense-data and an I that holds the elements of a proposition together in thought. Russell based this conclusion on the thought that propositions are not real unities and that the elements of a proposition can be held together only by some mind when it entertains the proposition. In agreement with Frege, Wittgenstein, on the other hand, was disposed to conceive of a proposition as a unity which does not depend on a thinking or judging subject. A proposition is essentially articulate and as such is "not a blend of words" (TLP, 3.141). In the proposition there exists, rather, a "nexus" between the signs. "Only in the nexus of a proposition does a name have meaning" (TLP, 3.3).

But why was Wittgenstein so confident that there is no such thing as the subject? While he does not always argue for the claims he makes in the *Tractatus*, he actually seeks to provide reasons for this one (TLP, 5.54–5.55). But even then his argument is highly condensed and quite difficult to figure out. The argument starts from the bold assertion that "propositions occur in other propositions only as bases of truth-operations" (TLP, 5.54). The truth or falsity of a complex proposition is, in other words, completely determined by the truth and falsity of its component propositions. As Wittgenstein had put it earlier in the *Tractatus*: "The expression of the agreement and disagreement with the truth-possibilities of the elementary propositions expresses the truth-conditions of the proposition" (TLP, 4.431). He credits Frege for this insight in this passage and this reference is useful because it draws our attention to the truth-functional logic of Frege's *Begriffsschrift*.

In that work Frege had shown how the truth-conditions of negative, conjunctive, disjunctive, and even hypothetical propositions can be explained in terms of the truth-conditions of their components, and he had extended this account even to universal and existential propositions. Frege had concluded from this that the concept of truth is fundamental to logic and that logic is concerned with unfolding the concept of truth. This was the point at which Wittgenstein most agreed with his mentor. In his notes to Russell in 1913, he wrote therefore of the "bi-polarity" of propositions (their capacity for being either true or false) as fundamental to logic. And in the *Tractatus* he said: "The proposition determines reality to this extent, that one only needs to say 'Yes' or 'No' to it to make it agree with reality. Reality must therefore be completely described by the proposition" (TLP, 4.023). But Wittgenstein was willing to go far beyond Frege in maintaining that all *logical* relations between propositions are truth-functional.

He has to admit, though, that "at first sight it looks as if it were also possible for one proposition to occur in another in a different way" (TLP, 5.541). He granted, in particular, that "certain forms of proposition in psychology" appear to contradict his thesis. Consider, thus, any proposition of the form "A believes that p" where "A" is meant to stand for a thinking and believing subject and "p" for a proposition. The truth or falsity of that proposition is certainly independent of that of "p." The most straightforward response to this situation would, of course, be to abandon the truth-functionality thesis or to restrict the scope of its validity. The latter was, in fact, the line of reasoning Frege had followed. He had argued that the truth and falsity of the complex proposition "John believes that p" is not a function of the truth and falsity of p but of what he called the sense of the proposition p. If p expresses the thought that it is raining, then "John believes that p" will be true, if John entertains that thought. But this required a distinction between the sense and the reference of a proposition that Wittgenstein was not willing to make. Instead, he insisted that the apparent counter-examples must be analyzed in accordance with the truth-functionality thesis. In order to maintain this one would have to distinguish, however, between the apparent and the real form of propositions. This was in tune with his earlier observation: "Language disguises thought. So much so, that from the outward form of the clothing it is impossible to infer the form of the thought beneath it" (TLP, 4.002). In discussing the apparent counter-examples to the truth-functionality thesis he contrasted what those propositions look like "if they are superficially considered" with their real logical form (TLP, 5.541 and 5.542). Superficially the proposition "A thinks that p is the case," he granted, looks "as if the proposition p stood in some kind of relation to an object A" (TLP, 5.541). But in reality that was not its true logical form.

Wittgenstein turned at this point to his critique of Russell's epistemology. "Modern theory of knowledge" of the kind endorsed by Russell takes the superficial appearance of these propositions to display their real logical form (TLP, 5.541). Such theorizing is tainted by a pervasive philosophical flaw since "most of the propositions and questions of philosophers arise from our failure to understand the logic of our language" (TLP, 4.003). Against Russell, Wittgenstein declares it to be clear "that 'A believes that p' and 'A says p' are of the form ' "p" says p' " (TLP, 5.542). In order to understand that remark we must note that the proposition " 'p' says p" expresses a relation between the proposition "p" and the situation p. But what kind of relation? Wittgenstein characterizes it elsewhere in the *Tractatus* in the words: "This proposition represents such and such situation" (TLP, 4.031). He also says that in order for the proposition "p" to succeed in this task of representation, it must have some structure to it. "It is only in so far as a proposition is logically articulated that it is a picture of a situation" (TLP, 4.032). In fact, the proposition and the situation must, in some way, be equivalent to each other. "In a proposition there must be exactly as many distinguishable parts as in the situation that it represents. The two must possess the same logical (mathematical) multiplicity" (TLP, 4.04). The articulated proposition is for Wittgenstein itself a fact – that is, something in which the elements hang together like links in a chain (TLP, 3.14). The sentence " 'p' says p" thus expresses for him a relation between a fact (i.e., the proposition) and a situation that has the same logical multiplicity. As he says in the passage under discussion, the sentence "does not involve a correlation of a fact with an object, but rather the correlation of facts by means of the correlation of their objects" (TLP, 5.542).

Two things follow from this analysis as far as Wittgenstein is concerned. The first is that the unity of the proposition cannot be sought in the thinking subject that Russell had postulated. Russell's account is unsatisfactory in particular because it cannot explain why only certain combinations of words form propositions. In Wittgenstein's words, "A correct explanation of the form of the proposition 'A makes the judgment p,' must show that it is impossible for a judgment to be a piece of nonsense. (Russell's theory does not satisfy that requirement.)" (TLP, 5.5421). Since for Russell the unity of the proposition is brought about by a subject holding its components together in consciousness, the elements "drinks," "eats," "merry" should under appropriate conditions form the content of a meaningful proposition, which they clearly do not.

Wittgenstein's second conclusion is that the subject cannot be conceived in Cartesian terms as both simple and representing (i.e., thinking, believing, judging etc.). These two characteristics, which the classical modern tradition from Descartes through Leibniz to Russell has taken to go together, are, in fact, not compatible. In order for some A to represent a state of affairs B, A must have the same complexity as B. And with this observation Wittgenstein cuts through the Gordian knot of the modern conception of the subject. But for Wittgenstein the alternative that the thinking subject might be complex is as absurd as the alternative that it might be simple. Since a representing, thinking subject can be neither simple nor composite, Wittgenstein sees himself justified in concluding "that there is no such thing as the soul" (TLP, 5.5421).

This can hardly be called a proof, since the premise that the soul cannot be composite is not argued for. And it is, in fact, not clear that Wittgenstein means to be giving a proof. When he says, "This shows too that there is no such thing as the soul," we need not understand the word "shows" to mean the same as "proves"; we may take the sentence instead to be saying that what he has argued makes once again evident that there is no such thing as the soul. Such a reading fits the fact that he ascribes belief in a soul to "the superficial psychology of the present day." And this "psychology" – which we may want to interpret literally here as a theory of the psyche, that is, of the soul or the subject – had already been dismissed earlier as irrelevant to philosophy.

But having reached this conclusion, Wittgenstein now adds, surprisingly, that there exists nevertheless a "metaphysical subject," "a philosophical I" as "the limit – not a part of the world" (TLP, 5.641). He links this commitment to a metaphysical self to a form of solipsism for which "the world and life are one" (TLP, 5.621). He says therefore also summarily: "I am my world" (TLP, 5.63). These formulations echo ones that are to be found in Schopenhauer's *World as Will and Representation*. They are also characteristic of ideas in Otto Weininger's *Sex and Character*, a book that served as another philosophical reference point to Wittgenstein. Wittgenstein derives his justification of this peculiar doctrine from the observation that the character of "the world" reveals itself to me only in and through language. This language is, however, (only) *my* language. *The* world turns out to be, therefore, *my* world. Wittgenstein imagines in this context a book with the title "The world as I found it" and he goes on to say that in this book we might be talking about everything in the world but there would be no mention of a thinking subject. "This would then be a method of isolating the subject or rather of showing that in an important sense there is no subject" (TLP, 5.631). The decisive point is, of course, that the book in question concerns the world "as *I* found it" and that this I reappears here therefore only as a "metaphysical subject" which is, however, "not the man, not the human body or the human soul" but precisely the limit of the world.

Even as he makes these pronouncements Wittgenstein is, however, fully aware of their dubiousness. They clearly belong to the senseless utterances in the *Tractatus*. And this for a number of reasons. First among them is that talk about the metaphysical subject requires us to speak of "the world" – which we have already recognized to be a pseudo-concept. Thus, everything we may want to say about the metaphysical subject turns out to be inevitably a pseudo-proposition. Wittgenstein concludes: "The key to the question, to what extent solipsism is a truth" is (as I have already quoted) that "what solipsism *means* is quite correct, only it cannot be *said*, but it shows itself" (TLP, 5.62). Here he seems to come close to the doctrine that there are unspeakable truths. But it should be noted that Wittgenstein does not say what it is that shows itself as the truth of solipsism. That "truth" may, after all, not be propositional in nature but instead lie embedded in the practice of our language.

It would be easy to dismiss all this as a piece of "metaphysical nonsense." But that leaves the question why Wittgenstein should have felt compelled to utter that nonsense in such an apodictic fashion. We must ask, rather, what drove him to make these peculiar assertions. The answer may be found in the following sentence: "That the world is *my* world, shows itself in the fact that the limits of the language (*the* language which I understand) mean the limits of *my* world" (TLP, 5.62). This suggests that it all comes down to the question in what sense the language I know is *my* language. This is not something for which the Wittgenstein of the *Tractatus* has a full answer because the book speaks of language for the most part as a wholly anonymous structure of signs. We hear almost nothing about who speaks this language, from where it has come, how it has been acquired, how it is used, how it is used in human intercourse. The language of the *Tractatus* hangs, so to say, in an airless space. Wittgenstein's remarks on solipsism in the *Tractatus* are perhaps in the end best understood as expressions of his inability in this period to come to terms with the reality of our language. It will be quite some time before Wittgenstein himself came to recognize this.

Ethics

The first proposition of the *Tractatus*, with its assertion that the world is everything that is the case, has important philosophical consequences. The most important of these is that values are excluded from the world. In other words, the world is, for Wittgenstein, a totality of "bare" facts. "In the world everything is as it is and happens as it does happen. *In* it there is no value . . . " (TLP, 6.41). The separation of fact and value is, of course, not Wittgenstein's invention. Both neo-Kantian and positivist philosophers had asserted it before him. The former took values to be transcendental while the latter thought of them as merely subjective colorings of the objective facts. The Wittgenstein of the *Tractatus* appears closer to the neo-Kantians than to the positivists on this point. According to him, "the sense of the world must lie outside the world" (TLP, 6.41) and "ethics is transcendental" (TLP, 6.421). But he draws more radical conclusions from that view than the neo-Kantians. They thought that the fact–value distinction cleared the way for a philosophical theory of value distinct from empirical science, that it made room for a philosophical science of value. Wittgenstein had no such illusions. He writes in a strictly anti-neo-Kantian spirit: "The true method of philosophy would be this. To say nothing except what can be said, i.e., the propositions of natural science, i.e., something that has nothing to do with philosophy" (TLP, 6.53). This was not meant, however, to dismiss questions of ethics and values. But there could on his view be no philosophical theory or science concerning these questions. To one correspondent he wrote: "My work consists of two parts: of the one which is here, and of everything which I have *not* written. And precisely this second part is the important one. For the Ethical is delimited from within, as it were, by my book; and I'm convinced that, *strictly* speaking, it can ONLY be delimited in this way."[7] Still later he would declare: "I can only describe my feeling by the metaphor, that, if a man could write a book on Ethics which really was a book on Ethics, this book would, with an explosion, destroy all the other books in the world" (LE, p. 40).

The *Tractatus* not only refuses to talk about values but it is also silent about other human things such as art, culture, or history; and it certainly tells us nothing about the troubles of the time in which Wittgenstein wrote his book: the bloodshed and murder of World War I, the madness and the suffering that Wittgenstein himself went through, the collapse of the entire historical order that he witnessed. Those were deliberate omissions. Hermann Broch, who lived through the same circumstances, was led to conclude in the end that the world has no logic.[8] The Wittgenstein of the *Tractatus* held on to the contrary belief. Behind all the madness he could still discern the same logic of the world that Parmenides and Plato, Leibniz and Russell had seen before him. "The life of knowledge," he wrote in his notebook, "is the life that is happy in spite of the misery of the world" (NB, p. 81).

How metaphysics, logic, and psychology are affected by the discovery that there are limits to what can be said was, no doubt, of interest to Wittgenstein. But the question of the limits of language gained its ultimate, existential significance for him only as he turned to ethics and aesthetics and to a concern with the meaning of life and the mystical. Those were, indeed, the topics to which the exposition of the *Tractatus* dramatically led up to in its final pages. "It is clear that ethics cannot be expressed . . . Ethics and aesthetics are one . . . The solution of the problem of life is seen in the vanishing of this problem . . . There is indeed the inexpressible. This *shows* itself; it is the mystical" (TLP, 6.421, 6.521, 6.522). It would, however, be a mistake to reduce the *Tractatus* to the status of an ethical treatise. We need to take equally seriously what Wittgenstein says in the course of the work about metaphysics, logic, psychology, and other philosophical matters. But its ultimate drift is clearly toward the ethical and toward the consequences for life that arise from the discovery that there are limits to meaningful language.

How strongly he felt on this matter is made evident in a "Lecture on Ethics" which Wittgenstein delivered at Cambridge in 1929, ten years after the completion of the *Tractatus* yet still very much under its influence. He says in that lecture that he wants to talk to his audience "about something I am keen on communicating" (LE, p. 39). His message is that "the tendency of all men who have ever tried to talk Ethics or Religion was to run against the boundaries of language," that this "running against the walls of our cage is perfectly, absolutely hopeless," and that ethics "so far as it springs from the desire to say something about the ultimate meaning of life, the absolute good, the absolutely valuable, can be no science" (LE, p. 44). In order to impress on his audience the implications of this thought, he added: "Our words used as we use them in science, are vessels capable of containing and conveying meaning and sense, *natural* meaning and sense. Ethics, if it is anything, is supernatural and our words will only express facts" (LE, p. 40).

His "Lecture on Ethics" makes clear that ethical thought, as he understood it, is not concerned with proposing normative principles of action. It concerns not the choice between specific and fixed alternatives but comprehensive views of the good. In this he was, once again, a faithful disciple of Schopenhauer, who had written of the ambitions of philosophy that "to become practical, to guide conduct, to transform character are old claims which with mature insight it ought finally to abandon. For here where it is a question of the worth or worthlessness of existence, of salvation or damnation, not the dead concepts of philosophy decide the matter, but the innermost nature of man himself, the daemon which guides him."[9] Schopenhauer's criticism had been aimed at Kant's categorical imperative. He did, of course, have a specific moral vision of his own, a belief that all life is suffering, that everything and, in particular, every sentient being – human or animal – deserves compassion, and that redemption is achievable only by overcoming the will to life and will to power within us. That view may have practical implications. But these are not assumed to derive from some normative principle (which would inevitably involve an affirmation of the will rather than its transcendence) but from a clear vision of what the world is like. Schopenhauer's ethics, we might say, is visionary rather than normative in character.[10]

The same thing can be said of Wittgenstein's ethics. He is evidently not concerned with moral rules such as the Ten Commandments, the golden rule, or Kant's categorical imperative. All such rules are, of course, fully expressible in language. Nor is he concerned with such concepts as duty and moral obligation. In the personal notebook Wittgenstein kept in World War I, we find the characteristic entry: "I still do not know how to do my duty because it is my duty and to reserve my whole human being for the life of the spirit" (GT, p. 27f.). Duty is, in other words, something merely external whereas ethics is focused on the inner life of the human spirit. Ethics is, in any case, not concerned with the will as Kant has it. We have to recognize, instead, that "the will as a phenomenon is only of interest to psychology" (TLP, 6.423). Wittgenstein illustrates what is at stake once again in his personal notebook by reminding himself: "I can die in one hour, I can die in two hours, I can die in a month or only in a few years" (GT, p. 28). Living constantly under the gun, he is keenly aware that he may have no future ahead of him. He concludes: "Man must not depend on accident. Neither on the favorable nor the unfavorable" (GT, p. 27). And his question becomes therefore: "How must I live in order to persist at every moment. To live in the Good and the Beautiful until life ends by itself" (ibid.). The only imperatives he can formulate for himself in this situation are: "Do not be anxious!" (ibid.). And: "Live happily!" (NB, p. 78). And to live happily means here to live in harmony with the world, with the facts as they are.

In his "Lecture on Ethics" Wittgenstein says therefore that ethics is really concerned with the question of living well or, as we might also say, the question of the meaning of life. These questions have no answers that can be put into scientific form. He goes on to illustrate how one might conceive of the meaning of life. His own ethical experience par excellence, he says, is that of "wonder at the existence of the world." But there is also the experience of "feeling *absolutely* safe," whatever may happen (LE, p. 41). And there is, finally, the experience of "feeling guilty" not because of anything one has done, but absolutely and existentially guilty in the face of God (LE, p. 42). Wittgenstein admits that, looked at scientifically, the verbal expression of these experiences will be nonsense. But our attempts to put them into words, he concludes, aim nevertheless at something of the greatest importance.

Commenting on Martin Heidegger's *Being and Time*, Wittgenstein told members of the Vienna Circle that he could well imagine what Heidegger means by Being and anxiety:

> Man has the drive to run against the limits of language. Think, for instance, of the wonder that anything exists. That wonder cannot be expressed in the form of a question and there is also no answer. Everything we might say can *a priori* be only nonsense. Nevertheless we run against the limit of language. This running-against has also been seen by Kierkegaard and he has even named it similarly (as a running against the paradox). This running against the limit of language is *ethics*.[11]

The remark throws light back on the *Tractatus* and its concern with the unsayable. The statements about metaphysics and logic that make up such large parts of that work must be understood to involve a similar running against the limits of language. As such these statements must fail, but that they fail is illuminating. Wittgenstein can thus write at the end of the *Tractatus*: "My propositions elucidate that he who understands me finally recognizes them as nonsensical, when he climbed through them, on them, beyond them. (He must, so to speak, throw away the ladder after he has climbed up on it.)" (TLP, 6.54). The nonsensical propositions thus serve a purpose. They are needed as elucidations of what can and cannot be said. While they are literally nonsense, we must take seriously what they aim at. This same attitude Wittgenstein would later evince toward religious statements – combining deep respect for them while ultimately seeing them as mere elucidations rather than dogmatic truths.

I must highlight two consequences. The first is that these considerations throw light on what Wittgenstein meant by saying in the *Tractatus* that certain things show themselves but cannot be said. Some readers have taken this to mean that he was talking about truths for which our words fail us. But from his remarks on ethics it becomes clear that what shows itself are not unsayable truths but certain practices of life in which we resolve or fail to resolve the problem of the meaning of our existence. Hence, the solution of the problem of life is found in the vanishing of the problem. Those to whom the meaning of life has finally become clear cannot then say in what that meaning consists because there is really nothing for them to say. And the same thing holds for metaphysics and logic. When we try to say something metaphysical or try to say something about logic, we are merely gesturing to the ways we find it plausible and possible to speak. We are gesturing at human practices, not at hidden truths.

The second consequence concerns Wittgenstein himself. Having reached the conclusion of the *Tractatus*, he could hardly turn to a normal academic career. Instead, he became a monastery gardener, a primary school teacher, and an architect. Even when he returned to Cambridge ten years later, he found it difficult to integrate himself in the life of the academy. Throughout the rest of his life he remained motivated by a profound moral seriousness which finds its most compelling expression, perhaps, in the last sentence of the *Tractatus*: "Whereof one cannot speak, thereof one must be silent."

notes

1   Friedrich Waismann, "Theses", in *Wittgenstein and the Vienna Circle*, edited by Brian McGuinness, translated by Joachim Schulte (Oxford: Blackwell, 1979), p. 233.
2   Gottlob Frege, "On Concept and Object," in *Translations from the Philosophical Writings of Gottlob Frege*, edited by Peter Geach and Max Black, 3rd edition (Oxford: Blackwell, 1980), pp. 42–43.
3   Frege, "On Concept and Object," p. 54.
4   Frege, "On Concept and Object," p. 43.
5   Frege, "On Concept and Object," p. 50.
6   Frege, "On Concept and Object," p. 54.
7   Ludwig Wittgenstein, "Letters to Ludwig von Ficker," translated by Bruce Gillette, in Wittgenstein: Sources and Perspectives, edited by C.G. Luckhardt (Ithaca, NY: Cornell University Press, 1979), pp. 94–95.
8   Hermann Broch, *Die Schlafwandler* (Frankfurt: Surhrkamp, 1978).

9   Arthur Schopenhauer, *The World as Will and Representation*, translated by E.F.J. Payne (New York: Dover Publications, 1969), vol. 1, p. 271.
10 On the topic of ethical vision see R.W. Hepburn and Iris Murdoch, "Vision and Choice in Morality," Aristotelian Society, Supplementary Volume 30, 1956.
11 *Wittgenstein and the Vienna Circle*, p. 68.

the prodigious diversity of language games

Wittgenstein's *Blue Book* reveals how far he has moved since completing the *Tractatus* 15 years earlier. While he has now abandoned many of his earlier assumptions concerning language, logic, and even philosophy itself, his work sparkles at the same time with a wealth of new and surprising ideas. The *Blue Book* is, indeed, one of Wittgenstein's most creative achievements and as such deserves to be put side by side with the *Tractatus* and the *Philosophical Investigations*.

Two things stand out in the work. The first is that Wittgenstein is more than ever committed to Mauthner's conception of philosophy as critique of language. If this critique differs methodologically from that of the *Tractatus*, that is due to a new thinking about language which is also now closer to Mauthner's than to Frege's or Russell's. Wittgenstein no longer wants to measure ordinary language by the standards of an artificial notation. We read: "It is wrong to say that in philosophy we consider an ideal language as opposed to our ordinary one. For this makes it appear as though we could improve on ordinary language. But ordinary language is all right" (BB, p. 28). Just as in the *Tractatus* the study of language is, for him, in no way an end in itself. He is certain, rather, that philosophers need only "deal with those points about language which have led, or are likely to lead, to definite philosophical puzzles or errors."[1]

The second thing to note in the *Blue Book* is Wittgenstein's retreat from the ethical and existential preoccupations of the *Tractatus*. Ethics is not a theme of the *Blue Book*. This does not mean that he has abandoned the moral seriousness that led him to write the final pages of the earlier book. But where he had previously *said* in so many words that we cannot talk about ethics, the Wittgenstein of the *Blue Book* (and after) seems determined to *practice* that radical conclusion. He has not, however, forgotten the lessons he has learned from his work on ethics. In the "Lecture on Ethics" he had sought to

wittgenstein, First Edition. Hans Sluga.
© 2011 Hans Sluga. Published 2011 by Blackwell Publishing Ltd.

show that the meaning of life reveals itself only in the practice of life. By 1933 he was applying that lesson to everything he had previously said about things that show themselves but cannot be said (whether in metaphysics, or logic, or in psychology). What shows itself, he now conceded, is not truths that must remain mysteriously silent. What shows itself is, rather, present in our practices, uses, and behaviors. What shows itself, in particular, is the way in which we use and abuse language.

Meaning as Use

Wittgenstein had returned to philosophy in 1929 with limited worries over the logic of the *Tractatus*. He first thought that he could resolve those matters quickly and then say goodbye to philosophy forever. But by 1933 his work had forced him to jettison large parts of Tractarian thought and to adopt a substantially new view of language. It was this that he sought to communicate in the *Blue Book*.

Unlike the *Tractatus* with its dogmatic assertions, the *Blue Book* begins characteristically with a question: "What is the meaning of a word?" Behind this odd-sounding query lie doubts about the entire *Tractatus* conception of meaning. Wittgenstein goes on to suggest that we replace this initial question with an inquiry into how we *explain* the meaning of a word. We will then discover that such explanations come in very different forms and this will make it easier for us to see that words have meaning in different ways. In the *Tractatus* he had maintained that our propositions can ultimately all be analyzed into "names" and that these all have meaning by standing for "objects." Against this simplistic view, he now holds that "if we had to name anything which is the life of the sign, we should have to say that it was its *use*" (BB, p. 4). And he declares it a mistake to look for the use of a sign "as though it were an object *co-existing* with the sign." Signs and the sentences made up from them get their significance, rather, "from the system of signs, from the language to which they belong"; our sentences have life only "as a part of the system of language" (BB, p. 5).

These remarks are widely taken to express a "use theory of meaning" in contrast to the supposed "picture theory" of the *Tractatus*. But the Wittgenstein of the *Blue Book* is no more committed to proposing a theory of meaning than the author of that earlier work. The formula that meaning is use provides us, in fact, with no substantive theory because Wittgenstein's concept of use is so multifaceted, open-ended, and undefined. We may even say that the formula is in effect a tautology. Certainly, if "meaning" means use – as Wittgenstein suggests – then the formula "meaning is use" means only that "use is use." And that is a plain tautology, not a substantive theory. For all that, there is something new being said about language. We can see that clearly when we look at the way Wittgenstein deals with the problem that had motivated his return to philosophy in 1929.

Language Games

That problem had been a peculiar consequence of the logical atomism of the *Tractatus*. Each atomic fact, he had argued in that work, must be logically independent of any other atomic fact. We can rephrase the issue in linguistic terms. If A and B are both elementary propositions, that is, propositions describing atomic facts, then the truth or falsity of A will be independent of the truth or falsity of B. If, on the other hand, for instance, A implies B, then at least one of those two propositions will not be elementary. Thus, "A and B" implies "B" and "B" implies "A or B" only because "A and B" and "A or B" are logically complex propositions. But now consider the propositions "A is red" and "A is green." They do not appear to be logically complex; they certainly do not, in their current form, contain any logical connectives – the usual sign of logical complexity. But they can also not both be true at one and the same time, if we mean to say that A is both red and green all over at one and the same moment. In the *Tractatus* Wittgenstein had drawn the conclusion that color propositions cannot therefore be elementary and he had sought to explain this with the help of the physical theory of light waves. But by 1929 he had come to see this as the wrong answer and was now considering a radically different solution of the problem. In December of that year he told members of the Vienna Circle:

> Once I wrote: "A proposition is laid against reality like a ruler. Only the end-points of the graduating lines actually *touch* the object that is to be measured." I now prefer to say that a *system of propositions* is laid against reality like a ruler . . . If I say, for example, that this or that point in the visual field is *blue*, then I know not merely that, but also that this point is not green, nor red, nor yellow, etc. I have laid the entire color-scale against it at one go . . . All this I did not yet know when I was writing my work.[2]

Wittgenstein remained fascinated for the rest of his life with this observation. He returned again and again to studying the language of colors. Why do we say that there can be a transparent red but not a transparent white? Why can there be no reddish green, or bluish orange, or yellowish violet? In notes from the last two years of his life he wrote: "We do not want to establish a theory of color (neither a physiological one nor a psychological one), but rather the logic of color concepts. And this accomplishes what people have often unjustly expected of a theory" (RC, 22). He also came to understand early on that besides color propositions there must be other such systems of propositions. Thus, he pointed out that number propositions also form a system of their own. "There are (exactly) three books on the table" implies, for instance, that there are not one or two or four and five books on the table. That system is, in turn, logically independent of the system of color propositions. That there are three books on the table tells us nothing about their color; and that there are red books on the table tells us nothing about their number. What we call language consists in this way of multiple systems of propositions or, as Wittgenstein was to say in the *Blue Book*, of multiple language games. He introduced that term there by explaining: "The study of language games is the study of primitive forms of language or primitive languages" and "Language games are the forms of language with which a child begins to make use of words" (BB, p. 17). Soon after, he was to say that language games are not incomplete parts of the language but "languages complete in themselves," that they are "complete systems of human communication." And to this he added: "The picture we have of the language of the grown-up is that of a nebulous mass of language, his mother tongue, surrounded by discreet and more or less clear-cut language games, the technical languages" (BB, p. 81). Still later he came to speak of "the prodigious diversity of all the everyday language games" (PI, p. 224). Among those language games he listed giving orders, and obeying them; describing the appearance of an object, or giving its measurements; reporting an event; speculating about an event; making up a story and reading it; guessing riddles; translating from one language into another; asking, thanking, cursing, greeting, praying (PI, 23).

The term "language game" had two advantages for Wittgenstein over that of "system." It suggested, first of all, that language was to be understood as an activity. Language games, he wrote later on, consist of "recurrent acts of play in time" (OC, 519). As such, they are dynamic and likely to change over time (OC, 256, 336). Instead of thinking about language as a formal structure, in the way the *Tractatus* had done, Wittgenstein asked now how children come to play a language game. "The child does not learn that books exist, that armchairs exist, etc. etc., – it learns to get books, to sit in armchairs, etc. etc. Later questions about the existence of things do of course arise" (OC, 476). The term "language game" also suggests that these activities are, like other games, governed by rules and that language games are characteristically distinguished by their specific rules. This does not mean that rules function in the same way in all of them. While there are some games, like chess, that have precise rules, others, like tossing a ball, do not. When we think of language "as a symbolism used in an exact calculus," what is in our mind is language as used in science and mathematics. But "our ordinary use of language conforms to this standard of exactness only in rare cases" (BB, p. 25). Condensing the resulting picture of language into a metaphor, Wittgenstein wrote later on: "We see that what we call 'sentence' and 'language' is not the formal unity that I imagined, but is the family of structures more or less related to one another" (PI, 108). And thus by analogy: "Our language can be seen as an ancient city: a maze of little streets and squares, of old and new houses, and of houses with additions from various periods; and this surrounded by a multitude of new boroughs with straight regular streets and uniform houses" (PI, 18).

Where the *Tractatus* had sought to show with the help of logic that language is a unity and that under its varying surface appearances it has a single underlying structure, the Wittgenstein of the *Blue Book* and the *Philosophical Investigations* was a determined pluralist. This shift in view had important consequences since Wittgenstein also considered language integral to our entire form of life. The pluralistic character of language thus bears directly on human culture, society and history, religion, science, and philosophy, on the ways we conceive ourselves and others. It follows, in other words, that the human condition in its various aspects is essentially pluralistic in character. In the *Philosophical Investigations* he captured that conclusion in the suggestive formula: "What has to be accepted, the given, is – so one could say – *forms of life*" (PI, p. 226).

But can we not envisage humanity as united in a single form of life, as speaking a single, unified language and thus engaged in one single language game? Wittgenstein allows for that possibility but he makes clear that the resulting form of life would be impoverished and almost sub-human. In section 2 of the *Philosophical Investigations* he imagines a group of actors engaged in just such a single language game:

> The language is meant to serve between a builder A and an assistant B. A is building with building stones: there are blocks, pillars, slabs and beams. B has to pass the stones, and that in the order which A needs them. For this purpose they use a language consisting of the words "block," "pillar," "slab," "beam." A calls them out; – B brings the stone which he has learnt to bring at such-and-such a call. – Conceive this as a complete primitive language.

If it were like that, we would be faced with a form of human existence in which interactions and language use are literally robotic. But can we not envisage a much richer but still unified language game? Had the author of the *Tractatus* not at one time assumed that there was, in a sense, only one language – a single underlying logical structure shared by all the different natural languages and by all invented notations? Have philosophers not again and again attempted to construct a singular, ideal language? The Wittgenstein of the *Blue Book* would respond to this kind of challenge by pointing out that different language games fulfill different needs and that "these needs can be of the greatest variety" (BB, p. 59). What is more, human needs are not only various in number, they also change over time, and they are unforeseeable. Who could have foreseen that we would find ourselves one day communicating electronically around the globe? The internet has, in fact, spawned a whole slew of new language games. The pluralism of language games is thus grounded in a pluralism of human needs and, we might add, in the pluralism of human interests and of ways of seeing ourselves and the world around us. There is, of course, always the possibility that we will let this pluralism slip out of our hands and that we end up with an utterly impoverished human existence. "Perhaps science and industry, having caused infinite misery in the process, will unite the world – I mean condense it into a *single* unit, though one in which peace is the last thing that will find a home" (CV, p. 63).

In order to appreciate how varied our everyday language games actually are, we may want to consider what Wittgenstein says from the 1930s onward about the mind–body problem, about mathematics, about myth, religion, and science, about culture, about our capacity for seeing things in different ways, and about the possibility of different world pictures.

Mind and Matter

The Wittgenstein of the *Blue Book* draws attention to the existence of two kinds of proposition in our language: "propositions of which we may say that they describe facts in the material world (external world)" and "propositions describing personal experiences" (BB, pp. 46–47). We can say, on the one hand, "the tulips in our garden are in full bloom," and, on the other, "I am in pain." The *Tractatus* had, of course, maintained that there are no legitimate propositions of the latter sort since the word "I" fails to stand for an object. Now Wittgenstein was willing to recognize their legitimacy; but he considered it essential that we interpret them properly. The distinction between the two kinds of proposition might lead us to think at first "that here we have two kinds of worlds, worlds built of different materials; a mental world and a physical world" (BB, p. 47). That interpretation must, however, be rejected. The same is true of another interpretation according to which "the mental phenomena, sense experience, volition, etc., emerge when a type of animal body of a certain complexity has been evolved" (ibid.). The same is true of a third interpretation, which holds that "personal experience, far from being the product of physical processes, seems to be the very basis of all that we say with any sense about such processes" (BB, p. 48). And it is true once more of a fourth metaphysical interpretation according to which "the whole world, mental and physical, is made of one material only" (ibid.). Wittgenstein rejects, in other words, Cartesian dualism, materialist emergentism, idealism, and neutral monism and, indeed, all metaphysical interpretations of the difference between the two kinds of proposition. Instead, Wittgenstein declares that the common-sense man, with whom he identifies, "is as far from realism as from idealism" (BB, p. 48). The key to the problem presented by two kinds of proposition is found, rather, in the observation that "the propositions 'A has a gold tooth' and 'A has toothache' are not used analogously. They differ in their grammar where at first sight they might not seem to differ" (BB, p. 53). The two propositions serve, in fact, different purposes, fulfill different needs. Language functions differently in them. We are dealing, in other words, with two different language games.

Wittgenstein takes the opportunity in the *Blue Book* to revisit the issue of solipsism. In the *Tractatus* he had maintained that solipsism was "quite correct" but that what it means cannot be said. Now, in the *Blue Book*, Wittgenstein argues that there are, in fact, two legitimate uses of the word "I." There is, as he puts it, its "use as object" and there is its "use as subject"

(BB, p. 66). We use "I" (or "my") to refer to an object when we speak of a human body and its bodily characteristics. In this class we have the propositions "My arm is broken" and "I have grown six inches." The word "I" is used as subject, on the other hand, when we speak of mental states, mental processes, and sensations. Wittgenstein's examples are: "I see so-and-so," "I hear so-and-so," "I try to lift my arm," "I think it will rain," "I have toothache" (BB, pp. 66–67). In the first kind of proposition, Wittgenstein says, an object (a body) is identified and something is said about it. In the second we are not referring to any object at all. "To say, 'I have pain' is no more a statement about a particular person than moaning is" (BB, p. 67). By uttering "I am in pain" I am not trying to state a fact; instead I am trying to attract attention to myself. By means of a number of thought experiments he seeks to show that in such utterances the word "I" certainly does not refer to a particular body. We can imagine for instance that I feel pain in your body rather than, as is normal, in my own. But even then that pain will still be *my* pain. "There is no question of recognizing a person when I say I have toothache. To ask 'are you sure that it's you who has pains?' would be nonsensical" (BB, p. 67). This does not mean that in such cases we are referring to something mental or spiritual. Wittgenstein concludes the *Blue Book* with the words: "The kernel of the proposition that that which has pains or sees or thinks is of a mental nature is only, that the word 'I' in 'I have pains' does not denote a particular body" (BB, p. 74). That negative fact does not justify the positive conclusion that we must be referring to something spiritual. Wittgenstein adds that "we feel that in the case in which 'I' is used as subject, we don't use it because we recognize a particular person by his bodily characteristics; and this creates the illusion that we use this word to refer to something bodiless, which, however, has its seat in our body" (BB, p. 69). This illusion, he argues, is the real source of the Cartesian belief in a metaphysically real, substantive I.

Wittgenstein concludes that the solipsist is not someone who has discovered a new fact about reality and the mind; he is rather a person who is "irresistibly tempted to use a certain form of expression" (BB, p. 60). This temptation arises because our ordinary ways of speaking hold the mind rigidly in one position and we sometimes feel cramped by that constraint. The solipsist wants to emphasize the difference between his own feeling of pain and someone else's more strongly than ordinary language allows for. He suggests therefore another way of speaking. There is, in principle, nothing wrong with what he proposes. We might even learn to go along with the solipsistic way of speaking and say "so-and-so is really seen" only when the solipsist sees so-and-so. "There is nothing wrong in suggesting that the others should give me an exceptional place in their notation; but the justification which I wish to give for it: that this body is the seat of that which really lives – is senseless" (BB, p. 66). The remark highlights how much Wittgenstein's picture of the relation of language to the world has changed from the one he had laid out in the *Tractatus*. It also reveals how much his picture of the world itself has changed. Wittgenstein writes of the solipsist:

He sees a way of dividing the country different from the one used on the ordinary map. He feels tempted, say, to use the name "Devonshire" not for the county with its conventional boundary, but for a region differently bounded. He could express this by saying: "Isn't it absurd to make *this* a county, to boundaries *here*?" But what he says is: "The *real* Devonshire is this." We could answer: "What you want is only a new notation and by a new notation no facts of geography are changed." (BB, p. 57)

Gone is Wittgenstein's earlier thought that the world itself has a determinate structure which is depicted in propositions replicating that exact structure. The conception here is of reality as a continuous surface that can be mapped differently for different purposes. While the post-Tractarian Wittgenstein shies away from making metaphysical claims, he still operates with an unspoken and informal understanding of reality. Gone is the idea that reality itself has a logical structure, that there is a unique order and organization to the world. The thought now is that we impose an organization on the world with the help of our language and that there is always more than one way of doing so, more than one language, more than one notation. This does not mean that our language games are detached from the world and that we can speak in any way we like. In his late notes Wittgenstein writes: "If we imagine the facts otherwise than they are, certain language games lose importance while others become important. And the use of the vocabulary of the language changes, gradually that is, in this way" (OC, 63). The mistake of the *Tractatus* had been to assume that the particular notation we adopt can be justified by reference to the logical order of the world, not in assuming that there is some connection between language and world.

Wittgenstein's new thinking modified also what he had previously said about the limits of language. On his new view he could allow that every particular language game had inherent limits. But he no longer thought of those limits as rigid and unmovable. Language games could, after all, change over time and accommodate new ways of speaking. And, as he had shown in his discussion of solipsism in the *Blue Book*, it was always possible to invent new language games to satisfy new needs and interests.

Mathematics and Other Sciences

I note in passing that Wittgenstein concerned himself extensively with two sets of questions in the 1930s. The first belongs to the philosophy of mind and concerns matters of the sort I have just discussed. The second deals with topics in the philosophy of mathematics. Wittgenstein had various reasons for pursuing this second set of questions. One of them was his desire to understand the nature of necessity. What do philosophers mean when they say that something is necessary? In what sense are mathematical propositions, for instance, necessarily true? How do the rules of mathematics necessitate their application? What necessity is there in the steps of a mathematical proof? In the *Tractatus* he had maintained that necessity (or "certainty," as he said at the time) manifests itself in a proposition being a tautology (TLP, 5.525). All necessity was thus for him logical necessity (TLP, 6.37). But this left an important question unanswered since he also believed both that the equations of mathematics are not tautologies and that they are necessary. What kind of necessity could they then exhibit?

There was, in addition, another interest that motivated his concern with the foundations of mathematics. As so often, he found himself at odds with his mentor Russell who had sought to reduce all of mathematics to logic. While Wittgenstein had disputed Russell's logicism in the *Tractatus*, he still subscribed to the idea that mathematics was a unified undertaking. Now, in the 1930s, he set out to show that this was not so, that mathematics consisted, in fact, of various language games, various distinct but related modes of thought. He wrote accordingly: "I should like to say: mathematics is a MOTLEY of techniques of proof. – And upon this is based its manifold applicability and its importance" (RFM, p. 176).

It makes sense to extend these considerations to other sciences and to natural science as a whole. Wittgenstein never developed a philosophy of the empirical sciences, but he would surely have opposed any belief in the unity of science. Instead, he would probably have argued that natural science is also a motley, just like mathematics. And this conclusion would have followed quite naturally for him from his observations about the mathematical motley since different empirical sciences use different parts of mathematics and do so in manifold ways. Wittgenstein would, presumably, have also been sympathetic to accounts of science, such as that developed by Thomas Kuhn, that emphasize the discontinuity of science over time. He granted, in any case, that there is more than one way to comprehend and speak about the world and that science, mythology, and religion do so in ways that employ very different and, indeed, incommensurable language games.

Science, Myth, and Religion

Wittgenstein came to these conclusions in the early 1930s when he read Sir James Frazer's *Golden Bough*, a treatise on magical and religious practices that counts as one of the great achievements of Victorian scholarship. In his notes on the book he sharply criticized Frazer for the reductive character of his account of those practices and the resulting unitarian conception of human understanding. He wrote that Frazer treats magic as "essentially false physics or, as the case may be, false medicine, technology, etc." (RF, p. 67). Wittgenstein, by contrast, thought it wrong to assume that "mankind does all that out of sheer stupidity" (RF, p. 61). "Why do primitive people engage in the rain dance?" he asked himself. Are they simply in error about the efficacy of their actions? Do they not know that eventually it will rain anyway? Frazer, he concluded, had failed to see that magic is not an attempted and mistaken science, that it does not operate with a notion of causal efficacy, but that it is based on the idea of symbolism and language (RF, p. 64). Magic involves a distinctive attitude toward the world which is radically different from that of science. "The form of the awakening spirit is veneration of objects" (RF, p. 73). As the human spirit awakens it brings about a separation from the original soil, the ultimate basis of life, and this separation gives rise to magical and religious rites. The magical and the scientific form of life are thus utterly different from each other. Magic has its own language, its own language games, and these are quite distinct from the language games played in science and in a world dominated by science.

Frazer's scientism extends to all religious belief. But Wittgenstein objects that Augustine was certainly not in error when he called upon God in his *Confessions*. Nor is the Buddhist with his very different religious views. Wittgenstein added elsewhere: "Obviously the essence of religion cannot have anything to do with the fact that there is talking, or rather: when people talk, then it is itself part of a religious act and not a theory. Thus it also does not matter at all if the words used are true or false or nonsense."[3] The language games of religion are in this way to be distinguished from the language games of scientific truth, just like those of magical thought. Magical and religious languages have life and meaning in their use which cannot be reduced to the narrow employment of language in describing and analyzing facts.

In the period in which he was reading Frazer's *Golden Bough* Wittgenstein also studied Oswald Spengler's *Decline of the West*. In that book Spengler sought to give a "morphology of world-history," arguing that each of the great historical cultures of the world has its own distinctive form. That form determines, according to Spengler, all aspects of the culture, from its religious rituals to its science and mathematics. It also sets the course of each culture from its birth to its decline. Wittgenstein was clearly intrigued by these ideas. This is apparent in one of his notes from the 1930s where he writes: "Our civilization is characterized by the word 'progress.' Progress is its form . . . Typically it constructs. It is occupied with building an ever more complicated structure" (CV, p. 7). The remark reflects Spengler's influence not only in suggesting that "our civilization" has a form that differs from that of other civilizations but also in relying on Spengler's distinction between culture and civilization – the latter being for Spengler the final phase in the evolution of a culture in which the culture becomes petrified and exhausted. In this spirit, Wittgenstein insists that we find ourselves now "in the great stream of European and American civilization" but no longer in "a time of high culture" (CV, p. 6).

Seeing Aspects

In the *Tractatus* Wittgenstein had written: "We make pictures of the facts for ourselves. The picture represents the situation in logical space, the existence and non-existence of states of affairs. The picture is a model of reality" (TLP, 2.1–2.12). According to this account, a picture depicts a fact by having exactly the same structure as the fact, that is, by being isomorphic with it. Propositions (and specifically elementary propositions) are, in this precise sense, logical pictures of facts. This is not an account he would maintain after the *Tractatus*. But the later Wittgenstein still maintained an interest in pictures and the picturing relation. He even continued to be attracted to the idea that propositions work in some ways like pictures. This becomes evident in section 11 of part 2 of the *Philosophical Investigations* where he writes at length about picturing and seeing and points out that "a sentence can strike me like a painting in words, and the very individual words in the sentence as like a picture" (PI, p. 215).

Once he had given up on logical atomism and on metaphysics in general he could, of course, no longer speak about pictures and propositions as having the same structure as the facts they represent. In the *Philosophical Investigations* the crucial observation is that one and the same picture can serve to depict different situations. A book may, for instance, contain the same illustration in a number of places but in each of them it may represent something different, "here a glass cube, there an inverted open box, there a wire frame of that shape, there three boards forming a solid angle" (PI, p. 193). The observation draws our attention to the kind of puzzle pictures that we can see in one moment as one thing and in the next as another.

Wittgenstein had been interested from early on in such pictures. In the *Tractatus* he had written of the Necker cube, a drawing of a cube in which we can see either one side or another as being in front. He had argued that we can have these two different views because "we really see two different facts" (TLP, 5.5423). The shifting perception is, in other words, not to be explained by saying that we see the cube in two different ways; it is rather that there are two perceptual representations which depict two different facts, two actually different positions of the cube in space. In accordance with the *Tractatus* conception, the perceiving subject thereby has dropped out of the account.

In the *Philosophical Investigations* Wittgenstein's favored puzzle picture is the "duck-rabbit," a drawing that can be seen alternatively as depicting the head of a duck or that of a rabbit. His discussion of this kind of picture makes clear how far he has moved beyond the simplicities of the *Tractatus*. In the *Philosophical Investigations* Wittgenstein asks himself: What is it to see one aspect rather than another one? What is it to see the drawing as depicting a duck's head or, alternatively, a rabbit's? And what happens when we learn to look at the drawing in one way or another? What happens when our perception switches from one way of seeing the drawing to another one? Wittgenstein understands now, moreover, that the issues that come to light in this discussion relate not only to puzzle pictures. They arise also when we come to recognize the face of a friend in a crowd, when we perceive or fail to perceive the similarity of two faces, and when we identify or fail to identify a facial expression, when, for instance, "someone sees a smile and does not know it for a smile, does not understand it as such" (PI, p. 198). The same issue arises when we see a drawing sometimes as flat and sometimes as three-dimensional, when we see a sphere afloat in a painting, or when we see the still photograph as depicting a galloping horse.

His discussion of all this is intricate, though perhaps not entirely conclusive. Two important points, nevertheless, stand out clearly in it. The first is that to see something as something means to see it in relation to other things. When I see the duck-rabbit as a rabbit, the picture stands for me in relation to rabbits but also to other rabbit pictures. It also stands in relation to things I and others will say: simple statements like "This is a rabbit" or exclamations like "Look, a rabbit!" or explanations of the form "If you look at the picture in this way, you will see a rabbit." The rabbit picture will also stand in relation to certain applications. Wittgenstein writes: " 'Now he is seeing it like *this*,' 'now like *that*' would only be said of someone *capable* of making certain applications of the figure quite freely. The substratum of this experience is the mastery of a technique . . . It is only if someone *can do*, has learnt, is the master of such-and-such, that it makes sense to say that he has *this* experience" (PI, pp. 208–209). We can express this conclusion in other words. While Wittgenstein does not use the term "language game" in this context, we may say that, according to him, seeing something as something, having the experience of something, is always part of a language game that involves words and images as well as their applications. That we can see different aspects in a picture illustrates once more the diversity of possible language games.

The second point that stands out in this discussion is that Wittgenstein no longer assumes that a picture by itself depicts any particular fact by its very structure. It is, rather, that we can use one and the same image for very different purposes and, indeed, see that image in very different ways. The *Tractatus* had been right in saying that we make pictures of facts for ourselves. But the pictures are interpretable; they can be seen in different ways and thus we cannot draw metaphysical conclusions from the pictures we make about the facts of the world. Wittgenstein gives us a dramatic application of this idea early on in the *Philosophical Investigations*. Consider that someone says "Bring me a slab." According to the *Tractatus* that proposition must have a definite (logical) structure corresponding to the structure of the fact of which it speaks. But "could we not mean this expression as *one* long word corresponding to the single word 'Slab'!" Wittgenstein now asks (PI, 20). The structure we ascribe to our proposition will depend on the other possible propositions in our language. The structure we ascribe to a proposition is, in other words, a function of the language game to which it belongs. Wittgenstein writes therefore: "Thought and intention [taken on their own, that is] are neither 'articulated' nor 'non-articulated'; to be compared neither with a single note which sounds during the acting or speaking, nor with a tune" (PI, p. 217).

World Pictures

Wittgenstein's discussion of aspect-seeing prepares the way to his reflections on systems of thought and world pictures. His notes on these topics, written in the last two years of his life, have been published under the title *On Certainty* and they reveal Wittgenstein to be once again moving in a new direction. Central to these final notes is Wittgenstein's conviction that "all testing, all confirmation and disconfirmation of a hypothesis takes place already within a system . . . The system is not so much the point of departure, as the element in which arguments have their life" (OC, 105). In other notes he adds that all our assumptions and convictions, everything we believe or doubt, are part of such a system. We also read that "our knowledge forms a large system. And only within this system has a particular bit the value we assign to it" (OC, 410).

The most comprehensive term he employs in this context is that of a "world picture" (*Weltbild*), which refers us back, on the one hand, to the picture language of the *Tractatus* and, on the other, to his discussion of Frazer's and Spengler's "world view" (*Weltanschauung*) in the 1930s. *On Certainty* argues that our world picture determines how we perceive things and how we speak of them. "Everything I have seen or heard gives me the conviction that no man has ever been far from the earth. Nothing in my world picture speaks in favor of the opposite" (OC, 93). This world picture can be described more or less fully in propositions (OC, 162). And these propositions form a system that serves "a role similar to that of rules of a game" for "the entire system of our language games" (OC, 95, 411). World picture, system, and language game are thus closely related to each other. In contrast to the atomism of the *Tractatus*, Wittgenstein's view of meaning, thought, and language is now thoroughly holistic. Aphoristically, he writes: "Light dawns gradually over the whole" (OC, 141).

This holism has significant philosophical consequences. Since all doubt presupposes a system, language game, or world picture, radical, all-inclusive philosophical doubt must be a monstrosity. "A doubt without an end is not even a doubt" (OC, 625). Our certainties, on the other hand, also guarantee nothing. They only constitute a "kind of mythology" that defines "the river-bed" of our thought. While they may seem completely indubitable to us we must not forget that "the mythology can change back into a state of flux, the river-bed of thought may shift" (OC, 97). Moore's attempt to prove metaphysical realism by drawing attention to the certainty of the proposition "I know that there is a hand here" leads, for that reason, to nothing.

Furthermore, we must be alert to the fact that all justification and argumentation can take place only within a system. It follows that the system itself has no justification. "You must bear in mind that the language game is so to say something unpredictable. I mean: it is not based on grounds. It is not reasonable (or unreasonable). It is there – like our life" (OC, 559). We come to our world picture not by being convinced of its correctness but by being brought up into it. And that picture of the world serves then for us as "the inherited background against which I distinguish between true and false" (OC, 94). Language, which "did not emerge from some kind of ratiocination" (OC, 475), is grounded, rather, in practices and habits inculcated in us in childhood. At the beginning was the deed not consciousness and reason. In one of the most illuminating passages of *On Certainty* Wittgenstein writes: "What kinds of grounds have I for trusting text-books of experimental physics? I have no grounds for not trusting them. And I trust them. I know how such books are produced – or rather, I believe I know. I have some evidence, but it does not go very far and is of a very scattered kind. I have heard, seen, and read various things" (OC, 600). The remark is, of course, by no means meant to undermine our trust in physics; it is intended to show us, rather, how much we rely on trust even in physics.

Wittgenstein often speaks in the singular of "my world picture" and our "system" in *On Certainty* but he assumes, in fact, that there are many possible world pictures and many possible systems of thought. Indeed, he plays constantly with the possibility that other people might see the world differently from the way in which modern human beings have come to see it. Thus he writes: "*Very* intelligent and well-educated people believe in the story of creation in the Bible, while others hold it as proven false, and the grounds of the latter are well known to the former" (OC, 336). Since all reasoning takes place within a system of thought, it follows, of course, that we cannot effectively use one system to undermine another. Where two world pictures meet, where two sets of principles really come into conflict, "each man declares the other a fool and a heretic" (OC, 611). Then we can only combat the other man; for what reasons could I supply to him? "At the end of reasons comes *persuasion*. (Think of what happens when missionaries convert natives" (OC, 612).

The Inner and the Outer

Wittgenstein's pluralism raises thorny questions. How do we differentiate between language games? It appears that the same words can appear in two different language games. (The word "I", for instance.) How are we to tell whether a proposition belongs to one language game or another one? What relations are there between different language games? How do they correlate and form what we consider to be one language? What dissociations, links, and possible transitions are there between different systems of thought and different world pictures? To what extent can one understand one world picture within another one? Are systems of thought or world pictures comparable with each other? How do we recognize that someone has a particular world picture? And so on.

Wittgenstein did not consider all of these questions but he did recognize their validity. That is illustrated by the way he went eventually beyond the *Blue Book* account of the difference between objective and subjective ways of speaking. There he had argued simply that the objective and the subjective way of speaking belong to two different language games but had said almost nothing about the relations between those language games. In the *Philosophical Investigations*, on the other hand, he returns to the topic and revises the view that the objective and the subjective language game are sharply separated from each other. Speaking of the difference between physical objects and sense impressions he writes: "Here we have two different language games and a complicated relation between them. – If you try to reduce their relations to a simple formula you go wrong" (PI, p. 180). His crucial new insight is now that "an 'inner process' stands in need of outward criteria" (PI, 580). Our recognition of the fact that someone is in pain is linked to his behavior and his speech – but in a complex fashion. " 'I noticed that he was out of humor.' Is this a report about his behavior or his state of mind? . . . Both; not side-by-side, however, but about the one via the other" (PI, p. 179). The behavior in question may be verbal, non-verbal or both at once. "The doctor asks: 'How is he feeling?' The nurse says: 'He is groaning.' . . . Might they not, for example, draw the conclusion 'If he groans, we must give him more analgesic' – without suppressing a middle term?" (PI, p. 179). Instead of groaning the patient might, of course, also have said: "It hurts here. The pain is awful." And this might have led the doctor and the nurse to draw the same conclusion.

It follows for Wittgenstein that "only of a human being and what resembles (behaves like) a living human being can one say: it has sensations; it sees; hears; is deaf; is conscious or unconscious" (PI, 281). Thus, we can imagine pain in the wriggling fly but not in the dead rock, unless we imagine in addition that a living being is hidden in the rock. This might make it appear as if Wittgenstein has now slipped back into the kind of materialist behaviorism he had tried to refute in the *Blue Book*. But just as in the *Blue Book* he dismisses disputes between idealists, solipsists and realists are being merely in disagreement about forms of expression and not about "facts recognized by every reasonable human being" (PI, 402). While the behaviorist is bound to deny that there is any difference between pain and pain behavior Wittgenstein continues saying: "What greater difference could there be?" And when he is challenged: "And yet you again and again reach the conclusion that the sensation itself is a *nothing*!" he replies: "Not at all. It is not a *something*, but not a *nothing* either! . . . The paradox disappears only if we break radically with the idea that language functions always in *one* way, always serves the same purpose" (PI, 304). With this puzzling remark Wittgenstein seeks to communicate that pain is not an object (e.g., an object *in* the mind) that we refer to when we say that we are in pain. The pain experience plays, rather, a very different role in our language.

We are led into a metaphysical interpretation of the nature of mental processes only because the first step in our thinking "is the one that altogether escapes notice" and thus, "the decisive movement in the conjuring trick has been made, and it was the very one that we thought quite innocent" (PI, 308). What then is the decisive first step in our thinking about the mind that takes us in the end all the way into either idealism, or Cartesian dualism, or into behaviorism? Wittgenstein's answer is short and decisive: "We talk of processes and states and leave their nature undecided . . . But that is just what commits us to a particular way of looking at the matter" (PI, 308). In physics we may observe certain things going on inside elementary particles that we do not understand. When we turn to mental processes we are inclined to talk in the same way. We speak of these processes as going on "in the mind" and then add that the mind is something difficult to understand. But on Wittgenstein's account that analogy comes quickly apart.

In order to see that, we must look closely at how statements about the human body are connected to psychological utterances. Here we must distinguish two cases: the case where we are speaking about a third person ("He is in pain") and the case where we are speaking in the first person ("I am in pain"). When I say of someone else that he is in pain, I depend entirely on the availability of outer criteria. I say that he is in pain because I see his pain behavior or hear his words. That does not mean, however, that I am making a statement simply about the pain behavior. There are a number of reasons for this. One is that the criterial relation connecting behavior and pain is not absolutely tight. It is possible that someone may feel pain and yet not show it and it is equally possible for someone to simulate pain, that is, to exhibit pain behavior without feeling actual pain. On the other hand, it is obvious that our practice of ascribing pain to others would not get off the ground if there were no general and natural relation between pain and pain behavior.

The case of first-person utterances like "I am in pain" provides us with another, and still more powerful, reason for denying behaviorism. When I say "I am in pain," I certainly do not do so on the basis of observing my own behavior. In this case, "words are connected with the primitive, the natural, expressions of the sensation and used in their place . . . the verbal expression of pain replaces crying and does not describe it" (PI, 244). For this practice to get going, for children to learn to say "I am in pain" as a replacement for crying, presupposes, of course, that there is a linkage between non-linguistic behavior and the utterance. For children are taught to say "I am in pain" by adults who speak the language and they will teach the child to use the utterance when they see the child's pain behavior. "A child has hurt himself and he cries; and then adults talk to him and teach him exclamations and, later, sentences. They teach the child new pain-behavior" (PI, 244). The first-person case makes clear the difference between a description of a behavior and a pain utterance. When I say "I am in pain" I am not describing anything, I am rather expressing pain. My utterance has a different function from a description. That holds true even in the third-person case. When I say of someone "I believe that he is suffering," I am not describing his behavior, though my ascription is surely based on his behavior; I am rather expressing an attitude toward him: "my attitude towards him is an attitude towards a soul" (PI, p. 178).

While behaviorism correctly diagnoses the existence of a connection between pain and the expression of pain (pain behavior), it misinterprets this fact when it argues that pain utterances are descriptions of behavior. To overcome behaviorism means to "make a radical break with the idea that language always functions in one way, always serves the same purpose: to convey thoughts – which may be about houses, pains, good and evil, or anything else you please" (PI, 304). This questionable assumption behaviorism shares, in fact, with Cartesian dualism, its apparent opposite. For that view also assumes that words have meaning by standing for something. Both behaviorism and dualism are thus driven into their mistaken metaphysics by their lack of failure to understand the diverse functions of language.

These considerations are at the heart of what is known as Wittgenstein's private-language argument. If we construe the grammar of the expressions of sensation and inner states on the model of "object and designation," we may become seduced into thinking that there are inner objects which our sensation language designates. But Wittgenstein seeks to show that such inner objects can play no substantial role in our language and thought. "The thing in the box has no place in the language game at all; not even as a something; for the box might even be empty" (PI, 293). If we construe meaning on the model of "object and designation," then "the object drops out of consideration as irrelevant" (PI, 293). He raises at this point the potential objection that we might be able to invent an essentially private language. "The individual words of this language are to refer to what can only be known to the person speaking . . . So another person cannot understand the language" (PI, 243). Such a language would be *essentially* private in the sense that what it talks about is in principle accessible only to the speaking subject. But the conception of such a language is incoherent, Wittgenstein argues, because it would have no criteria for determining whether one has properly identified a sensation or not.

A Field of Diversity

There emerges from all of this a picture of the human world as a field of utter diversity. The metaphysical pluralism of the *Tractatus* (or, at least, that of the pre-*Tractatus* phase) with its multiplicity of objects, states of affairs, and facts has given way to the idea of multiple uses of words, multiple language games, and multiple forms of human life. These are, in turn, seen to be linked to a variable diversity of interests, needs, and ways of seeing the world. This vast array of forms and formations is, moreover, unstable and shifts in the course of time in unpredictable ways.

The picture suggests an entirely new way of looking at the human condition. It stands in sharp contrast to our tradition in philosophy and science which has always, in one way or other, upheld an ideal of unity. On its view the palpable diversity of the human world is a mere surface phenomenon, a curtain behind which a principle of strict unity waits to be discerned by us. The name of that principle has, of course, varied from one system of thought to another; in one it is considered to be transcendental (God, the One, the Idea of the Good), in another empirical (the Big Bang); in one spiritual and in another material. The assumption that there must be such a principle has, however, always been tacitly presupposed. It has colored also how we conceive of human knowledge, of philosophy and science, and of human reason. In its light, reason has been generally understood as a capacity to look for a singular principle, as a capacity to unify. It is an assumption that has, finally, shaped also much of our thinking about society and politics.

Wittgenstein, on the other hand, seeks to teach us the inherent diversity and multiplicity of the human world. He tries to show us that the search for a unifying principle is not only hopeless but that such a principle would, in any case, explain nothing. And he touches here on one of the real difficulties of any monistic and reductive theory: its inability to tell a coherent story of how plurality can spring from an unconditioned unity. Pluralism of any kind (whether metaphysical or not) presents us, however, with a complementary question: how do the things postulated by the pluralistic conception hang together? If there is no connection between them, it becomes unclear how the plural items can form any totality such as the world or the human form of life. The Wittgenstein of the *Tractatus* finessed the problem (in part, at least) by holding that the objects that make up the world "hang together like links in a chain." While the world is a plurality of facts, the logic of the world is one and singular. But the later Wittgenstein was no longer willing to subscribe to this idea of a singular, underlying, sublime logic. In what sense are different language games then all part of one language and human forms of life part of human life as a whole? The question would have no positive answer, if language games and forms of life were disjoint. But as we saw from Wittgenstein's discussion of the distinction between the inner and the outer, he assumed, in fact, that there may be various relations between language games and, equally, between forms of life. Sometimes they may, indeed, be disjointed, but they can also build on each other, be embedded in each other, overlap, and be similar or dissimilar in various respects. In place of the picture of a world held together by an inalienable unity, Wittgenstein is promoting the idea of a modulated variety of relationships which bind language games and forms of life together. We will see in the next chapter how Wittgenstein mobilizes the notion of family resemblance to describe these multiple forms of relation.

To conclude this chapter, I need to add only that everything I have said here also bears, of course, on the question of how we should understand social and political phenomena. Here, too, it is not a question of unity or disjointedness, but of multiple forms of connectedness and disconnectedness. And these will have to be studied in their multiplicity, if we are to make sense of the social and political sphere.

notes

1 G.E. Moore, "Wittgenstein's Lectures in 1930–33," in *Philosophical Papers* (London: Allen and Unwin, 1959), p. 324.
2 *Wittgenstein and the Vienna Circle*, recorded by Friedrich Waismann, edited by Brian McGuinness, translated by Joachim Schulte (Oxford: Blackwell, 1979), p. 63f.
3 *Wittgenstein and the Vienna Circle*, p. 117.

further reading

Stern, David. "The 'Middle Wittgenstein': From Logical Atomism to Practical Holism." *Synthese*, 87, 1991.

families and resemblances

"You talk about all sorts of language games," Wittgenstein chides himself in the *Philosophical Investigations*, "but have nowhere said what the essence of a language game, and hence of language, is; what is common to all these activities, and what makes them into language or parts of language" (PI, 65). He grants that he has, indeed, abandoned the earlier, troublesome search for "the general form of the proposition" but defends himself with the observation that he has adopted a brand-new strategy in its place: "Instead of producing something common to all that we call language, I am saying that these phenomena have no one thing in common which makes us use the same word for all, – but that they are *related* to one another in many different ways. And it is because of this relationship, or these relationships, that we call them all 'language'" (ibid.). Our different language games share, in other words, a cluster of overlapping and crossing-cutting similarities and that makes them parts of our language. "I can characterize these similarities in no better way than through the word 'family resemblances'" (PI, 67).

This was to prove a fertile new strategy. Not that Wittgenstein had invented the concept of family resemblance. The German word *Familienähnlichkeit* had, in fact, been in use in literary contexts since the early nineteenth century;[1] and later on, in the 1880s, Nietzsche had spoken eloquently of a family resemblance of Indian, Greek, and German philosophizing.[2] But Wittgenstein was to give the term a philosophical weight that it had not previously had. The concept of family resemblance turned out to be handy, in particular, in combating all kinds of essentialism: from Plato's theory of ideas and Aristotle's doctrine of natural kinds to the *Tractatus* account of language, propositions, facts, objects, etc. It may also serve a useful purpose in social and political theorizing, where we tend to speak of races, classes, cultures, forms of government, and the like in an essentialist manner. Nothing comes, in fact, more easily to us than the belief that the world is sorted into sharply distinguished kinds, that individual things have essences whose necessary and sufficient conditions we can list in neatly formulated definitions.

wittgenstein, First Edition. Hans Sluga.
© 2011 Hans Sluga. Published 2011 by Blackwell Publishing Ltd.

Despite such obvious uses, the concept of family resemblance is, in fact, a hybrid notion – as should be apparent from its composite name. In order to make that point I will first of all separate what Wittgenstein says about family resemblance concepts from what he says about concepts more generally. I will also introduce the term "cluster concept" as an auxiliary notion. The broad conclusion I will seek to drive at is that we cannot simply appropriate Wittgenstein's concepts and methods and apply them unthinkingly to our own problems. In asking how we can use Wittgenstein in reflecting on our social and political existence, we attain not only a good understanding of Wittgenstein's work but also a critical one.

Games Form a Family

Wittgenstein used the notion of family resemblance for the first time when he read Spengler's *Decline of the West* in the early 1930s. In that book Spengler had argued that every one of the world cultures possesses an archetypal unity and also that all of them display the selfsame pattern of development. In his notes on the book Wittgenstein suggests that "Spengler could be better understood if he said: I am *comparing* different cultural epochs with the lives of families; within families there is a family resemblance, though you will also find a resemblance between members of different families; family resemblance differs from the other sort of resemblance in such and such ways, etc." (CV, p. 14).

Wittgenstein made his first substantial philosophical use of the term (or, rather, of the term "family likeness") subsequently in the *Blue Book*. This was occasioned by the observation that thinking is really operating with signs – an idea due to Leibniz. In his "Dialogue on the Connection between Things and Words" Leibniz had maintained that thought may not require words but that it cannot exist without some signs or other. "Ask yourself whether you can perform any arithmetical operation without making use of any number-signs. When God calculates and exercises his thought, the world is created."[3] Wittgenstein agreed that in thinking we always make use of symbols of one sort or another (words, numerals, pictures, etc.). And he also followed Leibniz in holding that we sometimes "think by writing" and at other times "think by speaking" and at yet others think silently "by imagining signs or pictures." In the first case, he said, the activity of thinking "is performed by the hand" and in the second "by the mouth and larynx" (BB, p. 6). That there is in such situations no gap between the inner process of thinking and the outer process of writing or speaking is, indeed, evident, and conforms to Wittgenstein's view on the relation between states of consciousness and external behavior.

In the *Blue Book* Wittgenstein goes on to say that his conception of thinking as "an operating with signs" might provoke the question: "What are signs?" (BB, p. 16). But instead of looking for a general answer to that question, he proposes that we should consider particular cases in which we use signs. For instance, when we go to the store with a shopping list containing the words "six apples" the assistant will compare the word "apple" with labels on different bins and then count from 1 to 6 as he takes out the apples. This makes evident that even in such an elementary case we use words in quite different ways. But we are likely to overlook this fact because of "our craving for generality" which results from a number of "tendencies" in our thinking. We tend "to look for something in common to all entities which we commonly subsume under a general term" (BB, p. 17). Thus, we assume something to be in common to all games. But games are like the members of a human family. "Some of them have the same nose, others the same eyebrows and others again the same way of walking; and these likenesses overlap" (BB, p. 17).

Wittgenstein will return to this point once more in the *Philosophical Investigations*, where he considers a variety of games ranging from chess to ring-a-ring-a-roses. These games, he argues, far from having one thing in common, exhibit, "a complicated network of similarities overlapping and criss-crossing" (PI, 66). There are physical and there are intellectual games; there are light-hearted and serious games; there are competitive and cooperative games; there are games played by one person alone, by two, three, or four players, or by whole teams. How then can we explain to anyone what a game is? Well, we can describe particular games and add: "This *and similar things* are called 'games'" (PI, 69). Such similarities are most accurately described as "family resemblances," for the resemblances between members of a family "overlap and criss-cross" in the same way as those between games. We can therefore also simply say that games form a family (PI, 67).

Wittgenstein admits that it might be possible to define games disjunctively as "x is a game if and only if it is either a, or b, or c, etc. . . . " But he dismisses this possibility as "merely playing with words" (PI, 67). That we can give a formal definition of a concept does not, in any case, prevent the concept from being a family resemblance concept with "blurred edges" because the concepts we use in the definition may in turn also have blurred edges. Thus, lots of games have to do with winning and losing. But winning in chess is related only by similarity to winning in football. For many purposes it may prove advantageous, moreover, to have family resemblance concepts. In mathematics and in the natural sciences we strive for precisely delimited concepts; but when it comes to human culture we may find it necessary to have family resemblance concepts available because we want to apply them to things in the future whose exact properties are as yet unforeseeable. This is true of the concepts of art, literature, philosophy, community, politics, and many others.

What Wittgenstein is after, of course, is an agreement that language, language game, and sign are family-resemblance concepts. Asking himself whether language can be understood as "a calculus according to definite rules" (PI, 81), he writes: "Doesn't the analogy between language and games throw light here?" We can certainly imagine people loosely playing around with a ball.

"And now someone says: the whole time they are playing a ball game and following definite rules at every throw" (PI, 83). The absurdity of the claim is meant to show us that language, too, may not always be played according to definite rules, that language games are not necessarily like operations in a formal calculus. From this follows that many other concepts must also be family resemblance concepts. In the *Philosophical Investigations* Wittgenstein concludes that the concepts of proposition and number are also family resemblance concepts. His earlier remarks on Spengler make equally clear that he conceives of human cultures and, indeed, the entirety of human culture as held together by family resemblance.

What Is Common to All These Leaves?

Wittgenstein evidently thought that there were many family resemblance concepts. That is clear, for instance, from what he said about proper names. In the *Philosophical Investigations* he suggested that we typically draw on such a concept whenever we use a proper name. He wrote:

> By "Moses" I understand the man who did what the Bible relates of Moses, or at any rate a good deal of it. But how much? Have I decided how much must be proved false for me to give up the proposition as false? Has the name "Moses" got a fixed and unequivocal use for me in all possible cases? – Is it not the case that I have, so to speak, a whole series of props in readiness, and am ready to lean on one if another should be taken from under me and vice versa? (PI, 79)

The idea that every proper name is associated with a family resemblance concept is intriguing in that it seeks to give new life to Frege's doctrine of sense and reference. According to that theory every referring expression must have a sense in addition to its reference. In order to know what a name like "Moses" refers to, we must connect a sense with that name. Wittgenstein had dismissed that doctrine in the *Tractatus* in favor of Russell's thesis that names have only reference. But in the *Philosophical Investigations* he can be seen to move closer again to Frege's view. He now holds that we must distinguish between the meaning and the bearer of a proper name. A name may have meaning, even if there is nothing it refers to. But, in contrast to Frege, Wittgenstein does not assume that the meaning of a proper name is fixed and determined. It may, instead, be given by "a whole series of props," by a family resemblance concept.

Because of their ubiquity in Wittgenstein's thinking, some interpreters have argued that he considers all concepts to be family resemblance concepts.[4] That strikes me as a serious mistake, as we can see from the fact that Wittgenstein makes quite explicit that we need to distinguish between family resemblance and other kinds of resemblance in his remarks on Spengler. But the mistake is understandable because Wittgenstein does not clearly separate his discussion of concepts in general from that of family resemblance concepts.

In the *Blue Book* the two topics are, for instance, thoroughly intertwined. In the relevant passage Wittgenstein introduces the notion of "family likeness" but then continues in a more general vein: "There is a tendency rooted in our usual forms of expression, to think that the man who has learned to understand a general term, say, the term 'leaf,' has thereby come to possess a kind of general picture of a leaf, as opposed to pictures of particular leaves" (BB, pp. 17–18). This belief is "connected to the idea that the meaning of a word is an image, or a thing correlated to the word" (BB, p. 18). The man who learns to understand the term "leaf" was shown different leaves and the thought is that "showing him the particular leaves was only a means to the end of producing 'in him' an idea which we imagined to be some kind of general image. We say that he sees what is common to all these leaves" (ibid.). There is no indication here that Wittgenstein assumes "leaf" to be a family resemblance notion. But even if we were to grant this, it would not follow that all concepts are family resemblance concepts.

That assumption would, indeed, lead to an infinite regress. For assume that we have a family resemblance concept F. Then the determination of whether something falls under that concept would depend on there being an appropriate cluster of similarities to other things we also call F. Now, take one of those similarities. There will then presumably be a concept G that applies to things having those similarities. But if G is also a family resemblance concept then there will be a cluster of other similarities that will determine whether something is a G. This will give rise to new concepts and if we assume that these must in turn also be family resemblance concepts, then we are in danger of slipping into an infinite regress. Clearly, at some point it will have to turn out that a new concept is not a family resemblance concept but marks a simple, non-family resemblance similarity.

Let us assume that the color concept red is such a concept and that I am taught that something is red by means of exemplars or paradigms. Someone shows me a red flower and calls it "red." Maybe he needs to repeat the lesson with other red objects before I catch on. But eventually I will be able to employ the term freely. When I do so, I am saying in effect that the things I now call "red" are similar to the original exemplars. This characterization of how general terms have meaning is related to Wittgenstein's account of family resemblance concepts. But now we are not speaking of family resemblance ("a network of overlapping and criss-crossing similarities") but simply of the resemblance or similarity of the things we call "red," and it is an essential feature of this account that "family resemblance differs from the other sort of resemblance," as he had said in connection with Spengler.

Wittgenstein indicates in the *Blue Book* that he considers this resemblance conception of general terms to have important philosophical implications.

From Socrates and Plato onward philosophers have always asked questions about terms like "knowledge" or "virtue." What they have typically looked for is the common element in all the particular applications of these terms, and what they have dismissed as irrelevant are "the concrete cases which alone could have helped [them] to understand the usage of the general term" (BB, pp. 19–20). In the *Philosophical Investigations* Wittgenstein adds that in philosophy we must bring the use of our terms back to the ground. Then we see, for instance, "that what we call 'sentence' and 'language' does not have the formal unity that I imagined, but is the family of formations that are more or less akin to each other" (PI, 108). In our search for the essence of knowledge or virtue we are suffering from a "bewitchment of our intelligence through the medium of our language" (PI, 109). When a philosopher uses words like "knowledge," "being," "object," "I," "proposition," "name" we must always ask: "is the word ever actually used in this way in the language game in which it is at home?" (PI, 116). This does not mean that we can't give these terms a new precise meaning, but we must always remember that this new meaning must ultimately be explained in terms that we have already available or that these terms are explained by reference to exemplars and paradigms. However we go about it, the fact remains that our use of general terms relies ultimately on the recognition of resemblances and similarities.

What Wittgenstein writes on this topic in the *Blue Book* is closely similar to some remarks of Nietzsche's in his essay fragment "On Truth and Lies in a Non-Moral Sense." Wittgenstein even uses, indeed, the same example as Nietzsche. The latter writes in the relevant passage:

> Every concept arises from the equation of unequal things. Just as it is certain that one leaf is never totally the same as another, so it is certain that the concept "leaf" is formed by arbitrarily discarding these individual differences and by forgetting the distinguishing aspects. This awakens the idea that, in addition to the leaves, there exists in nature the "leaf": the original model according to which all the leaves were perhaps woven, sketched, measured, colored, curled and painted.[5]

On Nietzsche's view, concepts are constructed on the basis of our perception of similarities. "Every word," Nietzsche writes, "instantly becomes a concept precisely insofar as it is not supposed to serve as a reminder of the unique and entirely individual original experience to which it owes its origin; but, rather, a word becomes a concept insofar as it simultaneously has to fit countless more or less similar cases – which means, purely and simply, cases which are never equal and thus altogether unequal. Every concept arises from the equation of unequal things" (ibid.). On this point, Nietzsche and Wittgenstein may both, in turn, be indebted to Schopenhauer, who had written in his *Parerga and Paralipomena* that concepts are grounded in recognitions of similarity: "*Similes* are of great value in so far as they refer an unknown relation to a known . . . Even the formation of concepts rests at bottom on similes in so far as it results from our taking up what is similar in things and discarding what is dissimilar."[6]

Expressions Constructed on Analogical Patterns

Because of this shared understanding of the origin of our concepts, both Nietzsche and Wittgenstein assign an important place to metaphor or analogy in human thought and language. In "Truth and Lies" Nietzsche argues that our thinking is through and through metaphorical and the Wittgenstein of the *Blue Book* asserts similarly that our thinking is everywhere analogical. Both maintain, moreover, that metaphors/analogies are also a source of philosophical illusion. For Nietzsche, "everything which distinguishes man from the animals depends upon this ability to refine [*verflüchtigen*] perceptual metaphors in a schema, and thus to dissolve an image into a concept" (ibid.). These schemata allow, in turn, "the construction of a pyramidal order . . . – a new world, one which now confronts that other vivid world of first impressions as more solid, more universal, better known, and more human than the immediately perceived world" (ibid.). Truth, he insists, is, indeed, nothing but "a movable host of metaphors."[7] And he concludes, perhaps rashly, that we must consider "truths" to be nothing but illusions and "lies" (in a non-moral sense). These illusions may nonetheless be useful and may even prove essential in the struggle for survival. But the theoretical outcome is still a negative one: "We believe that we know something about the things themselves . . . and yet we possess nothing but metaphors for things."[8]

Wittgenstein speaks similarly about analogy in the *Blue Book*. We get a good sense of this from what he writes on the concept of a person. He begins by asserting that "the *ordinary* use of the word 'person' is what one might call a composite use suitable under the ordinary circumstances." But if one assumes these circumstances to be changed, he goes on, the application of the term "person" or "personality" will also change. And he concludes: "If I wish to preserve this term and give it a use analogous to its former use, I am at liberty to choose between many uses, that is, between many different kinds of analogy" (BB, p. 62). The remark gives two indications that Wittgenstein thinks of concepts as grounded in analogy. When he speaks of the ordinary use of the term "person" as composite he means, presumably, not that the concept is defined through a conjunction of distinguishing marks but that we apply it to a series of distinct yet similar phenomena. Different uses of a term involve, in fact, different analogies. Wittgenstein rejects, in other words, the assumption that there is one single thing that all persons share. He holds, furthermore, that in forming a new concept out of an old one, such as a new concept of person, we extend and modify the existing concept analogically. Like Nietzsche, he believes, moreover, that proceeding in this way is of distinctive value to us. He writes: "The use of expressions constructed on analogical patterns may be extremely useful . . . Every particular notation stresses some particular point of view" (BB, p. 28). But reliance on analogies may also lead to errors. Wittgenstein notes that "where words in ordinary language have prima facie analogous grammars we are inclined to interpret them analogously" (BB, p. 7), and this can be the source of philosophical confusion. We must therefore always ask: "How far does the analogy between these uses go?" (BB, p. 23). Philosophical problems are made difficult because of "the fascination which the analogy between two similar structures in our language can exert on us" (BB, p. 26). Augustine's problems with the reality of time, metaphysical quarrels between idealism and realism, and confusions about the relations between body and mind are all due to our fascination with analogical structures. The method of philosophy must therefore be "to counteract the misleading effects of certain analogies" (BB, p. 28). This is not easy since, as already noted, analogy is essential to language and there is, moreover, "no sharp boundary . . . round the cases in which we should say that man was misled by an analogy" (ibid.). We must therefore study and assess the use of analogies case by case. For this purpose, we may sometimes find it helpful to construct new notations. In order to break the spell of old analogies we introduce "ideal languages," that is, symbolic notations – not for the purpose of replacing ordinary language, which on the whole is perfectly all right as it is, but to test the analogies built into our ordinary ways of speaking:

> Thus we sometimes wish for a notation which stresses a difference more strongly, makes it more obvious, than ordinary language does, or one which in a particular case uses more closely similar forms of expression than our ordinary language. Our mental cramp is loosened when we are shown the notations which fulfill these needs. These needs can be of the greatest variety. (BB, p. 59)

Talk of analogy is less prominent in the *Philosophical Investigations*. Instead, Wittgenstein speaks more frequently of metaphors, similes, similarities, objects of comparison, and, of course, family resemblances. Still, he comes back repeatedly to that notion. It is primarily ordinary language that we call language, he writes at one point, "and then other things by analogy or comparability with it" (PI, 494). Once again, we are also reminded of the possibility of misleading analogies, such as "misunderstandings concerning the use of words, caused, among other things, by certain analogies between the forms of expression in different regions of language" (PI, 90). A misleading analogy, Wittgenstein also writes, lies at the root of the idea that "willing" is the name of an action (PI, 613).

I emphasize this affinity between Nietzsche and Wittgenstein in order to point out that both are led by their respective view to reject any metaphysical theorizing. Thus, Nietzsche writes in "Truth and Lies" that his account of concepts means that reality itself is for us an inaccessible X. "Nature is acquainted with no forms and no concepts, and likewise with no species, but only with an X which remains inaccessible and indefinable."[9] There remains nevertheless an important difference at this point between Nietzsche and Wittgenstein. For Nietzsche allows himself in his later writings – despite a continued opposition to metaphysics – a great deal of speculation about the nature of reality. In his notes collected in *The Will to Power* he speaks of the world as a continuum of energies and forces, as "a play of forces and waves of forces," and as "a sea of forces flowing and rushing together." The view is summarized in the formula that the world is "will to power – and nothing else."[10] It is on this continuum of forces and energies, Nietzsche suggests, that we impose our concepts and erect the order of human understanding. The picture of reality that emerges in this way is pluralistic but not atomistic in character. Nietzsche seeks to reconcile this account of reality with his anti-metaphysical stance by arguing that every account of reality, including his own, is only an "interpretation." Even the picture of the world as will to power is only our "perspective" and to be understood in terms of this speculative picture as an imposition of our will. He writes, accordingly: "There are many kinds of eyes. Even the sphinx has eyes – and consequently there are many kinds of 'truths,' and consequently there is no truth."[11] Nietzsche scholars rightly worry whether this account can be made fully coherent. I mention it here precisely to bring out Wittgenstein's specifically different stance. There is nothing akin in Wittgenstein's post-*Tractatus* writings to Nietzsche's speculations. We might, nevertheless, still ask ourselves whether Wittgenstein's understanding of concepts does not implicitly commit him to something similar to the view to which Nietzsche gives expression. Isn't Wittgenstein, too, committed to some "world picture"? And is that picture not one of a pluralistic universe, a continuum of similarities extending in all directions on which we impose the precise order of our concepts?

I ask those questions because it appears that in our social and political life we always need to operate with some picture or vision of reality and of our own human place within it. Every political party is tied to (and often defines itself) in terms of such a picture – be it religious, materialist, naturalistic, or whatever. But do such pictures not amount to the possession of a metaphysics? Is all politics metaphysically grounded? Plato certainly thought so. But Nietzsche and Wittgenstein may be offering us a somewhat different story. While both reject metaphysics as a philosophical or quasi-science, they are both willing to recognize that our thinking involves at all times an "interpretation" of the real world or, in Wittgenstein's late terminology, a "world picture." That interpretation or world picture does, on their account, never possess the status of a scientific and testable truth. As Wittgenstein puts it in *On Certainty*, "I have a world picture. Is it true or false? Above all it is the substratum of all my enquiring and asserting. The propositions describ-

families and resemblances

ing it are not all equally subject to testing" (OC, 162). This does not mean for either Nietzsche or Wittgenstein that such interpretations or world pictures are arbitrary. When Nietzsche proclaimed "the universality and unconditionality of all 'will to power,'" he added: "Granted this too is only an interpretation – and you will be eager enough to raise this objection – so much the better."[12] But he insisted at the same time that the interpretations of the world we have operated with so far have now disintegrated and that his own interpretation is the best alternative available to us. It is on this interpretation, in particular, that he also hoped to ground his "great, new politics." Wittgenstein, too, understood that our modes of thinking and our language games change over time and that certain ways of thinking may come to prove unviable. "Certain events would put me into a position in which I could not go on with the old language game any further. In which I was torn away from the *sureness* of the game. Indeed, doesn't it seem obvious that the possibility of a language game is conditioned by certain facts?" (OC, 617).

The Human Form of Life

It is part of the human form of life, according to Wittgenstein, to see similarities and resemblances between things. It is also part of our form of life to recognize clusters of overlapping and crisscrossing resemblances. These capacities give rise to our distinctive use of language. They allow us to form both simple concepts and what I want to call cluster concepts. The story also explains why there are different language games, different languages, different systems of thought, and even different world pictures. Language games, systems of thought, and world pictures become differentiated because we are able to see or stress different similarities.

Compelling as this story is, it raises two serious questions. The first concerns the limits of our recognition of similarities. Everything can be considered similar in one way or another to everything else. Is there then no limit to the concepts we might form on the basis of our recognition of a similarity? The second question concerns how we get from the recognition of a similarity to a concept. Similarity is, after all, a comparative notion. There are always degrees of similarity. But our fundamental concepts are classificatory, not comparative in character.

Regarding the first question, Wittgenstein admits that one person may see a similarity where another one does not. He also grants that we may come to see a similarity where we had previously not seen it or, alternatively, see similarity at one moment but not at the next. When he asks himself why we have one concept rather than another one, why we play one language game rather than another, he advances three explanations. First of all, it is evidently the case that our language games depend on how things are. Secondly, there are human needs and interests and these may vary. Thirdly, there is how we see things and that also may change over time. Our needs, interests, and ways of seeing are, moreover, all grounded in our human form of life and that form of life does not vary so easily from one moment to another. Wittgenstein addresses this issue most vividly in his "Remarks on Frazer's *Golden Bough*." He asks himself there why we can understand ancient mythology even though we no longer think about the world in its terms. He suggests that there are certain common features of human life on which mythology builds and which we can still identify. "There are dangers connecting with eating and drinking, not only for savages, but also for us; nothing is more natural than the desire to protect ourselves from these" (RF, p. 66). We can also understand that "a man's shadow, which looks like him, or his mirror-image, the rain, thunderstorms, the phases of the moon, the changing seasons, the way in which animals are similar to and different from one another and in relation to man, the phenomena of death, birth, and sexual life, in short everything we observe around us year in and year out, interconnected in so many ways," may become the source of a particular way of speaking and thinking (RF, pp. 66–67). Wittgenstein comes back to this point in *On Certainty* when he writes: "You must bear in mind that the language game is so to say unpredictable. I mean: it is not based on grounds. It is not reasonable (or unreasonable). It stands there – like our life" (OC, 559). And to this he adds that language has not emerged from ratiocination. We must look at the creator of logic and language, rather, "as an animal, as a primitive being to which one grants instinct but not ratiocination" (OC, 475). What unites us are certain fundamental givens of the human form of life. They allow us to perceive different kinds of similarities and thus to form different concepts, engage in different language games, speak different languages, and have different world pictures. But they also delimit the ways we see things. And this agreement in the human form of life guarantees that there are similarities and family resemblances between different language games, languages, and world pictures. In consequence, we can recognize that there exist a variety of language games, languages, and world pictures. We can even come to understand these language games, languages, and world pictures even though they are not our own.

The second question I have raised is more difficult to answer. Why does our recognition of similarities give rise to classificatory concepts? Wittgenstein says nothing on this topic. Here Nietzsche may once again be of help. In "Truth and Lies" he suggests that there are pragmatic grounds for this shift from the comparative to the classificatory. And in *The Will to Power* he writes even more forcefully: "In the formation of reason, logic, the categories it was *need* that was authoritative: the need, not to 'know,' but to subsume, to schematize, for the purpose of intelligibility and calculation."[13] While this calls for elaboration, the remark may still help us to understand that for Wittgenstein, as for Nietzsche, our readiness to classify things into discrete units is grounded in human need or, more generally speaking, in the human form of life.

Clusters and Families

The notion of family resemblance may have served Wittgenstein well for his characterization of the unity and the diversity of language games, of language, and of the human form of life. But it may need more work, if it is to be an effective tool for characterizing other aspects of our existence.

There are certainly concepts that apply to groups of items simply because of overlapping and crisscrossing similarities. Wittgenstein may be right in thinking, for instance, that "game" is such a concept. Diverging from Wittgenstein's own terminology, I will call concepts of this kind "cluster concepts" and will speak of the things to which they apply simply as "clusters." Much of the time when Wittgenstein talks about family resemblance he is actually speaking of cluster concepts. We often use the word "family," indeed, as equivalent to what I am calling a cluster. But some families (such as, for instance, human families) are more than clusters. Their members are related to each other not necessarily (or not only) by overlapping similarities but by what I will call loosely causal relations. In a biological family, for instance, there exist causal relations of descent. When Wittgenstein speaks of family resemblance he seems to be speaking at times simply of clusters but at other times of things held together by causal relations. (I will speak here simply of "causal groups.") It appears, then, that Wittgenstein's use of the term "family resemblance" is systematically ambiguous because it does not allow us to distinguish between clusters and causal groups. Some such distinction is, however, essential when we examine social and political phenomena.

Consider, for instance, human families. Wittgenstein seems to think of them as clusters, that is, as individuals exhibiting "family resemblance" where the emphasis is on the word "resemblance." But is this sufficient? Take the case of a mother who gives birth to a seriously disfigured child. The newborn may in no way resemble other members of its family. We take it, nonetheless, to be part of the family. Similarity and dissimilarity have nothing to do with this. The decisive factor is rather that the child is born of this mother and is thus biologically and causally related to other members of the family. It is true that those who are biologically related often display certain similarities, but this is a consequence of their biological kinship. It is equally true that we can sometimes determine that two people belong to the same family because of certain shared similarities in look or behavior. But these do not *define* membership in the family; they only provide evidence for it. Membership in a human family is, of course, not exclusively determined in biological terms. A husband and a wife form a family even though they usually do not share a bloodline. An adopted child belongs to its adoptive family even though it has no biological relations to other members of that family. In some cultures an abandoned child or an abandoned wife are no longer counted as part of the family even though they are biologically related to those in the family. Again, none of this has to do with similarity or dissimilarity. The concept of the human family is a biological, cultural, and legal – and thus a causal – concept rather than a mere cluster concept. But all this is obscured by the term "family resemblance."

Or consider the notion of being German. Is it a cluster concept? Mere family resemblance is surely insufficient for establishing that two individuals are both German. If we discovered living beings on another planet who shared a cluster of similarities with today's Germans, these extraterrestrials would still not count as Germans. Things might be different, if it turned out that these extraterrestrials were actually the descendents of some long-lost German astronauts. This might suggest that shared biological descent determines German nationality. There was certainly a time when this belief was common. But who is to say that Otto von Bismarck and I, for instance, have common biological roots? (The idea strikes me as unlikely right now.) And yet we are both indubitably German. A student of mine in Frankfurt, on the other hand, is just as German as I am even though her family came a generation ago from Turkey and there is surely no close biological link between us. Being German is, first of all, a legal and political concept and secondarily a cultural and historical one. Biological factors may or may not be relevant for it. But resemblance has little to do with the matter. Being German is certainly not a cluster concept.

I am inclined to think, with Wittgenstein, that "language" is precisely a cluster concept. Imagine once again that we are traveling in outer space and encounter creatures who voice or draw signs that serve to refer to things and that can be used to make statements about them. If their practice was sufficiently similar to our linguistic behavior, we would certainly want to say that those Martians possess a language. But what then will we say of the concept of the German language. If "German" is a causal concept and "language" a cluster concept, we can go either way. Nietzsche seems to have had some such complex formation in mind when he spoke of the family resemblance of Indian, Greek, and German philosophizing. He meant to indicate that these different traditions exhibit overlapping and crisscrossing similarities. But he also wanted to say that their affinity was due to a common descent.

Wittgenstein uses the notion of family resemblance to convince us that there are no formal definitions of such terms as "language," "proposition," etc. We may agree with him on this point but conclude that this may have two different explanations. In the case of causal concepts, it seems, we may have no formal definition because we cannot say in advance who will in the future be considered a causal kin. Causal kinship relations are open-ended and are so specifically with respect to the future. Consider the concept of art as such a term. It is characteristic of art that its course is unpredictable, that we cannot say in advance what future works of art may look like. Historical concepts have this kind of openness (think of "culture," "religion," "politics," etc.) and they have for that reason no formal definition. We can, of course, arbitrarily limit their use by declaring that only this or that is to count as an instance. But the peculiar way in which we use historical and cultural terms to project into the future cannot be captured in this manner. Nietzsche was certainly right when he declared in his *Genealogy of Morals* that only what is unhistorical can be defined. But there is, in addition, another form of open-endedness and it manifests itself in cluster concepts. It is the kind of open-endedness to which Wittgenstein draws our attention when he says that in any survey of games "many common features drop out, and others appear." The indefinability of Wittgenstein's cluster terms is due to the fact that the range of relevant similarities is not fully determined. Cluster terms are, in other words, open-ended with respect to relevance rather than the future. Either way, Wittgenstein is right in pointing out that terms like "language," "sign," "family," "game," "number," and so on have no formal definitions. That this may be so for different reasons does not have to concern him in the argument in which he is engaged in both the *Philosophical Investigations* and the *Blue Book*. It is enough for him to have shown that for whatever reasons the terms "language," "sign," and "game" are among the indefinable terms. But there are other situations in which we must be clearer on this point and here is an example that will illustrate this.

Analytic philosophy is one of the dominant forms of contemporary philosophy – at least in the English-speaking world. But what exactly is to count as "analytic philosophy?" It appears that we can understand the concept in two quite different ways. We can treat it as either a cluster concept or a causal concept. Understood in the first way, analytic philosophy is everything that stands in an appropriate resemblance relation to what we are calling today by that name. It then turns out that Plato and Aristotle, Leibniz, Kant, and Hume were all (at least, in some parts of their work) analytic philosophers. On the other hand, if we take "analytic philosophy" to be a causal and kinship term, we will think of it as a specifically historical enterprise. To study analytic philosophy will then mean to study the work of philosophers who lived in a particular period of time, who knew each other, who interacted with each other, who read and responded to each other's writings. Questions of dependence and influence will then become important. In this case we will speak of thinkers like Frege, Russell, Moore, Wittgenstein, Carnap, and Quine as analytic philosophers but not of Plato and Aristotle or Leibniz and Kant.

In summary, we can say that cluster concepts are purely structural notions. Things that belong to a cluster are characterized by a shared feature that Wittgenstein identifies as family resemblance. This feature has three characteristics. It is trivially the case that every object in a family resemblance group stands in a family resemblance relation to itself. Second, if A stands in a family relation to B then B stands in that same family resemblance relation to A. Third, if A and B in a family resemblance group stand in a family resemblance relation and B and C in that same group stand in that exact family resemblance relation to each other, than A and C stand in that family resemblance relation. This third proposition holds, however, only under these precise conditions. It will not, of course, be the case that A and C stand in a relation of family resemblance if A and B stand in one relation of family resemblance and B and C in another one. More generally, then, we can say that family resemblance is a reflexive, symmetrical, and transitive relation. And this makes clear immediately why family resemblance or cluster concepts are insufficient for analyzing social and historical phenomena. The fact is that distinctly historical, temporal, and causal concepts are not all reflexive, symmetrical, and transitive. And we cannot do without such concepts. As a species we are, after all, a product of natural evolution. As twenty-first-century beings we stand at the end of a specific historical (cultural, economic, and political) development. The forces of the natural world bear upon us continuously. As agents we rely on causal regularities and exploit our knowledge of them. We exist in time and rely on our distinctive sense of past, present, and future. It is essential to who we are that we are born, live, and die; the horizon of our experience and thought is set by the moment in which we live.

Wittgenstein's attitude toward these aspects of our existence is, for the most part, one of benign neglect. That is most evident in his early work. From the exclamation "What has history to do with me? Mine is the first and only world" in his 1916 Notebook through the detachment of the *Tractatus* from the devastating conditions under which it was written, the early Wittgenstein displayed a resolutely unhistorical state of mind. That had changed, of course, by the 1930s when he read Frazer's *Golden Bough* and Spengler's *Decline of the West*. But even then he insisted on dealing with historical phenomena in structural rather than temporal and causal terms. In the "Remarks on Frazer's *Golden Bough*" he wrote accordingly: "The historical explanation, the explanation as an hypothesis of development, is only *one* way of assembling the data – of their synopsis. It is just as possible to see the data in their relation to one another and to embrace them in a general picture" (RF, p. 69). And it is clear from the tone of this remark that he much preferred the latter method.

Wittgenstein's resistance to historical (i.e., developmental and causal) explanation is a consequence of the way he thinks about human action. He tells us in the *Blue Book* that the word "why" in the question "Why did he act in such and such a fashion?" is ambiguous. It may be about the causes of the action but also about the reasons for it. The two cases, he declares, must be kept sharply apart. That claim has been disputed; Wittgenstein makes it, however, on two grounds: (1) while the chain of causes goes back indefinitely, the chain of reasons always comes to a determinate end; (2) our knowledge of the causes of our actions is always hypothetical, whereas our knowledge of the reasons for our actions is immediate and certain. In the *Brown Book* he concludes, accordingly: "Now this game of giving the reason why one acts in a particular way does not involve finding the causes of one's actions" (BB,

p. 110). And in another place he adds: "The causes of our belief in a proposition are indeed irrelevant to the question what we believe. Not so the grounds, which are grammatically related to the proposition, and tell us what the proposition is" (Z, 437). That may sound plausible at first sight, but we forget that we can often say only what someone believes when we know from whom he has learned the words he utters. Wittgenstein's most pointed rejection of causal explanations of human action is to be found in yet another remark: "No supposition seems to me more natural than that there is no process in the brain correlated with associating or with thinking . . . Why should this order not proceed, so to speak, out of chaos?" (Z, 608). He compares that possibility to the thought that "an organism might come into being even out of something quite amorphous, as it were causelessly" and concludes his remark with the words: "There is no reason why this should not really hold for our thoughts, and hence for our talking and writing" (Z, 608). It is natural then that he should also steer away from hypothetical, causal explanations when it comes to historical facts. In the "Remarks on Frazer's *Golden Bough*" he writes in consequence that "an hypothetical link should in this case do nothing but direct attention to the similarity, the relatedness of the *facts*." We should concern ourselves with it "only in order to sharpen our eyes for a formal connection" (RF, p. 69). The question is, of course, how much such a methodology can deliver.

We get a sense of what is at stake by turning our attention once more to what he wrote about Spengler in 1931. Wittgenstein remarked then that we can compare cultural epochs with families and that "within a family there is family resemblance, though you will also find a resemblance between members of different families." But what kinds of resemblance are we to expect in this latter case? The answer is surely that members of different families may be related to each other by a cluster of overlapping and crisscrossing resemblances and would thus be related to each by family resemblance. This suggests, in effect, that Wittgenstein has been using the term "family resemblance" in two different ways. In its first use, intended in the remark on Spengler, family resemblance is meant to characterize the relations between members of one and the same family, what makes them into one family. In its second use, family resemblance has nothing to do with family identity; it characterizes, instead, a similarity that may obtain also between members of different families. The confusion arises because we have used the word "family" in two different senses: once to characterize a kinship grouping (a causal group) and once to characterize a similarity grouping (a cluster). The ambiguity is embedded in our ordinary use of the word "family" and is captured in the disjunctive dictionary characterization of a family as "a group of things having a common source or similar features."

In describing what he means by family resemblance, Wittgenstein uses a second term that has, unfortunately, the same sort of ambiguity as the word "family" and that is term "*Verwandtschaft*" (kinship, relatedness). Thus, he writes that the phenomena we call languages have no one thing in common, but "are related [*verwandt*] to one another" and that it is "because of this relationship, or these relationships [because of this *Verwandtschaft, oder diese Verwandtschaften*]" that we call them all "language" (PI, 65). Unlike (or, at least, more strongly than) the English "relationship," the German "*Verwandtschaft*" carries two meanings. On the one hand, it may mean as little as the word "similarity"; on the other, it can also refer to a relationship of blood and common descent. It is not easy to say in each case whether Wittgenstein takes the word "*Verwandtschaft*" in one or the other of these two senses. But his examples suggest that he is playing on its ambiguity. When he insists, for instance, that in games "we will not see something that is common to *all*, but similarities, relationships [*Verwandtschaften*], and a whole series of them at that" (PI, 66), the words "similarity" and "relationship" may simply express the same idea twice; but it is also possible that Wittgenstein is tacitly appealing to our intuition that games are activities that have developed out of each other. When it comes to human families, "*Verwandtschaft*" in the sense of kinship is certainly not definitively established by "various resemblances between members of a family: build, features, colour of eyes, gait, temperament, etc. etc" (PI, 67).

A Case for Methodological Pluralism

Both kinship and similarity concepts have a place in our thinking. In history we are not only concerned with mapping similarities of one sort or another; we are also seeking to establish real connections, causal links, dependencies and "influences." Similarity terms prove insufficient for this kind of undertaking. Thus causal and kinship terms are essential when we are telling the history of philosophy but not when we are comparing types of philosophical thinking. Causal and kinship terms are similarly essential in the history of art but not in the comparison of styles. They also play a role in literary history but not the same in comparative literature.

The status of a term as either a causal/kinship or a cluster/similarity term is, however, not fixed once and for all. Something that starts as a kinship term may eventually become in our use a similarity term and the same thing will hold vice versa. Thinking in terms of relations of kinship, of descent, of developments, of family trees, etc. can satisfy certain intellectual needs. But once we have established connections and descriptions in this way we may want to shift attention to similarities and dissimilarities in the field of the phenomena so described. This permits us to ignore historical contexts and causes, questions of descent, and family trees and may open up a new way of seeing things. It is plausible, for instance, to think of our concept of language as originally a kinship notion. The ancient Greeks certainly pretended that only they and their kin spoke a real language and that everything else was incoherent noise. But for us today "language" is, undoubtedly, a similarity and cluster term. Anything that looks like, sounds like, or functions like language is for us language. Phenomenology, we might say, has triumphed here over genealogy.

But similarity concepts may also over time become causal concepts. When we speak today of a family tree of the Indo-European languages, when we postulate that these languages have developed out of each other, and that they refer us to a shared cultural (and perhaps even biological) heritage, then we do so because of the similarities that philologists have discovered between the various Indo-European tongues. The term "Indo-European language" has thus developed from being a similarity term to a causal and kinship term and this development marks an advance in our understanding. Our grasp of the phenomena becomes firmer when we think not only in terms of similarities but also in the richer and more suggestive vocabulary of a causal order. I close with another example to illustrate that point. Consider the fact that color terms are for us almost always similarity terms. Black is what looks like black. Blue looks similar to blue and red to red. But the painter knows that some black is created from blue and some from red. And anyone who understands these derivations will begin to see black itself in a new way. He will recognize, for instance, relations and differences between a cold and a warm black. Recognition of causal kinship can thus lead to sharpened perception of similarities and dissimilarities. But the reverse is also true. As the painter's power of visual discrimination sharpens, he may also learn to create and mix colors in new and different ways.

notes

1 Grimm's *Wörterbuch* cites its occurrence in the writings of Jean Paul and Tieck and suggests its derivation from the Latin *gentilis similitudo*. Jacob and Wilhelm Grimm, *Deutsches Wörterbuch*, vol. 3 (Leipzig: Hirzel, 1862), p. 1306.

2 Friedrich Nietzsche, Beyond Good and Evil, translated by R.J. Hollingdale (London: Penguin, 1973).

3 Gottfried Leibniz, "Dialogue on the Connection between Things and Words," in *Selections*, edited by Philip P. Wiener (New York: Scribner's, 1951), p. 8.

4 Renford Bambrough, "Universals and Family Resemblance," in George Pitcher, ed., *Wittgenstein* (London: Macmillan, 1968).

5 Friedrich Nietzsche, "On Truth and Lies in a Nonmoral Sense," in *Philosophy and Truth: Selections from Nietzsche's Notebooks of the Early 1870's*, translated and edited by David Breazeale (New Jersey: Humanities Press International, 1979), p. 83.

6 Arthur Schopenhauer, *Parerga and Paralipomena*, translated by E.F.J. Payne (Oxford: Clarendon Press, 1974), vol. 2, p. 550.

7 Nietzsche, "On Truth and Lies," p. 84.

8 Nietzsche, "On Truth and Lies," pp. 82–83.

9   Nietzsche, "On Truth and Lies," p. 83.
10 Friedrich Nietzsche, *The Will to Power*, translated by Walter Kaufmann and R.J. Hollingdale (New York, Vintage Books, 1968), p. 1067.
11 Nietzsche, *Will to Power*, p. 540.
12 Nietzsche, *Beyond Good and Evil*, p. 22.
13 Nietzsche, *Will to Power*, p. 515.

our unsurveyable grammar

From the Synoptic View to the Album

When Wittgenstein ruminated on the *Tractatus* in 1933, he told his students that a book on philosophy with a beginning and end was really "a sort of contradiction."[1] The *Tractatus* had, of course, had both: a decisive first sentence and an equally decisive last one. But such a book could be justified, he held now, only if one had a comprehensive, "synoptic" view of things. Clearly he did not think, when he said this, that he was in possession of such a view or that he had had the correct synoptic vision at the time of the *Tractatus*.

The search for a synoptic view had occupied Wittgenstein from his first notes for the *Tractatus* onward. "Yesterday I worked a lot but not *very* hopefully since I lacked the right *overview* [*Überblick*]," he wrote on September 21, 1914 in the first of his wartime notebooks (GT, p. 24). And four days later: "I am still lacking an overview and for that reason the problem appears unsurveyable [*unübersehbar*]" (GT, p. 25). And another four days on: "I still do not see clearly and have no overview. I see details without knowing how they will fit into the whole" (ibid.). And once more, two months later: "Again no clarity of vision [*Sehen*] although I am obviously standing in front of the solution of the deepest problems so that I almost bump my nose in it!!! My mind is simply blind for this right now. I feel that I am standing right at the gate but cannot see it clearly enough to be able to open it" (GT, p. 43). These frustrations were not to stop him, however, from completing his book. As he put the *Tractatus* together he must have felt – at least for a moment – that he had found the previously missing synoptic view and that he could deal now with "the (!) problems of philosophy," as the preface said, in the certainty that they "have in essentials been solved once and for all."

With his return to philosophy in 1929 he found himself forced, however, to reconsider the possibility of attaining such a view. The issue arose for him now from his new idea that the task of philosophy was to deal with "particular

wittgenstein, First Edition. Hans Sluga.
© 2011 Hans Sluga. Published 2011 by Blackwell Publishing Ltd.

errors or 'troubles in our thought' . . . due to false analogies suggested by our actual use of expressions."[2] The focus on particular errors and specific uses of expressions suggested a novel concern with the details of thought and language rather than with a grand overview. If there was anything synoptic in this approach it would involve, in Wittgenstein's words, "a 'synopsis' of *many trivialities.*"[3] Was there then no comprehensive philosophical overview to be attained? He still thought that our philosophical discomfort "is not removed until we have a synopsis of all the various trivialities. If one item necessary for the synopsis is lacking, we still feel that something is wrong."[4] There remained, in other words, the feeling, as he said in the *Blue Book*, that "no philosophical problem can be solved until all philosophical problems are solved; which means that as long as they aren't all solved every new difficulty renders all previous results questionable" (BB, p. 44). But the *Blue Book* also indicated that we might have to content ourselves with something less. The work of philosophy, Wittgenstein said now, might, in fact, have to be compared to the arranging of books in a library. Even though our ultimate goal may be to create a complete ordering of the books, we may actually succeed only at "taking up some books which seemed to belong together, and putting them on different shelves; nothing more being final about their positions than that they no longer lie side by side." Some of the greatest achievements in philosophy, he added, were just like that. In the face of our hankering after a synoptic view, the difficulty in philosophy was "to say no more than we know" (BB, pp. 44–45).

In 1914 he had blamed his failure to achieve the appropriate synoptic view on his own personal limitations. Now he thought that the problem was intrinsic to philosophy. He told his students: "We encounter the kind of difficulty we should have with the geography of a country for which we had no map, or else a map of isolated bits."[5] This forced one to travel repeatedly over the territory in order to discover how things are related to each other. "So I suggest repetition as a means of surveying the connections" (ibid.). And using the comparison of philosophy with an uncharted country again in the preface to the *Philosophical Investigations* he wrote that his reflections on "the concepts of meaning, of understanding, of a proposition, of logic, the foundations of mathematics, states of consciousness, and other things" had forced him "to travel over a wide field of thought criss-cross in every direction." Along the way he had certainly come up with a number of passable "sketches of landscapes" but he had been unable to give his thoughts "a single direction against their natural inclination." And this, he added "was, of course, connected with the very nature of the investigation." Ruefully, he conceded now that, unlike the *Tractatus*, his new book was in consequence "really only an album" (PI, p. ix).

Was this false modesty? It is true that the text of the *Philosophical Investigations* has no affirmative beginning and no decisive end. It starts casually with a quotation and a critique of the view that is quoted and it ends at no landmark point in the argument. The reader may also have the experience of getting lost in a myriad of minute questions. (How do children learn to count? What goes on when we read a text aloud? How do we speak about our pains?) It is difficult, for that reason, to summarize the book in a single all-encompassing thesis. One must get down to the particulars of the text and subject Wittgenstein's individual observations and remarks to the most careful scrutiny. And yet it is difficult to avoid the impression that he still cleaves to a comprehensive view of some sort or other. Does he not speak in general terms about "language," "meaning," "rules," "consciousness," "thought," etc.? And does he not often enough step back from the details to make very general claims about philosophy and the confusions of human thinking? Does he not, after all, suggest to us a specific synoptic vision of the entire human form of life? How then are we to reconcile this apparent hankering for generality with Wittgenstein's determination to devote himself to the particular?

"I don't know my way about"

In the early 1930s Wittgenstein occasionally called his method of examining particular uses of language by the name of "phenomenology." With this term he meant to distance his philosophy from both the empirical sciences, with their explanatory and predictive theories, and the logical purism of the *Tractatus*. The same conception of his undertaking is still evident in the *Philosophical Investigations*, where we read: "Philosophy simply puts everything before us, and neither explains nor deduces anything" (PI, 126). And: "We must do away with all *explanation*, and description alone must take its place" (PI, 109). But by then Wittgenstein had come to avoid the term "phenomenology." He characterized philosophy, instead, as supplying "remarks concerning the natural history of human beings" (PI, 415). Drawing on an older sense of the word "*Naturgeschichte*," in which a description of the night sky can be called "A Natural History of the Starry Heavens,"[6] he was, in other words, characterizing philosophy once more as a descriptive undertaking. But he also wanted to make sure that no one took him to be supplying a comprehensive phenomenology. Instead, he spoke of philosophy now as limited to "remarks" concerning natural history. And even this characterization he modified in the subsequent warning that "we can also invent fictitious natural history for our purposes" (PI, p. 230). The kind of philosophy he was after was not meant to be dedicated specifically to the description of "our actual use of expressions" but might extend to the description of invented – that is, fictitious but possible – situations (such as the imagined language game of PI, 2).

The stated purpose of such descriptions had been from the 1930s onward to resolve "muddles" in our speaking and thinking by making language and thought transparent. Behind this project lies the idea that philosophical problems are generated by our inability to get a clear view of what is at stake in them. They are, in other words, problems of confusion rather than problems of ignorance. We might compare philosophy here to a jigsaw puzzle. Even when we have all the pieces of the puzzle in front of us we may still be unable to arrange them into a coherent picture, and that for a number of reasons. If the number of pieces is large, we may easily lose an overview of them; the pieces may look very similar and yet prove to be not interchangeable; when we try to combine them a false start may prevent us from making further progress later on; certain preconceptions about how the puzzle will come out may stand in the way of actually solving it, etc. There are for Wittgenstein similarly many things that stand in the way of looking at our philosophical problems clearly. One of them is that an "ideal in our thinking" may have become "immovably stuck." "The idea sits, so to say, as a pair of glasses on our nose and whatever we look at, we see through them. We never have the thought to take them off" (PI, 103). Two apparently similar forms of expression may induce us to make misleading analogies. Also: "A metaphor that has been incorporated into the forms of our language generates a false appearance; that disquiets us. 'But *this* isn't how it is!' – we say. 'Yet, it must *be such*'" (PI, 112). Or we are like a fly in a trap. It doesn't occur to us that the way out is to retrace our steps rather than to forge ahead. The result is disorientation. Most generally we can say, "A philosophical problem has the form: 'I don't know my way about'" (PI, 123).

The Problem of Grammar

The crucial philosophical difficulty turns out to be that "our grammar lacks surveyability" (PI, 122). In order to appreciate the nature of this difficulty we must understand that "grammar" is meant to be here not a system of abstract grammatical rules but more generally the organized pattern of our linguistic practices. It is this actual structure or order of our language game that proves to be unsurveyable. In fact, we should not be thinking only about language and language games. The human form of life – our society, our culture, our history – each has its grammar and of each such grammar we must say that it lacks surveyability.

It helps to illustrate the abstract idea with a mundane example. There are mornings when I come into my office and look at my desk in despair. It is completely covered with papers. The bulging piles contain all sorts of things: student essays (some read), notes, letters, documents, notifications, etc. It is clear that my papers are a mess. The stuff on my desk has become entirely *unübersichtlich*, to use a convenient German word with no exact English equivalent. (Sometimes I think that it takes a nation dedicated to the idea of order to have a precise word for something whose order escapes us.)

Wittgenstein draws our attention to this sort of totality in section 122 of the *Philosophical Investigations* when he writes (in my translation) that "we do not survey the use of our words" and that "our grammar lacks surveyability." Since he considers language central to the entire human form of life, it follows that our form of life must also be unsurveyable. No wonder then that unsurveyable wholes raise for him issues "of fundamental importance." That we do not survey the use of our words, our grammar, language, and form of life he declares to be, indeed, "a main source of our lack of understanding." He goes on to suggest that we need "a surveyable representation" that can generate "the comprehension that consists in 'seeing connections.'" The concept of a surveyable representation, he adds, "signifies our form of representation, how we see things." And he closes the section with the somewhat puzzling question: "Is this a 'world-view'?"

There is, indeed, much to puzzle about in this passage. That is one reason why it proves so difficult to translate. Our published English version is certainly unsatisfactory and in summarizing section 122 I have, therefore, found it necessary to modify the translation in various respects. But even in its original German, the section confronts us with difficult questions. For one thing, Wittgenstein never explains what he means by "*übersichtlich.*" Though section 122 clearly marks a nodal point in his thinking, he uses the word "*übersichtlich*" in an entirely informal fashion. It and its cognates occur, in fact, only seven times in the entire *Philosophical Investigations* and four of these are to be found in section 122. That the term is nonetheless important is shown by its reappearance at a number of other places in Wittgenstein's work. It belongs, moreover, to the vocabulary of visual terms that dot Wittgenstein's prose everywhere, from the *Tractatus* to his last notes. Like the rest of this vocabulary Wittgenstein uses the term "*übersichtlich*" almost always in a metaphorical fashion. Only occasionally does he employ it in its literal meaning. He does so, for instance, when he speaks of the color-octahedron as being "a surveyable representation of the grammatical rules" of our color concepts (PR, p. 52). The color-octahedron is certainly a visual object and I can perceive the colors on it at (more or less) a single glance. Similarly, when he writes in his *Remarks on the Foundations of Mathematics* that "a mathematical proof must be surveyable" (RFM, p. 143) Wittgenstein sometimes appears to have the kind of proof in mind that can be laid out diagrammatically on a single sheet of paper. But not every valid mathematical proof is of this kind. When he claims quite generally that every mathematical proof must be surveyable, he must then be using the term in a metaphorical fashion. The same holds of the assertion that our grammar lacks surveyability. The grammar of our language is certainly not a visual object like my desk. Perhaps Wittgenstein means to say by this remark only that our grammar is not organized in a fashion that we can fully grasp or that is easily or intuitively accessible to us. We might say, for instance, in this metaphorical sense that the arrangement of the books in the Berkeley library is surveyable. That does not mean that we can take it in at a single glance; it means only that there is an intuitively graspable system of organization that allows us to locate books very easily. If we understand that system, there will be no confusion over where a book belongs on the shelves.

Here is what Wittgenstein himself says about the issue in the context of a discussion of the contradictions that appeared in Frege's and Russell's logic.

In section 125 of the *Investigations* he writes: "It is not the business of philosophy to solve the contradiction by means of a mathematical, logico-mathematical discovery. But to make the state of mathematics that troubles us surveyable, the state *before* the solution of the contradiction." He is suggesting, in other words, that Frege and Russell did not have an entirely clear view of the mathematics that generated the contradiction. That's why the contradiction came to them as a surprise. They laid down rules for their deductive game but when they applied those rules, things did not turn out as they had anticipated. Wittgenstein suggests that we need to understand this peculiar situation of being entangled in one's own rules. It is clear from the context that he does not mean to say that we can literally see our entanglement in those rules at a single glance; he means rather that we can make the nature of that entanglement intuitively evident to ourselves.

But why should anyone ever have thought that the grammar of a language could be intuitively evident like a well-ordered library? Anyone who has ever struggled with a second language will know how opaque, how arbitrary, how unfathomably complex grammar can be. Did Wittgenstein not learn this when he acquired his English? What then is surprising and philosophically interesting in the observation that our grammar lacks surveyability? The answer is that the Wittgenstein of the *Tractatus* once thought that the logic of our language was intuitively evident and in this sense surveyable. That is why he had written at the time that the logic of our language shows itself and that there can therefore never be surprises in logic (TLP, 6.1251). Wittgenstein's observation that our grammar lacks surveyability is, thus, directed first and foremost at the *Tractatus* conception of language and logic.

What then follows for Wittgenstein from the discovery that our grammar is unsurveyable? Early on, in section 5 of the *Investigations*, he writes that "the general notion of the meaning of a word surrounds the working of language with a haze which makes clear vision [*das klare Sehen*] impossible. It disperses the fog to study the phenomena of language in primitive kinds of application in which one can survey the aim and functioning of the words." To show us such primitive applications of language is the function of the simple language games Wittgenstein constructs in the *Investigations*. We can illustrate the point also with a remark from Wittgenstein's notebook from 1914. He writes there: "In the proposition a world is as it were put together experimentally. (As when in the law-court in Paris a motor-car accident is represented by means of dolls, etc.)" (NB, p. 7). The physical model of the accident in the courtroom serves here as a representation of the actual happening which is no longer directly accessible to us and as such not surveyable. The model, on the other hand, is surveyable in the straightforward sense that we can look down on it from above and see it at once in its entirety. The model represents in an immediately visible fashion the items (cars, people, houses, etc.) that are presumed to have been involved in the incident and it spatially represents their supposed actual relations. The model is, moreover, relatively permanent and can be studied from different angles, whereas the accident itself was a momentary happening and would have been perceived by different people on the scene from different points of view. The model focuses our attention, finally, on what is essential in the accident by not depicting what is irrelevant to the incident. The model thus gives us a fully surveyable representation of an inherently unsurveyable situation.

I have chosen this particular illustration because it brings out a distinction that we need to be clear about, if we are to understand what Wittgenstein is after in section 122 of the *Philosophical Investigations*. It is the distinction between (a) something being itself surveyable and (b) something having a surveyable representation. In the case of the car accident, it is clear that the courtroom model provides a surveyable representation but the event remains nonetheless unsurveyable in so far as it cannot be retrieved from the past and was, in any case, never fully surveyable even as it happened. Consider also once more my office desk. I can easily make a drawing that shows the piles of paper neatly labeled and organized. But the desk does not become a bit more organized by this surveyable representation. It remains just as unsurveyable as it was before. When Wittgenstein writes in section 122 that our grammar lacks surveyability he does not mean, then, that our grammar lacks a surveyable representation. And when he adds that we need a surveyable representation, he does not mean to say that this would make the grammar itself surveyable. The surveyable representation is needed, rather, because our grammar is and remains unsurveyable, just as we need the surveyable courtroom model because the accident itself is and remains unsurveyable. Surveyable representations may, in other words, serve various functions. They may, in the simplest case, provide a representation of a totality that is itself surveyable. A surveyable representation may also function as a plan for making a totality surveyable. Third and last, and philosophically most important, is that a surveyable representation may serve as a tool for dealing with wholes that are (and will remain) intrinsically unsurveyable.

The courtroom model draws our attention to the danger inherent in this methodology of constructing surveyable representations for unsurveyable wholes. For our model may actually misrepresent the relevant features of the incident; it may oversimplify and thereby distort the actual situation; it may represent features that do not bear on the question of responsibility for the accident and leave out others that are essential. Our means for dealing with the unsurveyability of grammar is, thus, at the same time a potential means for misunderstanding grammar. For when we have constructed a surveyable model of something inherently unsurveyable, there is always the danger that the model does not capture the significant characteristics of the unsurveyable totality. Thus, the *Tractatus* had once sought to make the working of language transparent but it had considered, in fact, only a very specific and limited use of language. In the *Philosophical Investigations* Wittgenstein writes that the *Tractatus* had treated the formula "This is how things are" as if it were the general form of the proposition (PI, 114). This "surveyable representation" had produced, however, a distorted picture of language and meaning.

In order to avoid such misapprehensions we must understand how survey-able representations can help us to deal with our unsurveyable grammar. These models provide us in each case only with particular and "primitive applications" of our words. That is why they may prove to be illuminating but why they can also prove misleading. The method of constructing "survey-able representations" is thus not to be fully trusted. Only if we understand this will we achieve a proper reading of the second half of section 122 of the *Investigations*. Wittgenstein seems to speak there as if we could have a complete surveyable representation of our grammar. But when he writes that "the concept of surveyable representation is of fundamental significance for us and that it designates our form of representation, the way we look at things," we should not assume automatically that he means to include himself in the "for us" and the "our." He is saying, rather, that in our contemporary culture, for us moderns, it is evident that we can represent everything in a surveyable fashion. That assumption is fundamental to how we look at the world. And the same assumption is fundamental also to how the author of the *Tractatus* once looked at the world. It may, indeed, express a distinctively modern world-view. Hence, the concluding question of section 122: "Is this a *'Weltanschauung'*?"

The mock quotations around the word *"Weltanschauung"* should alert us to the possibility that Wittgenstein intends to distance himself from this particular world-view. That conjecture is confirmed by an earlier version of section 122 from 1931. In his "Remarks on Frazer's *Golden Bough"* Wittgenstein had already noted the importance that the concept of surveyable representation has "for us" but he had concluded the passage not with the parenthetical question "Is this a *'Weltanschauung'*?" but with the straightfor-wardly dismissive sentence: "A similar kind of *'Weltanschauung'* is appar-ently typical of our time" (RF, p. 69). The remark revises, in turn, a still earlier indictment against "our civilization" as obsessed with the ideas of progress and construction. In contrast to the great stream of European and American civilization, Wittgenstein had written in 1930, he himself was concerned only with "clarity, transparency [*Durchsichtigkeit*]" (CV, p. 7). Soon after that he must have come to the conclusion that universal transparency was itself a treacherous ideal. Section 122 of the *Investigations* must thus be read as a critique of the idea that there could be comprehensive surveyable representa-tion of our grammar or of anything else.

If the method of constructing surveyable representations is both useful and dangerous, the question is how we are to make effective use of it. The answer suggested by the practice of the *Philosophical Investigations* is that for each unsurveyable totality we must generate a large number of different surveyable representations, not just a single one, as the *Tractatus* had done. We must, according to section 5 of the *Investigations*, look at various "primitive kinds of application" and various "primitive forms of language" (note the plural in both phrases). Referring to the numerous "clear and simple language games" he had described in the early sections of the *Investigations*, Wittgenstein writes also that they "are not preparatory studies for a future regularization of language – as it were first approximations, ignoring friction and air-resistance. The language games are rather *objects of comparison* which are meant to throw light on the facts of our language by way not only of similarities, but also of dissimilarities" (PI, 130). And the "essence of language" is to be found in these similarities and dissimilarities.

Essential Complexity

We can usually take a situation in at a glance, when it is sufficiently simple. If there are just three people in a room, I may be able to survey that situation in a single glance as I enter. If the room is crowded, however, with dozens of people, I may not be able to see right away what is going on. But even when there are only three people present, I may find the situation opaque. Assume that I have interrupted the three in a heated argument or that there is an awkward silence in the room as I enter. Finally, I can't take in at a glance a situation that is too volatile, in which, let us say, people stream incessantly in and out of the room.

When Wittgenstein speaks of the unsurveyability of our grammar, he seems to have these three characteristics in mind. Our grammar is unsurveyable because it so complex, because its uses are so opaque, and because it is so volatile. He stresses these characteristics in section 23 of the *Philosophical Investigations* where he asks, "How many different kinds of sentence are there?" To this he answers: "There are *countless* kinds: countless different kinds of use of what we call 'symbols,' 'words,' 'sentences.' And this multiplicity is not something fixed, given once and for all; but new types of language, new language games, as we may say, come into existence, and others become obsolete and get forgotten." And in section 18 of the *Investigations* he adds to this an illustration that makes much the same point: "Our language can be seen as an ancient city: a maze of little streets and squares, of old and new houses, and of houses with additions of various periods; and this surrounded by a multitude of new boroughs with straight, regular streets and uniform houses."

One characteristic of unsurveyable wholes like our grammar, then, is that they contain a large number of items. But this is surely not a sufficient condition. If there were lots of pages stacked on my desk but they were all blank paper of the same size neatly bundled together, there would be nothing unsurveyable about the desk. A second characteristic of an unsurveyable totality is then that the items in it are characteristically of different kinds and are related to each other in multiple ways. This certainly fits the case of my desk as well as of language. In our language there are different kinds of sentence, as Wittgenstein reminds us, different kinds of use, different kinds of "houses." To this, he adds that language is unsurveyable also because (just like my desk where new papers flutter in all the time and old ones are discarded) our language is not a closed totality. New types of language and new uses of language are constantly coming into existence while old ones fall by the wayside. We end up then with three characteristics of unsurveyable totalities. None of the three characteristics is, however, necessary for something being an unsurveyable whole. A totality may consist of only a few items but if these are linked by an exceedingly complicated web of relations, the totality may still be unsurveyable. Thus a soccer game may prove unsurveyable even though there are only 11 players on each side. And even if there are only a few items that make up the totality and these are related in relatively simple ways, the totality may still be unsurveyable if it is sufficiently unstable in its composition. Chaotic events are typically unsurveyable. On the other hand, even a closed totality may prove to be unsurveyable as long as the items in it are sufficiently large in number or there are sufficiently many different kinds of relations between them. That is why the grammar of a dead language may be just as unsurveyable as that of a living one.

I will call totalities or wholes that have these three characteristics "essentially complex" or sometimes "complex." This allows me to distinguish between the epistemic condition of something being unsurveyable and the characteristics that make it so – two things which Wittgenstein does not explicitly keep apart. We may say that the fact of complexity explains the epistemic situation of unsurveyability. I am aware, of course, that the word "complex" has no sharply defined meaning in ordinary usage and that no theorist of complexity has ever offered a precise characterization of its meaning. How large does a totality have to be, how many kinds of items does it have to contain, how diverse must the relations between the items be, how open-ended must the totality be? Perhaps it is necessary to distinguish between degrees of complexity as well as between types of complexity. The physical universe, for instance, is very large but we may still be able to construct a surveyable representation of certain of its properties. That is why we can formulate general laws of physics that have both an explanatory and a predictive power. The human world, on the other hand, is only a small part of the physical universe but since we are interested in a vast array of diverse and shifting relationships, the human world turns out to be unsurveyable. And because of this, we find ourselves unable to formulate anthropological, social, or historical laws. Biology, finally, seems to fall between these two cases. The facts that concern biochemistry may be fully surveyable, but the actual course of biological evolution may be not.

The Practice of Language

But how we can cope with the grammar of our language, if it lacks surveyability? And how do we orient ourselves in our society, in our culture, and most generally in the human form of life, if they, too, lack surveyability? Don't we have a grasp of the grammar that allows us to speak our language fluently? Don't we have an understanding of human life, as we live it?

There are two answers available at this point on how we may get a grasp on a totality that lacks surveyability. The first is suggested by the state of my desk. I could after all organize my papers – given will, time, and energy – by sorting and arranging them according to a certain plan. An unsurveyable order can, in other words, be made surveyable. But language (and, more generally, the human form of life) presents us with a different problem. We may, of course, consider the possibility of reforming language in order to make it more surveyable. And it is true that such reforms are regularly instituted or proposed. Every so often someone tries to construct a simple, transparent language as an alternative to our essentially complex one. But such attempts never succeed. For good reasons we retain, in the end, our essentially complex, unsurveyable grammar. I emphasize this because Wittgenstein might be misunderstood on this point. In section 92 of the *Investigations* he speaks as if we could treat the unsurveyability of language in the same way in which I have suggested I can deal with the unsurveyability of my papers. He speaks there of the mistaken view that "the essence of language" is something "that lies *beneath* the surface"; this view, he adds, "does not see the essence as something that already lies open to view and that becomes *surveyable* through ordering [*durch Ordnen*]" (my translation). Does he mean to say then that we can make language surveyable by reorganizing it just as I can do with the papers on my desk? Surely this is not what he can be after, for he also maintains that "philosophy may in no way interfere with the actual use of language" (PI, 124). The task of the philosopher is certainly not, according to Wittgenstein, to reform or reorganize language in the name of surveyability.

The suggestion that we might replace the language we speak by another one with a surveyable grammar (English, for instance, with Esperanto or with a logical notation) faces, in any case, two major obstacles. The first is that we would have to explain the new language in the one we already know and since the latter is, by assumption, unsurveyable, it is not clear that the new one could be anything else. I am not sure how serious this obstacle is. Isn't it true that we have invented various surveyable systems of notation (in mathematics, logic, science, technology, and business) and that we explain their use routinely by means of our unsurveyable ordinary language? Can't we ever create order out of chaos, transparency out of obscurity, and hence, the surveyable out of the unsurveyable? It remains true, of course, that the new notation will not provide us with a literal translation from the old one. It will not make the unsurveyability of our original language disappear. And so the question remains how we can come to grasp that original and unsurveyable language. But why should this bother us, if the new surveyable notation is an adequate substitute for the original language? Only – will any such new notation ever actually do that job except under narrowly circumscribed conditions?

This gets me to the second and more serious objection to the idea that we could replace our unsurveyable language with a surveyable one. We can certainly invent a language with a simpler and more transparent syntax than that of English; but when Wittgenstein says that the grammar of our language is unsurveyable, he does not mean that its syntax is so. He uses the word "grammar," instead, for the entire system of use we make of our words. And similarly, when he employs the word "language," he does not mean simply a notation with precise rules but the entire activity of using signs. And it is far from obvious that we could invent a language that can serve all the uses of language in this broad sense and still have a surveyable grammar. This should dispose of the objection of linguists who have argued that behind the irregular surface structure of our language lies a precise and completely regular syntax and that this syntactic deep structure may even be innate to the human mind. Wittgenstein's considerations bypass this objection. We may or may not hold that our language has a surveyable deep syntax (the assumption strikes me as arbitrary). Wittgenstein's point stands, however, in any case. Such a syntax will not uniquely determine the use we make of it in the activity of speaking. Wittgenstein must be right in saying that this system of use is unsurveyable.

What exactly, then, is achieved by constructing a series of models or surveyable representations for an unsurveyable totality? What is the relation between these models and the totality? Two very different answers suggest themselves. The first is that each of the many surveyable models will represent a part of the totality we are dealing with. On this account the unsurveyable totality is made up of surveyable parts and each of those can, of course, be captured in a surveyable representation. The totality is unsurveyable only in the sense that it requires an unsurveyable series of representations to represent it completely. The second possibility is that each surveyable representation will give us only an approximate picture of the totality and we can get an understanding of the totality only by having a number of more-or-less adequate pictures of the whole. We can call the first the "part–whole view" of unsurveyability and the second the "approximation view." Wittgenstein recognizes both but does not explicitly distinguish them because he considers language to be unsurveyable in both ways at once. Thus, if we think of language as comprehending both the language of everyday life and the logical notations of the propositional calculus and other precise systems of notation, it may turn out that some parts of language can be represented precisely and others only approximately. Our misunderstanding of language may then rest on the false idea that the parts of language which can be represented only approximately are like those which can be represented precisely. We are then victims of a part–whole fallacy. There may be other totalities, though, which can be represented only by approximations. If we think that any such representation must be a full representation we are guilty of false understanding of the idea of representation; it is the fallacy of which the author of the *Tractatus* was guilty, the belief that in order for an A to represent a B, A and B must have precisely the same structure. This view is incompatible with Wittgenstein's recognition in the *Philosophical Investigations* that one and the same picture can represent completely different things: "here a glass cube, there an inverted open box, there a wire frame of that shape, there three boards forming a solid angle" (PI, p. 193).

Two things follow from this. The first is that our capacity for using words, the command we have of our grammar, our ability to participate in the human form of life cannot be due to our possession of a surveyable representation of the use of our words, of our grammar, or of our form of life. There are no such representations to be had. We acquire our linguistic capacities and our ability to participate in human life rather by imitation and habituation, by drill and practice. In section 5 of the *Investigations* Wittgenstein writes that when we teach children the first, primitive forms of language, "the teaching of language is not explanation, but *Abrichten*." Our translator has piously rendered the last word as "training," but Wittgenstein is speaking here of the kind of conditioning to which we commonly subject circus animals. By means of punishments and rewards we manage to get them to perform all kinds of tricks. One easily thinks here of the harsh methods that the schoolteacher Ludwig Wittgenstein used to get his peasant children to learn, methods that were to get him into trouble with both the parents and the school authority. An important part of such conditioning, Wittgenstein writes in the *Investigations*, "consists in the teacher's pointing to the objects, directing the child's attention to them, and at the same time uttering a word . . . This kind of teaching by indication can be said to establish an associative connection between the word and the thing" (PI, 6). Similarly, the teacher may show the students a table with words and pictures and the student "learns to look the picture up in the table through conditioning and part of this conditioning consists perhaps in the student learning to pass with his finger horizontally from the left to the right in the table" (PI, 86). We get a grasp of the grammar of our language through such simple things as learning to direct our attention, practicing the voicing of sounds so that uttering them becomes easy, establishing associations between words and objects, memory training, learning to use our fingers and to coordinate finger and eye movements, etc. In *On Certainty* Wittgenstein adds that "language did not emerge from some kind of ratiocination" (OC, 475). He proposes, instead, that we should look at man, rather, as an animal, "a primitive being to which one grants instinct but not ratiocination." When the child learns words like "book" or "armchair," it does not learn that there are such things but it learns to get the book or to sit in the armchair. The human language game is not based on knowledge but on practice. "The child, I should like to say, learns to react in such-and-such a way; and in so reacting it doesn't so far know anything. Knowledge only begins at a later level" (OC, 538).

We thus acquire a grasp of our grammar as a practical capacity, not by having a surveyable representation of it. And this practical capacity is itself essentially complex and hence unsurveyable. Eventually we learn, of course, also to reflect on our grammar and it is at this point that we learn to understand, use, and even construct surveyable representations of it. But these will always be partial or approximating representations since our practical capacity to use language is and remains essentially complex and hence unsurveyable. Surveyable representations of our grammar may nevertheless serve a number of purposes. They may prove helpful at times in teaching a language – we all know that from learning a second or third language as adults. But we also know that the grammatical rules we are taught in such contexts will have numerous exceptions and are never sufficient for establishing a fluent capacity to use the language. Surveyable representations of grammar may also serve as tools for normalizing and regularizing our linguistic practices. National academies, like the French Academy, often engage in such normalizing activity. Surveyable representations may, finally, also help us to overcome grammatical confusions. Wittgenstein is convinced that these confusions are the source of our philosophical dilemmas. In order to resolve what troubles us philosophically, we will therefore find ourselves constructing various surveyable representations of our grammar. But in doing so we must remain alert to the fact that such constructions can, in turn, give rise to new philosophical confusions. What representations we construct and for what purpose will depend, once again, on more than one factor.

Hyper-complexity

Wittgenstein's interest in the use and the limitations of the method of surveyable representation went beyond his concern with language. That is evident from his "Remarks on Frazer's *Golden Bough*" and his comments on Spengler's *Decline of the West*. In criticism of Frazer's attempt to explain magical and religious practices in evolutionary terms, Wittgenstein suggests that these phenomena can be adequately understood only through the method of surveyable representation. The representations of individual magical and religious practices, and more broadly of individual primitive cultures, will make their specific "logic" or "grammar" apparent. Those representations will reveal to us also family resemblances between various magical and religious practices and cultures. They will establish finally the existence of a gulf between those practices and cultures and our own scientific civilization. The goal of this application of the method of surveyable representation is, thus, to make explicit that magic and religion have their own characteristic grammar and that they produce language games that differ "grammatically" from those generated by our scientific and technological mode of thinking. To make those important points does not require that we should be able to give total representations of either magic, religion, or science, and Wittgenstein certainly does not assume that we could give a synoptic representation of them. His ultimate message is, rather, that we cannot construct an adequate synoptic representation of the human form of life as a whole.

In his comments on Spengler, Wittgenstein objects similarly to the idea of a single surveyable "morphology of world history." Spengler had allowed that individual cultures are incommensurable organic wholes and that we can understand them only in terms of their own internal logic. But he had maintained also at the same time that we can establish a common morphology of all culture. At the heart of Spengler's book we find, thus, a table that is meant to provide an overview over the great world cultures. It is intended to show that all cultures follow the same course of internal development and pass through precisely corresponding phases. We may think of that table as a paradigm of a surveyable representation – but of one that fails in Wittgenstein's eyes. While Wittgenstein's notes express sympathy for Spengler's approach, he remains critical of the idea that human cultures can be understood in terms of a single model of organic development. Contrasting Spengler's view to his own, he writes in 1937 that one can prevent general assertions (about language, culture, the human form of life) from being empty or unjustified only by looking at the ideal, that is, the surveyable representation, as "an object of comparison – so to say as a measuring-rod – instead of as a preconceived idea to which *everything* must conform. For in this lies the dogmatism into which philosophy slips so easily." The words anticipate section 131 of the *Philosophical Investigations*. They go further, however, than this later version in adding: "The ideal loses nothing of its dignity, if it is put forward as principle of the form of representation. A good measurability" (CV, pp. 26–27).

Once we expand the idea of unsurveyability from grammar and language to history, culture, society, and politics we must pay attention, however, to the different kinds of complexity and hence of unsurveyability that these totalities exhibit. The totalities in question are, of course, all essentially complex in that they all consist of large numbers of items of a large number of kinds that stand in a large number of diverse relations. They are all, moreover, open-ended totalities. They differ nevertheless in their type of complexity because of the nature of their constituent elements. While we can say roughly that grammar and language consist of words and sentences and suchlike, history, culture, society, and politics involve human beings – and human beings not just as bodies or as biological organisms, but as agents who have views about themselves, about their surroundings, and indeed about the history, culture, society, or political system of which they are a part. The views of these agents are, moreover, not incidental to those totalities but actually define them, and this gives to human history, culture, society, and politics an entirely new type of complexity.

If I were to give an account, for instance, of politics in the United States I would have to talk, first of all, of a large array of material facts: the state of the economy, budgets and deficits, climate, landscape, resources, industrial and military hardware, populations, poverty and wealth, and so on. It should be clear from this short list that even this material component of the political culture of the United States is essentially complex and thus, in principle, unsurveyable. But in order to characterize American politics I will also have to talk about the views of Republicans and Democrats, about the peculiar beliefs of certain fundamentalists, about the aggressive nationalism of some neo-conservatives, and about the mildly ineffective liberalism and humanism of many other Americans. This adds a whole new level of complexity to the structure of the political system. Each of the varying viewpoints of these different parties concerns, moreover, not only the material aspects of the political system but the views that others have of the system. Thus, Republicans have political views not only about the state of the economy but also about the views of their Democratic opponents. And the same is true, in reverse, of the Democrats. It is easy to see that each of these political views will, in fact, be unsurveyable. I am not saying here that these views are, in principle, inaccessible to us. In his reflections on the nature of human consciousness, Wittgenstein has shown that this would be an absurdity. If it were in principle impossible for me to say anything about the views of others, then I would have no reasons for ascribing any views to them whatever. As Wittgenstein puts it vividly: if I have a beetle in a box which only I can see and about which it is in principle impossible to say anything to others, there might as well be no such beetle. Nonetheless, it is true that, in practice, I cannot provide an adequate synoptic representation of any political viewpoint. My representation will be only a partial account of the other's view or a loose approximation, and most likely both.

It follows a fortiori that the totality of political viewpoints within the American political system will also be unsurveyable. We have thus, a cascade of levels of unsurveyability. And the same holds for totalities such as a human society, a human culture or civilization, and, of course, the human form of life as a whole. They all exemplify a type of complexity that goes far beyond that of grammar and language. In order to distinguish them I will call them hyper-complex.

Essentially complex totalities present us with distinctive epistemic challenges since we can't ever comprehend them in the way in which we can comprehend surveyable totalities. There are additional epistemic difficulties when we are dealing with hyper-complex totalities. These manifest themselves in all theorizing about the human form of life. Recognition of that fact is, however, still lagging. Our social theorists remain, on the whole, committed to the search for a synoptic view of human life. If representations of complex and hyper-complex totalities are, however, inherently problematic, one must ask why they remain so stubbornly committed to the project of constructing synoptic representations. Wittgenstein recognizes, of course, the valid function of partial and approximating representations of our grammar and our language and, presumably, also of our forms of life. He is, indeed, convinced that such representations can serve important philosophical functions. But he also maintains that the attempt to construct a synoptic representation of our grammar, our language, and our form of life lacks purpose. He assumes that this project is motivated by the mistaken assumption that the confusions generated by unsurveyable totalities can be resolved only by constructing surveyable representations. But since the totalities are inherently unsurveyable, Wittgenstein concludes, that project will prove impossible to carry through. The result is that we will end up with ever more complex theoretical constructs and ever more elaborate schemes that will all, in the end, prove unsuccessful. We should therefore abandon the attempt to construct a synoptic representation of unsurveyable totalities and look, instead, for surveyable representations of those specific aspects of such totalities that initially generated our confusion.

But how satisfactory is this conclusion? It may be adequate when it comes to grammar and language. But when we are concerned with hyper-complex totalities we find ourselves in a different situation. The reason is that the agents within such a hyper-complex totality require a comprehensive view of that totality. In order to act politically, for instance, agents require a comprehensive view of the political system. In order to engage in a culture, agents need to have an overall view of that culture. In order to participate in a historical course of actions, agents need to have a historical perspective. These views will, of course, be generally schematic but they will, nonetheless be synoptic in character. This is not the case in language. In order to speak a language I do not need an overall view of that language. The question that remains at this point then is what it is for us to be agents within hyper-complex totalities.

notes

1 "Yellow Book," in *Wittgenstein's Lectures: Cambridge 1932–1935*, edited by Alice Ambrose (Chicago: University of Chicago Press, 1979), p. 43.
2 G.E. Moore, "Wittgenstein's Lectures in 1930–33," in *Philosophical Papers* (London: Allen and Unwin, 1959), p. 257.
3 Moore, "Wittgenstein's Lectures," p. 323.
4 John King and Desmond Lee, *Wittgenstein's Lectures. Cambridge 1930–1932. From the Notes of John King and Desmond Lee*, edited by Desmond Lee (Chicago: University of Chicago Press, 1980), p. 34.
5 Wittgenstein, "Yellow Book," p. 43.
6 For example, Franz Gruithuisen, *Naturgeschichte des gestirnten Himmels* (Munich: E.A. Fleischmann, 1836).

visible rails invisibly laid to infinity

You say you must; but cannot say what compels you.
Ludwig Wittgenstein, *Remarks on the Foundations of Mathematics*

R ules play an indispensable part in our lives. We know them as laws, regulations, and technical instructions, as prudential and moral principles, as the rules of games, of fashion and etiquette, and also, of course, as logical, mathematical, and grammatical rules. For all that, a history and philosophy of rules – of how we devise and use them, how they get taught and justified, what place they occupy in our practices, of how they have come to be so pervasive, of their status as divine commandments, principles of rationality, as built into the nature of things or as mere conventions – is still to be written. Consider, for instance, the peculiar rule that rules are there to be broken. Why should we need a rule to question the rules we have, a rule to constrain but not necessarily undermine our use of rules? Philosophical reflection on these matters is still in its infancy, but we can say with confidence that Wittgenstein has helped to bring it to birth. The challenge for us is how to expand on the questioning Wittgenstein has begun.

Proceeding According to Rules

We can trace Wittgenstein's interest in rules and rule-following, like so much else in his work, back to his critical engagement with Frege and his logic.

One of Frege's notable innovations had been a sharp distinction between the formulas of his symbolism and the rules of inference we apply to them. Traditional logic, from Aristotle to the late nineteenth century, had never made much of such a distinction. For Frege, on the other hand, rules of inference constituted the foundations of the symbolic system of his new logic. In

wittgenstein, First Edition. Hans Sluga.

order to emphasize their distinctness he wrote in the first exposition of his new logic, the *Begriffsschrift* of 1879, that unlike the formula truths these rules "cannot be expressed in our *conceptual notation.*"[1] They belong, we would say, to the meta-language of the conceptual notation. Frege went on to argue that such rules of inference were needed "because we cannot enumerate the boundless numbers of laws that can be established, we can obtain completeness only by a search for those which, *potentially*, imply all the others." It was necessary for this purpose to give logic an axiomatic form, starting with nine "judgments of pure thought" in order to "deduce the more complex . . . judgments from the simpler ones" with the help of rules of inference. In this way, Frege wrote, it could be shown how some judgments "are implicitly contained in others"; how, in particular, the content of the axioms includes, "though in embryonic form," the content of all the derived formulas. With the help of the rules of inference one could thus "elucidate all the interconnections of the laws of thought."[2] On Frege's views, the rules of inference were, thus (in Wittgenstein's memorable phrase), "visible rails invisibly laid to infinity."

Frege returned to this connection between rules and our capacity for grasping a "boundless number of laws," and more generally infinite totalities, in the second volume of his *Basic Laws of Arithmetic* (1903). He was motivated at this point by his wish to defend once more his thesis that arithmetical formulas express logical truths. His opponents at this point were "mathematical formalists" who maintained that these formulas were, in fact, only meaningless configurations of symbols – comparable, in this respect, to arrangements of chess pieces on a chessboard. They sought in this way to avoid any talk about abstract entities like numbers and sets but also specifically about infinite totalities. Frege argued against them that they could not, in fact, avoid the use of meaningful language in arithmetic since they would still have to formulate rules for the operation of their (supposedly) uninterpreted calculus. Even if one assumed that arithmetic was merely a game with uninterpreted symbols one would have to distinguish "the theory of the game . . . from the game itself"; the real logical and mathematical interest would then shift to that theory and the infinite would inevitably reappear in this theory because it would be in this theory that rules with their infinite extension would have to be formulated. To avoid that conclusion the formalists had argued that the operational rules of arithmetic should be identified with constellations of symbols or with moves in the game. To this Frege responded: "The actions within the game proceed admittedly according to rules; the rules are, however, not items in the game but the foundations of the theory of the game." And to this he added that "no constellation of the chess figures and no move expresses a rule; for the job of the figures in the chess game is not at all to express something but only to be moved according to rules."[3]

The Wittgenstein of the *Tractatus* was fully familiar with Frege's considerations but not particularly sympathetic to them. His views were, in fact, closer to the formalists than to Frege in this area. We have seen already that he considered arithmetical equations to be "pseudo-propositions" and as such strictly meaningless. More broadly speaking, he was following Russell's neglect of what Frege had been saying about the indispensability of rules of inference. The *Tractatus* had, in effect, very little to say about rules. This was motivated largely by his surprising lack of concern for the deductive side of logic. In order to distance himself from both Frege's and Russell's preoccupation with the axiomatization of logic and mathematics, he had thus written: "All propositions of logic are of equal rank. There are not some which are essentially primitive and others deduced from these" (TLP, 6.127). He had held, instead, that every proposition of logic is a tautology and could as such show itself directly without the need for any deductive argument. In logic, he wrote, "every proposition is its own proof" (TLP, 6.1265). He had also expressed no particular interest in the rules of syntax, a topic which Frege had also neglected. He believed, rather, that the signs of which propositions are composed determine by themselves how they can be combined. "The rules of logical syntax must go without saying, once we know how each individual sign signifies" (TLP, 3.334). Once again in tune with Frege, he had also said nothing about semantic rules (of ordinary language or the system of symbolic notation). The meaning of our propositions must instead show itself directly. Wittgenstein was, finally, quite definite about rejecting any need for and any possibility of a meta-language. When a notation is properly set up, he insisted, "there is *in it* a rule" according to which propositions are constructed. And: "These rules are equivalent to the symbols and in them their sense is mirrored" (TLP, 5.514).

Around 1930, however, as he discarded the assumptions of the *Tractatus*, he came to an altogether new appreciation of rules and their place in our thinking and practice. It was at this point also that he criticized Russell for having treated the axioms of *Principia Mathematica* as being "at the same time the basic configurations and the rules of progression. But in this he was wrong, and this was shown by the fact that he himself had to add further rules . . . This was already explained by Frege."[4] The remark amounted, in fact, to a kind of self-criticism and showed how far he had moved from his own earlier position on rules. Moore noticed it when he attended Wittgenstein's lectures in the early 1930s. He reports that Wittgenstein was insisting at the time that understanding the grammatical rules of our language would help us to resolve a host of philosophical problems. And this is, of course, in accord with his remark in the *Blue Book* that every metaphysical proposition, in fact, "hides a grammatical rule" (BB, p. 55). It is not easy to say what motivated this shift. A clue may, perhaps, be found in the lecture notes of two of Wittgenstein's students at that time. According to them Wittgenstein was saying in the spring of 1931 that "there must be rules, for language must be systematic. Compare games: if there are no rules, there is no game, and chess, for example, is like a language in this sense. When we use language we choose words to fit the occasion."[5] In the preceding term, Wittgenstein had also said that "if a proposition is to have sense we must commit ourselves to the use of the words in it. It is not a matter of association; that would not make lan-

visible rails invisibly laid to infinity

guage work at all. What is essential is that in using the word I commit myself to a rule of use."[6] There must be rules, then, because language is systematic; there must be rules, because language is like a game and games must have rules; there must be rules because in using words we enter commitments or (to say it in a more contemporary idiom) there is a normative aspect to our use.

Rules and Regularities

When Moore attended those lectures he had found it difficult to follow what Wittgenstein was saying. It occurred to him at the time that Wittgenstein "was not using the expression 'rules of grammar' in any ordinary sense," but he felt "unable to form any clear idea as to how he was using it."[7] Moore must have sensed that Wittgenstein's thinking about rules was, in fact, very much in flux at that moment. At first, he appears to have thought that language was circumscribed everywhere by precise grammatical rules. But by 1933–1934 he was complaining that to conceive of "language as a symbolism used in an exact calculus" was to be misled by the example of scientific and mathematical notation. "Our ordinary language conforms to this standard of exactness only in rare cases" (BB, p. 25). Still later, in the *Philosophical Investigations*, he was to argue that there was, indeed, an analogy between language and games but that not all games are played according to rules. There are also those in which we play "aimlessly" or "make up the rules as we go along." Wittgenstein concluded that "the application of a word is not everywhere bounded by rules" (PI, 84). The claim has remained a sore point for some of Wittgenstein's readers – among them some of the most prominent twentieth-century linguists and logicians. It clearly needs further attention since it bears also very much on how we should conceive our social and political existence.

The first thing to note is that there are, of course, always uses of language that do not accord to grammatical and deductive rules. It is obvious that in poetic language the normal rules of syntax and semantics are often suspended. Likewise, there are "ungrammatical" uses of language by children, by careless speakers, and by those who are not fully competent in a language. But all these cases might be considered marginal to the regular, rule-bound use of language. More decisive is the observation that our language is not a fixed system; our linguistic practices are, instead, constantly changing. It is implausible to assume that at each moment in this process there exist precise rules that precisely govern the practice of language at that moment. We can generalize this consideration by noting that only what is regular can be regulated by a rule. Unique events cannot be said to be rule-governed. Some parts of our use of language are, of course, governed by precise rules. These will concern regular and predictable situations. But language is not restricted to that kind of use. We also employ it in radically new situations and in order to express entirely new thoughts. In doing so, we produce syntactic and semantic forms that have never before existed. It is surely fiction to believe that these uses of language are all predetermined by a fixed set of rules.

Even when our linguistic practices are completely regular, we should not assume that they are necessarily guided by rules. Wittgenstein argues that we need to distinguish between actions and processes in which a rule is followed and those actions and processes that merely accord with a rule. There is, of course, an evident difference between an agent consulting a rule and then acting on it and a merely mechanical process which we can describe in terms of a rule. In calculating the sum of 145 and 387 a human calculator may consciously apply the familiar rules of addition; meanwhile an adding machine may churn out the same result mechanically, not because it follows any rules but because it has been constructed to produce the correct result mechanically. But what are we to say of an agent who performs a calculation without consciously appealing to the rules of addition? Are we to think of him in terms of the deliberately rule-following agent or in terms of the mindless computer? Wittgenstein's methodological stance after 1930 inclined him to resist the assumption of hidden, "unconscious" processes. Phenomena were to be taken *as* phenomena and philosophical difficulties to be removed not by finding mechanisms, structures, or processes hidden behind them but by attending carefully to what is in principle "open to view" but often not seen because we are so close to it. "What is hidden," he wrote in the *Philosophical Investigations*, "is of no interest to us" (PI, 126). It is the same attitude that made him insist in the *Blue Book* that a rule is involved in a calculation only if "the symbol of the rule forms part of the calculation" (BB, p. 13). This still leaves us with the case of an agent who at first applies certain rules in order to carry out a task but later on becomes so adept at his job that he no longer needs to invoke any rules. Is that agent now following those rules "unconsciously," or should we say, as is perhaps more plausible, that his action has now become so "habitual" or even "mechanical" that he no longer follows a rule but has learned to act in a manner that merely accords with the rule?

Wittgenstein maintains, in fact, that regularity of behavior is a more fundamental phenomenon than rule-following. He argues that we could not learn to do anything, if we had first to learn rules for acting. In the *Blue Book* he illustrates the point by saying that teaching can be conceived in two very different ways. When we teach a student, for instance, the word "yellow," such teaching may, in the first instance, involve a drill (BB, p. 12). This kind of teaching can be compared to "installing an electric connection between a switch and a bulb." But the teaching of the word "yellow" may also, instead, supply the student with a rule "which is itself involved in the processes of understanding, obeying, etc." It is easy to read this passage as if Wittgenstein favored the second story over the first as an account of teaching. But he is saying, in fact, that in actual teaching both things happen and that the first and more elementary situation is presupposed in the more sophisticated situation of learning with the help of rules. For this reason he also writes in the

Philosophical Investigations that a child's learning is initially a drill or conditioning. In his final notes he asserts in the same vein: "Rules are insufficient for establishing a practice, one also needs examples. Our rules leave loop-holes open, and the practice has to speak for itself. We do not learn the practice of making empirical judgments by learning rules: we are taught *judgments* and their connection with other judgments. A *totality* of judgments is made plausible to us . . . Light dawns gradually over the whole" (OC, 139–140).

Disputes have erupted between "individualists" and "collectivists" over how exactly Wittgenstein's account of rules is to be understood. While the one side has argued that Wittgenstein considers rules to be "standing intentions" that can be entertained, in principle, by a single individual, the other side maintains that he thinks of rules as shared, social conventions and of rule-following as participation in an institution and as the adoption of a custom or convention. David Bloor, who has made a vivid case for the "collectivist" reading, writes about rule-following: "The real source of constraint preventing our going anywhere and everywhere, as we move from case to case, are the local circumstances impinging upon us: our instincts, our biological nature, our sense experience, our interactions with other people, our immediate purposes, our training, our anticipation and response to sanctions, and so on through the gamut of causes, starting with the psychological and ending with the sociological."[8] Much of this appears right as an account of what Wittgenstein was after. The only point to disagree with is Bloor's insistence that such observations amount to a theory. Wittgenstein was certainly not concerned with constructing any kind of theory. His stated purpose was, rather, to bring our thinking back from philosophical theorizing to that of "the common-sense man" (BB, p. 48), and this is what he was surely also after in his characterization of how rules work.

The Uses of Rules

We must have specific skills to construct, communicate, understand, and use rules, but that we possess such skills is not inevitable. There are certainly sentient creatures that lack them. And so we need to ask how a human child comes to understand what the teacher wants when she says, for instance: "Please, open the door." In the *Blue Book* Wittgenstein writes: "If I give someone the order 'fetch me a red flower from that meadow,' how is he to know what sort of flower to bring, as I have only given him a *word*?" (BB, p. 3). How can a word, or a drawing, or a gesture be action-guiding? In the *Philosophical Investigations*, Wittgenstein adds: "Following a rule is analogous to obeying an order. We are conditioned into doing so" (PI, 206). But there is no guarantee that such conditioning will succeed. What are we to say if the student fails to catch on? "Such a case would present similarities with one in which a person naturally reacted to the gesture of pointing with the hand by looking in the direction of the line from fingertip to wrist, not from wrist to fingertip" (PI, 185). But human beings usually know to look in the right direction or can learn to do so. Even that is not something to be taken for granted. Some dogs learn to understand that you are pointing at something in the distance with your outstretched finger; others will look helplessly at your fingertip. If human beings had proved unable to understand how words, signs, or gestures can be intended to guide actions, the practice of having rules and following them would never have got off the ground. "A rule stands there like a sign-post . . . But where is it said which way I am to follow it; whether in the direction of its finger or (e.g.) in the opposite one?" (PI, 85). If signposts are to work for us, we must have the ability to understand them *as* signposts as well as the ability to understand *how* they are meant to serve in directing our behavior.

In the *Philosophical Investigations* Wittgenstein concludes: "If language is to be a means of communication, there must be agreement not only in definitions but also (strange as this may sound) an agreement in judgments. What we understand by 'measuring' is actually in part determined by a certain constancy in results of measurement" (PI, 242). That we agree, to a considerable extent at least, in the application of our rules "is not agreement in opinions but in form of life" (PI, 241). At the base of our capacity to follow rules lies, thus, "a common human way of acting" (PI, 206). This fact is obscured as long as we look only at the rules themselves; but as soon as we pay attention to how we apply them we come to understand that "to obey a rule, to make a report, to give an order, to play a game of chess are *customs* (habits, institutions)" (PI, 199). Suggestive as this formulation is, we must not ignore, however, that some customs and habits develop out of using rules and that some institutions are set up by means of rules (states, for instance, with the help of constitutions) and that they operate only through the use of rules. Nonetheless, Wittgenstein is right in maintaining that our practice of having rules and following them relies on more basic forms of behavior. Regularity of action, we may summarize, is more basic than acting on rules. And this point is of interest not only when we think about language, logic, and mathematics but also when we try to understand social and political phenomena.

But what do we gain from using rules, what contribution do they make to our form of life? What progress does a child make when it learns to understand and apply rules? What does society gain when it issues rules? There is no simple answer to those questions because rules come in very different forms and perform, accordingly, very different functions. Wittgenstein fully understood this. In his extensive discussion of rules in the *Brown Book*, he declined therefore to say altogether what a rule is and preferred, instead, to list "different applications of the word 'rule'" (BB, p. 98). The concept of rule turns out to be, in other words, a family resemblance concept. At one end of the field of resemblances rules get close to individual orders, commands, requests and the like; at the other end they include universal prescriptions and commandments (of the sort, for instance, that moralists proclaim). While some rules impose requirements, others are permissive and there are all kinds of gradations in the strictness of the requirement and degrees of permissiveness of rules. While some rules are precise in what they demand, others are only loosely suggestive; while some appear to determine their application with iron necessity, others are open to interpretation; while some rules can be expressed in the words of everyday language, others require the precise terminology of the law or some specialized notation; while some rules come in the form of propositions, others take the form of "tables, ostensive definitions, and similar instruments" such as drawings or gestures (BB, p. 90). And while some rules regulate actions, others – like the rule that rules are there to be broken – serve to regulate other rules (BB, p. 91).

Many forms of complex human behavior would not be possible without our possession and use of rules. This holds, in particular, in mathematics, technology, and science. Just as important is that many of our social undertakings (whether financial, economic, cultural, or political) would not be possible without our possession and use of rules. The law, systems of regulation (such as those that regulate traffic or those that tell us how to assemble things), and all kinds of institution, from religious to political, exemplify this point. Rules help us to standardize our actions, that is, to make them more uniform and hence more calculable, more predictable, and thus more transparent to others. They help us, in this way, also to coordinate our actions more effectively and to engage in large-scale and long-term undertakings.

Three Questions about Rules

Wittgenstein considered, in particular, three questions about rules: first of all, and most extensively, the inexorability with which applications of a rule seem to be determined; second, the generality typical of rules; and, third, their "normative" character.

(1) I will say here relatively little on the first of these topics even though it proved to be of great importance for Wittgenstein from the mid-1930s onward. A detailed discussion would lead us into complexities that lie well beyond the scope of this book. In addition, there exists now a large body of literature on this topic, much of it inspired by Saul Kripke's imaginative treatment of it in his book *Wittgenstein on Rules and Private Language*. It would certainly be impossible to reconstruct and do justice to that discussion in this chapter. I can refer readers who are particularly interested in this issue only to this specialized literature. A further thought is that the inexorability at stake is of great concern in fields like logic and metaphysics but much less so when one is focused on the social, cultural, and political aspects of the human form of life. Nonetheless, something needs to be said on the topic of inexorability.

In the *Philosophical Investigations* Wittgenstein makes his imagined interlocutor say that "the rule, once stamped with a particular meaning, traces the lines along which it is to be followed through the whole of space" (PI, 219). But Wittgenstein himself considers this claim to be problematic. He grants that one wants to say: "The steps are *really* already taken, even before I take them in writing or orally or in thought," and that all those steps are "in some *unique* way predetermined, anticipated – as only the act of meaning can anticipate" (PI, 188). But he tries to show through a multiplicity of illustrations how questionable that claim really is. The difficulty is only that to deny it would seem to lead us to the equally unacceptable conclusion that "no course of action could be determined by a rule, because every course of action can be made out to accord with the rule" (PI, 201). This touches on problems that philosophers from Plato onward have grappled with and that have led them at times to excesses of metaphysical speculation. Wittgenstein seeks to deal with this issue by asking what our criterion is for saying that a formula determines such and such an application. And he replies straightforwardly: "It is, for example, the kind of way we always use it, the way we are taught to use it" (PI, 190). We may be tempted, of course, to say that we intuit the meaning of the rule "in a flash." But Wittgenstein objects that we have "no model for this extravagant fact" and that we are here seduced into using a philosophical "super-expression" (PI, 192). He is, however, under no illusion about what it will take to convince his readers that he is right. He spends, for that reason, a great deal of philosophical resources both in the *Philosophical Investigations* and in the *Remarks on the Foundations of Mathematics* on trying to make this conclusion stick. Interpreters, particularly since Kripke, have debated vigorously whether and how Wittgenstein succeeds in resolving this apparent "paradox." Whatever his resolution may be, it is certainly part of his longer-term project, already announced in the *Tractatus*, to strip modal terms like "necessary" and "must" of their metaphysical aura.

"Inexorable" rules are typical for logic and mathematics. We assume, for instance, that the rule to "add 2" to a given number specifies "inexorably" that we ought to write 1002 after 1000. When Wittgenstein considers the case of a student who stubbornly writes 1004 after 1000 claiming that he is applying the rule of adding 2, he makes the teacher say: "But I already knew, at the time when I gave the order that he ought to write 1002 after 1000." The problem is, however, that the teacher presumably did not actually think of the transition from 1000 to 1002 at the time he gave his order and even if he did think of *this* step, he still did not think of other ones such as the transition from, let us say, 1006 to 1008. Wittgenstein responds therefore to the teacher's remark: "When you said 'I already knew at the time . . . ' that meant something like: 'If I had been asked what number should be written after 1000, I should have replied 1002.' And that I don't doubt" (PI, 187). The problematic thing is the assumption that "the act of meaning the order had in its own way already traversed all those steps: that when you meant it your mind as it were flew ahead and took all the steps before you physically arrived at this or that one" (PI, 188).

(2) In order for us to be able to use rules at all it must be the case that the world is sufficiently regular. Rules are, in contrast to individual commands, characteristically general in content. The principle "Do not lie" would lose its character as a moral rule if there ever was only one occasion for lying. Wittgenstein observes correctly: "It is not possible that there should have been only one occasion on which someone obeyed a rule" (PI, 199). Moreover, if the regular were to become the exception and what is exceptional were to become regular, our normal, rule-governed language games would lose their point. Hence: "It is only in normal cases that the use of a word is clearly prescribed" (PI, 142). Generality is, we might say, of the essence of rules and that rules prove useful to the human form of life is due, first of all, to the fact that the world is sufficiently regular and, secondly, due to our ability to recognize and act on this regularity. Assume that I try to drill an elephant to stand on his hind legs at the appropriate signal in the circus arena. That drill would not succeed if the elephant was never brought back into the arena or if he was unable to recognize the signal and the circus arena again. The same holds when I try to teach the child the word "yellow" in the presence of a yellow object. My expectation is in that case that there will be other occasions for using that word and that the child will recognize them as such.

That we are capable of grasping such generality is again surely not something to be taken for granted. Assume that I try to teach a child to construct a series of numbers starting from 0 by always adding 2 to the previous number. The rule to be learned is that of the addition of 2. Now the teacher may train the child into applying the rule by giving him examples. He writes down, let us say, the series 0, 2, 4, 6, 8. But however many examples the teacher provides, however far she constructs the series, the child will eventually have to go at it independently. The child must, in other words, come to understand that the rule applies beyond the examples the teacher provides; he must get to understand how to continue the series by himself. But what if the child continues the series up to 1000 in the standard way but then continues: 1000, 1004, 1008, 1012. Wittgenstein writes: "We may say to him: 'Look what you have done!' – He doesn't understand. We say: 'You were meant to add *two*: look how you began the series!' – He answers: 'Yes, isn't it right? I thought that was how I was *meant* to do it.' – Or suppose he pointed to the series and said: 'But I went on in the same way'" (PI, 185). In order to apply the rule of adding 2 correctly, the child must, in other words, be aware of what he has already done. He must be able to determine what it is to go on "in the same way." Again, we assume that we possess those capacities. But what if we didn't? Or, if we suddenly ceased to have them?

(3) The pedagogic role of such rules is said to be buttressed by their "normative" force. Talk of the normativity of rules is currently fashionable in philosophical circles but must be considered with caution. Some rules are certainly used normatively but many others are not. The kind of drawing we find in assembly manuals illustrates this point. The drawing shows us what

the assembled item is meant to look like; it provides us with a rule for assembling the item. But the drawing has a "normative" function only in the weak sense that, unless I follow the instructions, the product will not be put together in the way the manufacturer intended it to be and may not perform its promised function. But this kind of "norm" is not really normative. There is no sanction attached to it. No one will punish me if I do not follow the instructions. My failure to do so will certainly have consequences; the assembled item may not work. On the other hand, I may have reasons for assembling the piece in my own way; I may not be interested in making the machine work in the suggested manner. A consequence of not applying a rule is, in any case, not the same as a sanction that will be imposed if I fail to follow the rule. Wittgenstein is therefore right when he speaks only occasionally of the normative function of rules.

The term "norm" is best limited to rules involving sanctions. Such rules are, of course, pervasive in social and political life. Some would say that there could be no society and no politics without normative rules. Hobbes once said, famously, that the social contract without the threat of the sword to enforce it would be empty. But even here the normativity function works in different ways. One important difference is that the sanction is sometimes specified in the rule itself while at other times it is extrinsic to the rule. The first is illustrated by the police officer who issues a ticket to a speeding driver, the second by the teacher who scolds a student for failing to apply a rule of grammar. Both the teacher and the policeman are using rules normatively. But the grammatical rule by itself has no normative content. It specifies what is grammatically correct, but does not prescribe a sanction for speaking ungrammatically. A consequence of breaking a grammatical rule may be that we will not be understood. But that is not a sanction, just as getting wet is not a sanction for failing to bring my umbrella. Driving regulations, on the other hand, do not merely tell us how to drive, they also specify sanctions of the sort the policeman applies. Any rule can, of course, be *used* normatively. That is how the scolding teacher uses the grammatical rule. But driving regulations are, in addition, normative in content. Failure to apply them may also lead to undesirable consequences (it may, for instance, lead to an accident), but those consequences must be distinguished from the sanctions prescribed by the regulations. Moral and aesthetic principles, rules of prudence and fashion are in this respect typically like rules of grammar, whereas laws, administrative regulations, and the rules and orders of authority are typically like driving regulations. Both kinds of rule have their use.

The normative use of rules of either kind establishes a social ordering between those who apply the sanction and those to whom the sanction is applied. The possibility of this kind of social ordering is grounded in the evident inequality of power inherent in human relationships. That inequality manifests itself in the relation between a parent and a child, a teacher and a student, a rich man and a poor one, a physically strong and a physically weak person. When such inequalities are taken as inevitable and even legitimate we speak of such power as authoritative. Power and authority are certainly more fundamental than a system of normative rules. But it is also true that normative rules both give expression to power differentials and reinforce them.

Rules and Interpretations

There are, of course, always instances in which disputes break out over how a rule is to be applied. Think, for instance, of how they occur regularly in competitive games and how in some cases such disputes have escalated into actual wars. Disputes over rules are, in fact, common in social and political life and perhaps even characteristic of this domain. Wittgenstein is certainly right when he points out that in other parts of human life there are no such disputes. He writes: "Disputes do not break out (among mathematicians, say) over the question whether a rule has been obeyed or not. People don't come to blows over it, for example. That belongs to the scaffolding from which our language operates" (PI, 240). But even in mathematics there are occasionally disagreements over how certain rules are to be applied, as Wittgenstein knew well from the lecture by the Dutch mathematician Brouwer that had inspired him so much in 1928. In that lecture Brouwer had attacked the use of the principle of the excluded middle in certain parts of mathematics. But it is characteristic of mathematics that we do not fight over applications of, let us say, the rules of addition. If someone were to doubt that 2 + 2 = 4, we would not treat him as a dissident mathematician but as an incompetent.

Wittgenstein also understood, however, that outside logic and mathematics our rules are widely open to interpretation and that disputes may therefore always arise over their application. In a passage that precedes the discussion of rule-following in the *Philosophical Investigations* Wittgenstein compares a rule to a signpost and then asks himself: "Does the sign-post leave no doubt about the way I have to go?" And he answers by allowing that the signpost "sometimes leaves room for doubt and sometimes not" (PI, 85). In other words, rules sometimes leave doubts about how they are to be used and sometimes not. Immediately after this remark Wittgenstein also observes that one may say to someone "Stand roughly here" and that this instruction may work perfectly well in the context in which it is uttered (PI, 88). But the person who is given this instruction will, of course, have to decide for himself where exactly he is to stand. He will, in other words, have to interpret the instruction and make a decision on how to act.

We should note furthermore that Wittgenstein begins his systematic discussion of rule-following in section 143 of the *Philosophical Investigations* by considering various "inexorable" mathematical rules, but interpolates into this passage a series of remarks (PI, 156–184) that deal, in fact, with interpretable rules. This has been largely overlooked by the interpreters of the *Philosophical Investigations*. Because Wittgenstein himself is so preoccupied with the question of the inexorability of the rules of logic and mathematics, and because contemporary analytic philosophers are so much concerned with logic and mathematics, they have failed to see that Wittgenstein is also interested in interpretable rules. Thus, the question he raises in section 156 concerns "the activity of rendering out loud what is written or printed" (PI, 156). Wittgenstein asks in what way the written text can be said to "guide" our speaking. This kind of guidance is surely different from the one that a mathematical rule provides to the calculator. The rules of addition demand that we continue a series of numbers in one, and only one, way. We are given no choice in the matter; there is no room for interpretation and decision. But when we read a text aloud we always have different options. (Think of the very different ways in which an actor may speak the words of Shakespeare's Hamlet!) That Wittgenstein recognizes this is clear from his additional remark that cases he is interested in include "writing from dictation, writing out something printed, playing from a score, and so on." We must surely remember at this point that Wittgenstein was keenly attuned to music and knew very well what it means to play music from a score. He understood that such playing always requires an interpretation of the score. One of the standard complaints in the Wittgenstein family about Paul Wittgenstein, Ludwig's brother, the professional pianist, was that he played his music too mechanically.

When we say that a musical score requires interpretation, we must be clear about what that means. In the *Philosophical Investigations* Wittgenstein suggests that "we ought to restrict the term 'interpretation' to the substitution of one expression of the rule for another" (PI, 201). An interpretation in this sense might, for instance, involve the translation of a rule from one language or one idiom into another. Wittgenstein notes that when we take the term "interpretation" in this sense, it becomes clear that interpretations will inevitably reach an end. There is always a last interpretation, even though it will, of course, always remain possible to provide a further one. And this has an important consequence for how we should think about the application of a rule:

> In the course of our argument we give one interpretation after another; as if each one contented us at least for a moment, until we thought of yet another standing behind it. What this shows is that there is a way of grasping a rule which is *not* an *interpretation*, but which is exhibited in what we call "obeying the rule" and "going against it" in actual cases. (PI, 201)

But we use the word "interpretation" also in another way which is evident from the concept of musical interpretation. Such an interpretation is a particular rendering of the score, a specific use of it, not a translation of it into another idiom. Likewise, the actor who speaks the words of Hamlet on stage is giving us an interpretation. But this does not mean that he is substituting one expression for another; he is, rather, using Shakespeare's words in a particular way. Wittgenstein was aware that the word "interpretation" has these two different meanings. In the *Blue Book* he says, on the one hand, that an Englishman might "interpret" the German word "Buch" as "book." But he also allows that the man who makes the right choice when he is asked to pick a banjo from an array of instruments "has given the word the word 'banjo' the correct interpretation" (BB, p. 2). What justifies us in speaking of interpretations in the rendering of a score, the voicing of Shakespeare's text, and in responding to the request to pick a banjo is that in each case the application of the score, the written words, or the spoken request is not uniquely determined. In each case we are faced with interpretable rules and such rules lack the inexorability characteristic of the rules of logic and mathematics.

Interpretable rules are ubiquitous in social and political life. The law, for instance, consists entirely of such. Judges and juries, officials and citizens are therefore forced to ask themselves over and over again: how is the law to be understood? How does it apply to this or that situation? In trying to answer those questions, we have to interpret the law, use our "judgment," make decisions. To facilitate this process we have invented umpires, review boards, appeals courts, a Supreme Court, ombudsmen, oversight committees, etc. None of these set-ups are needed in logic and mathematics; but they are characteristic and even definitive of social and political life. Interpretations of interpretable rules are, of course, themselves typically guided by rules. An appeals court, for instance, will review the actions of a lower court according to law. Such laws will typically refer to the law; we are dealing in this case with rules that are meant to apply to rules and their application. Wittgenstein, as I have pointed out, recognized the existence of such "higher order" rules in the *Brown Book* (BB, p. 91) but he did not make much of this matter. The rule that rules are there to be broken, which I mentioned at the beginning of this chapter, is such a higher-order rule. Rules of this kind are of the greatest importance in social and political life. We may even say that our social and political institutions typically involve complex hierarchical systems of rules.

Rules and Intentions

In the *Philosophical Investigations* Wittgenstein makes an interlocutor say of the student who was supposed to continue a number series by adding always 2: "But I already knew, at the time when I gave the order that he ought to write 1002 after 1000." And to this Wittgenstein responds: "Certainly, and you can also say that you *meant* it then; only you should not be misled by the grammar of the words 'know' and 'mean'" (PI, 187). And in trying to identify the mistake, he adds in the next remark: "Your idea was that of meaning the order had in its own way already traversed all those steps: that when you meant it your mind as it were flew ahead and took all the steps before you physically arrived at this or that one . . . And it seemed as if they were in some *unique* way predetermined, anticipated – as only the act of meaning can anticipate reality" (PI, 188). This had, of course, been Frege's view of his rules of inference when he had said that the rules of inference allow us to trace an infinity of logical connections that are, in some peculiar sense, already there.

If we are to attend properly to the grammar of the word "mean" in this context, we must attend to the fact that the word is used in two different ways (the same holds for its German equivalent "*meinen*"). We speak, in one sense, of the meaning of a sentence and of what someone means by uttering a sentence. This kind of meaning can be rendered by another sentence, for instance, in another language. On the other hand, we can also say that the teacher "means" the student to go on in a particular way. In expressions of the form "A means to . . . " and "A means B to . . . "the word "means" is, in fact, equivalent to "intends." Wittgenstein writes, in this sense: "In a law-court, the question might be raised how someone meant a word . . . It is a question of *intention*" (PI, p. 214). The question in the court of law is: what did the person intend when he said . . . ?

This returns us to the issue of rule-following. How should we understand the idea that when the teacher told his student to continue the series of numbers in a certain way, he intended him to . . . ? Is it that the intention in some ways determines what is to count as a correct application of the rule? In order to consider this point further, we need to distinguish two different situations. In the first, I form an intention to do something at some later point. I can say to myself, "Tomorrow I will go for a walk," and when tomorrow comes I go for that walk. Here we have two separate things: the intention, on the one hand, and the subsequent action, on the other. Antecedent intentions of this sort must be distinguished from what we may call active intentions. The latter manifest themselves directly in the action itself. How do I know, for instance, that an animal intends to hunt its prey? Not because it has told me what it plans to do later on. It is, rather, that its intention finds "natural expression" in its predatory behavior. Wittgenstein reminds us: "Look at a cat when it stalks a bird; or an animal when it wants to escape" (PI, 647). But in this case there are not two separate things going on: the intention and the action. "The intention *with which* one acts does not 'accompany' the action any more than the thought 'accompanies' speech" (PI, p. 217). We are certainly not aware of two things going on when we speak fluently – first the thought and then the speech – and similarly we are not conscious of a separation between an active intention and the action in which the intention manifests itself. Wittgenstein writes therefore that in such cases, "Thought and intention are neither 'articulated' nor 'non-articulated'; to be compared neither with a single note which sounds during the acting or speaking, nor with a tune" (ibid.). The intention is in this case not a separable ingredient but an aspect or feature of the action. But if this is so, then it makes no sense to say that the intention determines the action, that how we apply the rule is fixed by our intention.

But what then about antecedent intentions? Here there exists a manifest difference between the intention and its execution in action; the one may precede the other and sometimes, indeed, by a very long time. Antecedent intentions are of interest when we are dealing with interpretable rules. When we are uncertain about how such a rule is to be applied we may find it helpful to ask how the rule was originally intended. That question can be asked, of course, only when the rule has an identifiable point of origin or at least a definite and identifiable history. There is no point in asking what is the original intention behind the golden rule. There are, on the other hand, situations in which an identifiable authority has issued a rule. In that case it may be important to ask how that authority meant the rule. Take the case of a mother who warns her child not to leave the house while she is away. What is the child to do if the house unexpectedly catches fire? Knowing its mother's original intention in issuing her rule – the intention, that is, to keep the child safe – the child may decide that in this situation it should not remain in the house. But even in cases where a particular authority has issued a rule it may be impossible to determine its original intention. When a law is passed, for instance, by majority vote in a parliament, we cannot really speak of the original intention of the lawgiver. The parliamentarians who voted in favor of the law may have had quite different intentions in passing it. We sometimes speak in such situations of "the will" of the lawgiver or the authority. Wittgenstein himself considers this possibility when he writes: "Might it not even be imagined that several people had carried out an intention without any one of them having it? In this way a government may have an intention that no *man* has (Z, 48). But such formulations call for explication. Taken literally, they express no more than a convenient fiction. There is, literally, no such thing as a "general will."

Even if there is a clear expression of an antecedent intention, there remains the question what significance we ought to attach to it. According to Wittgenstein our words have meaning because their use is embedded in the practice of our lives. We can say much the same about the expression of an original intention. What that intention means can be assessed only by considering the practices into which its expression is embedded. Wittgenstein is therefore rightly critical of the idea that one could intend to play a game of chess in a world in which there exists no chess, and therefore of the idea that "the existence of a custom, of a technique is not necessary." In such a world someone might, of course, utter the words "Let's play chess!" But we must ask: "Where is the connection effected between the sense of the expression 'Let's play a game of chess' and all the rules of the game?" And the answer is: "Well, in the list of rules of the game, in the teaching of it, in the day-to-day practice of playing" (PI, 197). We must understand, in other words, that "an intention is embedded in its situation, in human customs and institutions. If the technique of the game of chess did not exist, I could not intend to play a game of chess" (PI, 337). Hence, when we ask after the original intention behind an interpretable rule, it will not be enough to find out what words the makers of the rule uttered or in what ways they expressed their intention; we must look at how they used the rule in order to determine the actual content of their original intention. As Wittgenstein puts it succinctly, in a formula that has multiple uses, "An 'inner event' requires external criteria" (PI, 580).

Even when we can determine the original intention behind an interpretable rule, it does not follow that we must use the rule only in the way it was originally intended. To understand this we must consider once more the difference between inexorable and interpretable rules. Inexorable rules are useful in a context of high regularity. When a domain of things is highly uniform, it becomes possible to formulate an inexorable rule. And this brings us certain benefits such as regularity, predictability, and precise application. But in domains that are fluid and highly diverse and, in particular, in what I have called complex and hyper-complex totalities, inexorable rules prove to be of limited value. In order to apply interpretable rules in such situations we must also often set aside the original intention behind them. We are fully used to this in the field of technology. The makers of inventions have often specific intentions with respect to their use. But later on, we may use those inventions in ways not anticipated by their inventor. No one will feel constrained in their use of gunpowder by being told that its inventors meant it to be used only for making fireworks. Why should we proceed differently when it comes to other interpretable rules?

Contested Rules

It is regrettable that Wittgenstein paid so little attention to the contestation to which rules and their application can be subject. This is understandable given that such contestation is rare in logic and mathematics. But we cannot get very far in talking about social and political phenomena without considering the contestability of rules. This applies even to the social phenomenon of what Wittgenstein calls "everyday language." Certain questions about everyday language will not come into view if we do not take the contestability of its rules into account. We cannot fully explain, for instance, in what sense that language is "everyday." Similarly, we cannot explain what it is for "our" language to be "ours." Sometimes, the answers to such questions are highly contested and inflammable. What if there is more than one language that lays claim to being the common medium of communication? What if the linguistic group is stratified by social and class divisions? Who is then speaking "everyday" language? Whose language is it then? What happens when one language claims to have a higher standing than that of everyday? The phrase "our everyday language" suggests a whole set of linguistic practices held together by a set of grammatical rules. As with all rules of social life, we need to ask of these rules: whose rules are they? What authority do they possess? What do they demand from us? The grammatical rules of what we call "everyday" language are taught to us by our parents and teachers and also by other users of the language. Some of these figures possess an authority over us that is rati-

visible rails invisibly laid to infinity

fied by society and the state. Though grammatical rules carry with them no inherent sanctions, our teachers may nevertheless use the threat of sanctions to inculcate them. But from where have my teachers (parents, other language users) got the rules that they teach me? It would be naïve to assume that the grammatical rules of our everyday language have evolved spontaneously. It is, rather, that teachers are given instructions by higher authorities as to what they are supposed to teach. There are all kinds of institutions that regularize our everyday language (academies, textbooks, bureaucracies, churches, etc.) and there are all kinds of ways in which our language becomes regularized as, for instance, through the writings of great authors, through movies and other media. At every given moment there exists, in fact, more than one everyday language. Different social groups employ these languages. Some of those languages have more prestige than others. The balance between these languages often shifts over time. Slang becomes high language, standard language becomes outmoded. There are generational, ethnic, and class differences in the way we speak. The everyday language of highly trained philosophers differs naturally from that of everyday men and women.[9]

Finally, what happens when contestable rules become actually contested? Wittgenstein considers at one point that we might be attracted to the idea that in such situations an intuition may be needed about how the rule is to be applied. But he adds: "It would almost be more correct to say, not that an intuition was needed at every stage, but that a new decision was needed at every stage" (PI, 186). When rules are actually contested, it may, indeed, be necessary to make decisions about how they are to be applied. Decision making is, indeed, of the essence of all social and political life and is an essential part of the life of rules in such contexts. We cannot say that Wittgenstein has recognized this sufficiently.

notes

1 Gottlob Frege, *Conceptual Notation and Related Articles*, translated and edited by Terrell Ward Bynum (Oxford: Clarendon Press, 1972), p. 136.
2 Frege, *Conceptual Notation*, p. 136.
3 Gottlob Frege, *Grundgesetze der Arithmetik*, 2nd, unaltered, edition (Heidelberg: Georg Olms, 1962), p. 114.
4 *Wittgenstein and the Vienna Circle*, recorded by Friedrich Waismann, edited by Brian McGuinness, translated by Joachim Schulte (Oxford: Blackwell, 1979), p. 123f.
5 Ludwig Wittgenstein, *Lectures, Cambridge 1930–1932*, from the notes of John King and Desmond Lee, edited by Desmond Lee (Chicago: University of Chicago Press, 1980), p. 48.
6 Wittgenstein, *Lectures*, p. 40.
7 G.E. Moore, "Wittgenstein's Lectures in 1930–33," in *Philosophical Occasions, 1912–1951*, edited by James Klagge and Alfred Nordmann (Indianapolis: Hackett, 1993), p. 276.

8 David Bloor, *Wittgenstein, Rules and Institutions* (London: Routledge, 1997),
p. 20. The opposing, individualist view is defended by Colin McGinn, according
to whom understanding "is an unmediated propensity to act." (McGinn,
Wittgenstein on Meaning: An Interpretation and Evaluation (Oxford: Blackwell,
1984), p. 43). This propensity exists in us naturally as individuals and
Wittgenstein is therefore "insofar as he has a view on the individual/social
opposition, . . . an individualist" (ibid., p. 200).

9 Ernest Gellner, *Words and Things: A Critical Account of Linguistic Philosophy
and a Study of Ideology* (London: Gollancz, 1959).

further reading

Bloor, David. *Wittgenstein, Rules and Institutions*. London: Routledge, 1991.
Kripke, Saul. *Wittgenstein on Rules and Private Language*. Cambridge, MA:
Harvard University Press, 1982.

visible rails invisibly laid to infinity

what is the use of studying philosophy?

> Wisdom is cold and to that extent stupid. (Faith on the other hand is a passion.)
>
> Ludwig Wittgenstein, *Culture and Value*

The first half of the twentieth century – the period of Wittgenstein's adult, philosophical life – was a time of extraordinary violence in Europe. In a two-phased war (1914–1918 and 1939–1945) the old political, economic, and social order of Europe was torn apart.[1] Wittgenstein himself had come out of the first phase of that war as a debilitated and disillusioned veteran. It took him 10 years before he was ready to return to philosophy and even then he continued to suffer from what we would now diagnose as post-traumatic stress syndrome.[2]

In 1918 the Austro-Hungarian Empire had collapsed and Viennese culture – of which the Wittgensteins had been such an integral part – began to dissolve. A politically unstable republic vegetated on for 20 more years until Adolf Hitler clawed it into his arms. As the tide of anti-Semitic repression and persecution rose, the Wittgensteins must have felt increasingly anxious even though they had long left their ancestral faith behind them. In 1938 Wittgenstein wrote to G.E. Moore of "the great nervous strain" he was feeling because he realized, "My people in Vienna are in great trouble."[3] At the time, Wittgenstein also considered it incumbent on him to "confess" his Jewish ancestry to friends and acquaintances alike since he thought that they "took him to be three-quarters Aryan and one-quarter Jewish" (when the proportion was, in fact, the reverse) and he had "done nothing to prevent this misapprehension."[4] But neither the external circumstances nor their own anxieties were sufficient to move the members of the Wittgenstein family to engage in

wittgenstein, First Edition. Hans Sluga.
© 2011 Hans Sluga. Published 2011 by Blackwell Publishing Ltd.

political activity. Luck and family wealth protected them, no doubt, from hardships to which others – Jews, Austrians, other Europeans– were subjected. From 1930 onward, Wittgenstein himself was moreover safely back in Cambridge where he became – reluctantly, though,– a British subject in 1939. Too old for military service, he volunteered to work in a hospital as the war resumed– first as a porter and then as a lab assistant.

After the war, in 1945, he was to write eloquently of the "poverty" and "darkness" of his time, which would make it unlikely that his work could bring light or enlightenment to anyone (PI, preface). His reservations about the age in which he lived went deep. Already before the war he had called the spirit of European and American civilization, its "industry, architecture, and music, . . . its fascism and its socialism," utterly "alien and uncongenial" (CV, p. 6). That civilization had been built on the promises of science and technology. With their help Europe had become rich, world dominating, and modern. But all this had come at an extraordinary price. European and American civilization, he wrote, was characterized through and through by its preoccupation with progress. It sought to build ever more complex structures – houses, industries, societies, and dominions as well as theories and ideologies. This system of progress appeared to him inherently unstable and flawed. By contrast, he – the ex-engineer and one-time architect – insisted that he was no longer interested in building machines, or houses, or even theories. His only goal now was, as he put it, to achieve clarity of vision and transparency of thought.

Such thoughts reveal once more the extraordinary hold that Schopenhauer had on Wittgenstein's imagination. Schopenhauer's despair of the world and his hope for redemption from it had, in fact, accompanied Wittgenstein since his youth. It was a pessimism that veered between the personal and the cosmic but held little regard for the social and political realities in between. Like Schopenhauer, Wittgenstein lacked an eye for political matters. And when it came to making political choices, he tended, like Schopenhauer (and, indeed, many pessimists), toward conservative conclusions. He was certainly in no way a political thinker. While his writings range over a wide arc of topics – from metaphysics to psychology, from logic to language, and from mathematics to aesthetics – politics has no significant place in them. Already in the *Tractatus* he had expressed the profoundly anti-political view that good and bad willing can affect only the limits of the world, not any specific facts. And in the spirit of Schopenhauer he had sought redemption there in a "life of knowledge," not in active engagement. The *Philosophical Investigations* were similarly apolitical in spirit. In contrast to Marx's thesis that philosophy must set out to change the world, not just to understand it, he held that philosophy can teach us only to see things clearly in the hope of redeeming us from our illusions. In the face of the grossest forms of inhumanity it might teach us, for instance, that there exists in us a natural compassion for the suffering of others.[5] But this Schopenhauerian thought was for Wittgenstein once again a specifically personal insight, not one that would lead him to political action.

Wittgenstein's apolitical stance is tied to a conception of philosophy that insists on a sharp demarcation between itself and everything else. His characterization of that boundary changed, of course, over time; but he always remained committed to a separation of disciplines directly due to Schopenhauer but ultimately Kantian in spirit. In asserting that philosophy had only a specific and narrow task to perform he did not, of course, mean to say that only philosophy mattered. His famous and controversial claim that philosophy "leaves everything as it is," (PI, 124) does not imply that human beings should leave all things as they are – as incautious readers have surmised. The words are intended to highlight merely the distinctive job of philosophy. They do not tell us that there must be no social or political change. And even in philosophy, they do not call for the status quo. We must remember that in the same passage Wittgenstein also speaks of philosophy as "a battle against the bewitchment of our intelligence by means of language," as a means for "the uncovering of one or another piece of plain nonsense," and as a tool for "avoiding ineptness or emptiness in our assertions." And later on he adds that his aim in philosophy is "to show the fly the way out of the fly-bottle," that is, to show human beings how to escape from the traps in their thinking by retracing the steps that have brought them there (PI, 309). None of this sounds quietist. Philosophy must admittedly, in Wittgenstein's view, leave the facts as they are, that is, acknowledge those facts for what they are – including the facts of language. But this acknowledgment is conceived to be transformative in nature. Still, Wittgenstein's words also make evident that social and political matters were far from his mind. Politics is, after all, a field in which the distinction between the factual and conceptual is constantly broached. There is certainly no genuine political thought with a claim to the kind of conceptual purity that Kant and his followers have espoused for philosophy.

A Political Moment

Once, in 1939, when Norman Malcolm told Wittgenstein that he considered the British too noble to have plotted an assassination attempt on Hitler, Wittgenstein exploded with anger. Malcolm writes in his *Memoir*: "He considered it a great stupidity and also an implication that I was not learning anything from philosophy. He said these things very vehemently, and when I refused to admit that my remark was stupid he would not talk to me any more." The incident obviously rankled in Wittgenstein's mind, for five years later he reminded Malcolm once more of it, adding: "What is the use of studying philosophy if it does not improve your thinking about the important questions of everyday life?"[6] For Wittgenstein himself those important questions were certainly not in the first instance political but personal and individual in nature. His "Lecture on Ethics" shows that his ethics was, primarily, an ethics of the self: of how the existence of the world can strike one with wonder, how one can feel absolutely safe or absolutely guilty. Individual honesty and personal integrity were, moreover, his personal moral guidelines, as he made clear on many occasions.[7] Such individual virtues do, of course, have social and political repercussions. Wittgenstein made that evident in his dispute with Malcolm. Yet in questioning Malcolm's political judgment he was still primarily concerned with his student's readiness to face reality in an honest fashion. He was questioning, in other words, whether philosophy had succeeded in shaping Malcolm's personal character.

But what if "the important questions of everyday life" turned out to be more directly social and political in nature? How might Wittgenstein's thought help us then? The question poses itself because we can see today – more clearly perhaps than Wittgenstein – how deep the knives of twentieth-century politics have cut into the flesh of the human condition. Does it not look increasingly as if the blood of the whole modern era was running into the gutter? And with it perhaps also what has given life and vitality to modern philosophy? And so we find ourselves forced to ask: has the moment not come when philosophy can no longer afford to evade the question of politics? Cannot afford to, that is, as a practice of asking the most fundamental questions? Are we perhaps not back to a time like Plato's when political thought was and had to be first philosophy? That leaves us to ask of what use Wittgenstein might be to us when the issue is no longer simply that of rebutting the epistemological, ontological, and logical views of a Descartes or Kant, of a Frege or Russell. Hanna Pitkin, one of the first to raise the question of Wittgenstein's relevance to political thought, has claimed that Wittgenstein's thinking was, indeed, "continually centered on the problem of the contemporary human condition."[8] But how far does this get us with Wittgenstein's actual philosophical work? What can it tell us about our contemporary human condition? We can only say once more that Wittgenstein was, first and foremost, a man at the crossroads. He was obviously much preoccupied with such characteristically "modern" philosophical themes as the logical structure of the world, the question how thought or language represents reality, the nature of the self and its relation to the world. But he was perhaps also gesturing at the same time beyond the limits and limitations of the modern philosophical sensibility.

"Could there be such a thing as a Wittgensteinian political theory? What might it look like?" Pitkin has asked. She suggests that such a theory would be as radically different from traditional political theorizing as Wittgenstein's thought is from traditional philosophy. It "would presumably share his suspicion of broad systematic generalization, his therapeutic stress on the particular case, on the investigating and speaking self, and on the acceptance of plurality and contradiction."[9] The words imply that Wittgenstein's thought might be used, first and foremost, for the purpose of a critical assessment of political theories. And it is not difficult to see how his concepts might be employed in the critique of the science model of political theory and, in fact, of all attempts at constructing comprehensive explanatory accounts of politics.[10] Even so-called "critical social theory" is not immune to a Wittgensteinian critique. James Tully has shown how to wield it in dissecting, for instance, Jürgen

what is the use of studying philosophy?

Habermas's reliance on the concept of reason and Charles Taylor's trust in that of interpretation.[11] But in her seminal book *Wittgenstein and Justice* Pitkin anticipates also a more positive role for a political theorizing in the spirit of Wittgenstein. This, she writes, would have to draw on his thoughts on language, grammar, and meaning; on the ordinary, the commonsensical, the everyday; on his insights into the diversity of language games and forms of life; on his understanding of concepts and family resemblances, and so on. Her list suggests that Wittgenstein's work can be utilized in more than one way in political theorizing.[12]

Since this is a book about Wittgenstein and not about political philosophy, I can only sketch some of these lines of thought. I will have to leave it to another occasion to show how it might actually be possible to construct a political philosophy with the help of Wittgenstein's methodological considerations.

Action, Words, and Concepts

The first question in political philosophy perhaps is what, if anything, such philosophizing can contribute to actual politics. Is the relation of political philosophy and political theory to actual politics that of astronomy to the stars? Astronomy may be able to describe and explain the heavens to us but it cannot change their course. Was Hegel right, in other words, when he said that philosophy "as the thought of the world" appears only when the world has completed its formative process? As, literally, an afterthought? Politics concerns, in the first instance, specific action in response to a concrete, substantive, practical problem. A group of citizens demands, for instance, that their needs, interests, or rights be respected. Government responds by delivering or denying their demands. What can philosophers contribute to this situation? Certainly few of them have the wherewithal to be effective political agents. But they are needed nevertheless, we are told, to provide norms of political action: principles of justice, characterizations of the good life, constitutional plans, the claims of freedom, equality, and community. This only elicits the question whether any such norms can be justified by purely philosophical – that is, extra-political – means. And, once reached, can we apply them without having once again to employ political means? At both ends, the gap between theory and practice remains.

Such worries multiply when we speak of a political philosophy in the spirit of Wittgenstein. It seems unlikely that this kind of political philosophy could ever come up with normative principles. Wittgenstein never speaks of such principles, not even in his lecture on ethics. And his passing political references give us no whiff of any normative rules. Wittgenstein's thinking proceeds, in fact, at a level of abstraction that makes it difficult to see how it could be applied directly to our political reality. At most, we can envisage it having methodological implications, implications for how to think and speak about political matters. But then we are back to the question what bearing that would have on actual politics. To get a more adequate view we must reassess the conception of politics as being essentially local action in equally local circumstances. It is here where the normative political philosophers get something right. They understand that in demanding or delivering political action we usually draw on broader considerations of what is right and hence on something that extends beyond the local condition of the action itself. Political action is, we might say, through-and-through relational in character. It concerns a weighing of different and sometimes competing priorities and claims. To award a benefit to one group means commonly to deny a benefit to another group. To make one political choice prevents another one. There are options to be considered, claims to be compared and adjudicated, risks to be calculated. Ultimately, the question will be faced regarding what kind of goods political action is meant to deliver, the extent and the limits of the political as against, for instance, the personal or the moral. It is here where philosophical questioning gets its traction in politics.

Politics is, in other words, a process of mediation between groupings of human beings. And this mediation will be carried out characteristically not only in physical action but also in words. Language is, in fact, so fundamental that one might be tempted to reduce politics to communicative interaction. But this would, of course, mean underestimating what one might call the physiological element in politics, the fact that it is grounded in the realities of the human body. Still, it is true that these bodily realities are negotiated in words and have an immediate political function. And this justifies us in saying that the examination of those words is itself a genuinely political undertaking. How we conceive of our political language has, in fact, immediate bearing on our political reality. It is here that Wittgenstein's reflections may prove useful to us politically. We use words in politics to name and to describe, to classify and to relate, but what all this comes to is by no means evident. There exists a whole mythology of naming and describing, of classifying and relating, and our attachment to that mythology produces numerous miscalculations, political and otherwise. With Wittgenstein's help I single out three of them.

In a famous and notorious essay, *The Concept of the Political*, Carl Schmitt complained around 1930 that "one seldom finds a clear definition of the political."[13] For practical purposes, "the political" is usually explained by reference to the state but that notion has itself become problematic as its boundary to society has turned blurry. In consequence, Schmitt writes, "the equation state = politics" has become "erroneous and deceptive."[14] His own attempt to find a new way to characterize the essence of the political is motivated not so much by a desire to bring conceptual clarity into the discussion, but in order to bring home to us that politics is inescapable from our being fully human. Hannah Arendt began her own work in political philosophy similarly with the question "What is politics?" In a note from 1951 she called for a new kind of thinking on this question: "What is remarkable among all great thinkers is

what is the use of studying philosophy?

the difference in rank between their political philosophies and the rest of their works – even in Plato. Their politics never reaches the same depth. This lack of depth is nothing but a failure to sense the depths in which politics is anchored."[15] In reflecting on the concept of the political she wants, like Schmitt, to bring home to us the dignity and importance of politics that, she fears, we have largely forgotten. In the 1970s Michel Foucault, finally, declared once more in a kindred spirit that "political analysis and criticism have in large measure still to be invented." He rejected the idea that the primary task of political philosophy was to supply us with standards for choosing between forms of institutions, principles of justice, and courses of action. The problem was for him "not so much that of defining a political 'position' (which is to choose from a pre-existing set of possibilities) but to imagine and bring into being new schemas of politicization." And to that end, he considered it essential to establish what sense to give to the word "political."[16] For Schmitt, Arendt, and Foucault the concern with political concepts has, in other words, an urgently practical meaning.

A political philosophy in Wittgenstein's sense would certainly hold that active political engagement requires clarity about the concepts of politics and, in particular, about the concept of the political. To this extent such a philosophy would be in sympathy with Schmitt's, Arendt's, and Foucault's attempted analyses of the concept of the political and of more specific political concepts such as those of sovereignty, democracy, liberalism, dictatorship, judgment and decision, friendship and enmity, freedom and authority, labor, work, and action, the public and the private, the political and the social, power, discipline, and government. In a note on the mathematician F.P. Ramsey, Wittgenstein wrote metaphorically that Ramsey was a "bourgeois thinker" who only meant to clear up "the affairs of some particular community," that is, that of traditional mathematics. In expanding that metaphor, he offered us at the same time a hint as to what political philosophy in his sense would have to deliver. Wittgenstein wrote that Ramsey "did not reflect on the essence of the state . . . but on how *this* state might be reasonably organized. The idea that this state might not be the only possible one in part disquieted him and in part bored him" (CV, p. 17). The remark suggests that political philosophy will have to concern itself with the "essence" (i.e., the concept) of the state and, presumably, of other basic political realities. It would have to get us to understand that our existing state is only one among possible others and, presumably, also that all other existing political institutions are variable in character. By contrast, the task of determining the reasonable organization of any particular state is said to take merely second place. Such considerations clearly align Wittgenstein with theorists like Schmitt, Arendt, and Foucault.

It would be disappointing, however, to have to conclude that a Wittgensteinian form of political philosophy amounted only to an alignment with work done already by others. But that is not how it is. Wittgenstein's thought is bound to make a significant contribution to political philosophy with the realization that the basic concepts of politics are likely to be family resemblance concepts. Neither Schmitt, nor Arendt, nor Foucault seems to have considered that possibility. Schmitt, perhaps, comes closest to it when he speaks of the historical variability of our political concepts. "All concepts of the spiritual sphere," he writes, "can only be understood in terms of concrete political existence."[17] He rejects for that reason any formal definition of the concept of the political and allows only for the possibility of a "determination of its content."[18] But he still falls short of the insight that the concept of the political must be a family resemblance concept, for he goes on to argue that all our variable conceptions of the political share a single, invariable form and insists that "the specific political distinction to which political actions and motives can be reduced is that between friend and enemy."[19] Arendt is caught in an even more evident essentialism when she asserts, without qualification, that "the meaning of politics is freedom."[20] And Foucault ends up similarly when he speaks of politics simpliciter as an exercise of power on power relations. A Wittgensteinian political philosophy will look at all such essentialist and reductive formulas with suspicion and propose instead a series of specific descriptions of different embodiments of the political and of the resemblances and kinship relations between them.

This does not mean that we can apply Wittgenstein's methodology in an uncritical manner to the analysis of our political concepts. We must recall here the reservations I expressed in Chapter 5 about Wittgenstein's use of the notion of family resemblance. Wittgenstein employs that notion to highlight resemblance relations but family relations are also causal in character and this is crucial when we consider political phenomena. They are related to each other, after all, not only by degrees of similarity but also by causal relations. Among these are, first of all, relations of biological descent, relations that establish and maintain family bonds, tribal communities, ethnicities, races, and nations. We need to consider also causal factors like geography and climate, propinquity and distance in space and time. Finally, there are historical facts to consider – that is, relations of dependence and influence, of developments, progresses, and retreats, and above all relations of power. Our political order consists, in fact, of a web in which affinities and causal strands are inextricably woven together.

The Pluralism of the Political

There is a second respect in which Wittgenstein may be thought able to make a decisive contribution to our understanding of politics. Schmitt, Arendt, and Foucault have all set themselves up against an understanding of politics for which the idea of unity is the grounding notion and ideal. Instead, they have all argued that politics is based in one way or another on the fact of human plurality. In the Wittgensteinian spirit just sketched, I want to argue that their position should not be understood as seeking to isolate an invariant feature of all politics but as saying that in our current world situation a pluralistic conception of politics is appropriate for us. Together with the idea of political plurality go the notions of communication and mediation, of translation and interpretation – but equally those of misunderstanding, disagreement, and conflict and of the overcoming and controlling of them. All those concepts are certainly essential for us in characterizing our current political situation. But in what is the pluralism of the political grounded and how is communication in the field of diversity nonetheless possible? Here Wittgenstein will once more prove helpful.

I will try to explain this by reference to Arendt. In her criticism of classical political philosophy she insists that the tradition has failed to recognize the essential plurality of the human condition and has thus proved unable to generate an adequate concept and conception of the political.[21] This is a startling accusation and one that is particularly unfair, so it seems, to Aristotle. For in his *Politics* Aristotle speaks explicitly of human plurality as a condition of the possibility of political life. What then is missing in Aristotle's account, according to Arendt? Her answer is that Aristotle conceived only of an objective plurality of human beings. According to him there can be a polis only if human beings are organized into separate families, individually own things, have different occupations and different social and political positions. The pluralism Arendt envisages is of a different order. She holds that each human being comes into the world at a unique point in space and time and perceives and understands the world thus from a singular location. The politically fundamental feature of human plurality has, for Arendt, in other words, a subjective dimension. This pluralism constitutes, according to her, a "chaos of difference" from which politics must emerge. In Arendt's picture, politics consists in the effort to commensurate initially incommensurable perspectives that human beings bring to the world. Politics is, in her language, free action – that is, a free interaction of human beings in which they reveal themselves to each other in their plurality and define themselves in their distinctness.

But Arendt never asks how such free interaction is to be achieved in a chaos of difference. If you and I do, indeed, see the world from entirely different points of view, how can we ever come to understand each other? How, indeed, can we ever come to understand that there are different world-views? It is here that an appeal to Wittgenstein's thinking proves useful. Like Arendt, he allows that human beings may have different world pictures. But he realizes, in contrast to Arendt, that these are from the start embedded in – and indeed are part of – the common language we speak. Our thoughts about the world take shape only in the medium of language. And this language exists always and only in the public world; it is socially created and maintained, not embedded in the folds of an individual consciousness. Where Arendt leaves a gap between world-views and their commensuration, a gap that she cannot effectively close, Wittgenstein understands the interconnectedness of our seeing the world and communicating about it.

Arendt's account is subject to the further difficulty that she cannot easily explain the connection between our different world-views and our actions and interactions. How do world-views manifest themselves in the social and political sphere? Historical materialists argue that ideologies are mere super-structures, that they have no causal efficacy, that they are mere by-products of solid, material circumstances. Arendt, it appears, has nothing to say in response to this kind of challenge. Wittgenstein, on the other hand, can explain to us that historical materialism misconceives the distinction between the material basis and the ideological superstructure. It assumes a sharp sepa-ration between the inner and the outer, the material and the ideological – a distinction which it has, in fact, inherited ultimately from Descartes and his dualism. But Cartesian dualism cannot be maintained, as Wittgenstein force-fully reminds us, since "inner" phenomena require "outer" criteria.

Arendt would, of course, have agreed that the commensuration of world-views must take place in the public sphere and that it is largely carried out in language. Politics and speech are, indeed, so intimately linked for her that she appears on occasions to identify them. To the extent to which she does, she fails once more to appreciate fully that language is rooted in human practice and that the meaning of a word is its use both in the language and in the context of the world. Wittgenstein helps us to understand not only why human beings have different world-views but also how these views connect to and matter in the public sphere. This is so because world-views and lan-guage games are integrally related. The multiplicity of our language games is, in turn, grounded in the complexity of the world, in our inability to survey that complexity, and the resulting partiality of all human understanding. Aware of the diversity of our needs and interests, Wittgenstein understands that these needs and interests do not form a single overall system. Human pluralism is for him a consequence of our diverse capacities and of multiple limitations to our understanding.

Natural Affinities

Given that there are different world-views, how do we ever achieve a common understanding? Wittgenstein offers us two insights in this regard. The first is, as I have just indicated, that we come to our views of the world only by inter-acting with others, by learning to share a language, and not in strict privacy. Wittgenstein also understands that our various language games and hence our various individual world-views are linked, from the start, by an intricate web of resemblances. World-views form families and together they constitute a shared human form of life, a single family. Because of the multiple overlapping relations in this family structure, human world-views are always in principle accessible and understandable to us. In his "Remarks on Frazer's *Golden Bough*" Wittgenstein writes in a crucial previously quoted passage:

what is the use of studying philosophy?

There are dangers connected with eating and drinking, not only for savages, but also for us; nothing is more natural than the desire to protect oneself from these . . . It goes without saying that a man's shadow, which looks like him, or his mirror image, the rain, thunderstorms, the phases of the moon, the changing of seasons, the way in which animals are similar to and different from one another and in relation to man, the phenomena of death, birth, and sexual life, in short everything we observe around us year in and year out, interconnected in so many ways, will play a part in his thinking (his philosophy) and in his practices, or is precisely what we really know and find interesting. (RF, pp. 66–67)

To this we might add that there are also shared psychological states and experiences such as dreams, mental absences, lunacy, states of sudden insight and illumination, anger and joy, unhappiness and depression. And there exists in us perhaps also a shared repertoire of biologically coded behaviors and behavioral responses. These givens can all be worked up by us into different world-views and can be spoken of and seen in different ways. Different as these world-views may be, they are at the same time linked by a web of family resemblances that makes communication and mutual understanding possible. Wittgenstein's account also explains, moreover, why there are degrees of such understanding, since the resemblances between world-views may be more or less great and the phenomena on which they draw may be assembled in different ways. But even when there is great distance between two world-views, he shows us, we can still always strike connections between them by tracing them back to their shared roots.

Words and Their Contexts

Wittgenstein's reflections on language tell us much about how we should go about reading and interpreting words, sentences, speeches, and texts. "The sign (the sentence) gets its significance from the system of signs, from the language to which it belongs. Roughly: understanding a sentence means understanding a language," he writes in the *Blue Book* (BB, p. 5). The language in question must be conceived, moreover, as typically consisting of a large number of distinct language games related to each other by resemblance and kinship relations. These language games have also, in addition, relations to our non-linguistic actions and practices and to things in the world. Wittgenstein is thus not espousing a "linguistic idealism" – as is sometimes claimed – according to which we can never get out of our language. This should be clear, for instance, from the language game of the builders in section 2 of the *Philosophical Investigations*. The language game described there relates the words of the builders directly to their activity of building and to the physical materials needed for that purpose. Without those relations their verbalizations would have no meaning at all.

It should be clear, then, that a political philosophy in the spirit of Wittgenstein will concern itself with the language we speak both in politics and in our reflections on politics in a very specific way. It will certainly encourage us to look at particular uses of words and sentences in politics, but it will insist at the same time that these must be considered in relation to the system of signs to which they belong. While Wittgenstein encourages us to focus on particulars and to avoid quick generalization, he also wants us, on the other hand, to look at the particulars holistically, that is, in relation to their larger context. A Wittgensteinian political philosophy will, moreover, avoid treating political language as if it were a single whole; it will seek, instead, to identify lines of demarcation between the different political language games. It will think of politics, in other words, not as a single totality, but as a fissured, yet interconnected field of differences and resemblances. The same word (e.g., "democracy") or the same verbal formula (e.g., "man is political by nature") may thus play very different roles in different contexts. Finally, it should be clear that a political philosophy in Wittgenstein's spirit will certainly not reduce to linguistic analysis. It will concern itself just as much with our non-linguistic actions and practices and with the things of the world.

Language games are for Wittgenstein characteristically social undertakings. They typically involve a number of participants who propose and oppose, who question and answer, who demand or command and are, in turn, obeyed or resisted. When we think about words and sentences in the context of language games we must understand that those words and sentences are generally not spoken into the blue and that there is always a before and an after to them. Thus, when a speaker asserts a proposition we are entitled to ask to whom it is addressed and whether it is intended, for instance, as an answer to a question, or as a challenge, as a truism, or as an affirmation of a shared belief, etc. It is important to recall that the words even of the greatest theorists and philosophers have such contexts.

Wittgenstein's view of meaning implies that we should, in general, not expect to be able to list necessary and sufficient conditions for the use of our terms. This implies that we should not expect to be able to give formal definitions of those terms. Our conceptual analysis of political language will, instead, have to be descriptive and piecemeal, devoted to the particular; also to the historically specific rather than to large-scale, speculative generalizations. There are certainly areas of human knowledge in which it is useful to construct formal definitions of terms (e.g., in mathematics and logic). And we can, of course, always draw an arbitrary line around the use of a word and on this basis construct a formal definition. Thus, Wittgenstein writes in the *Philosophical Investigations:* "I *can* give the concept 'number' rigid limits . . . that is, use the word 'number' for a rigidly limited concept, but I can also use it so that the extension of the concept is *not* closed by a frontier" (PI, 68). We often think that we need such definitions in order to prevent deviant uses of our terms. But Wittgenstein points out that "any general definition can be misunderstood, too" (PI, 71). Unless we make our definitions purely stipulative, we must, moreover, test their adequacy against how our words are actually used. Even when we have formal definitions of a term there remains always the question of how the term is actually used.

Wittgenstein took the exegetical context of his language games to be rather narrowly circumscribed. He never looked closely at actual historical uses of language even though he believed that meaning is use; and he never seriously considered the social dimension of our uses of language. From the perspective of political philosophy, that must be considered a serious limitation. But we need to remain conscious at the same time of the danger in speaking about the context of our words and sentences too indiscriminately. A language game certainly has no one single context in which it is at home. But when we look at it from too far away, when we make the context of the language game too large, there is the possibility that the specific contours and conditions of our language game begin to blur. Whenever we are engaged in the exegesis of a particular language game we need to consider carefully which context needs to be taken into account and avoid both an overly narrow and an overly wide view of this context.

Rules, Decisions, Authority

Rules are essential to all the more complex forms of social and political life. We are familiar with them as regulations and as laws. The latter are issued by governments and states. The former may be issued by both private and governmental bodies but they are usually, in turn, backed up by law. Our modern political institutions are now all governed by law – even the so-called "lawless" and "unlawful" regimes. There are, for that reason, in all our societies also law makers, law interpreters, and law enforcers. Law is, indeed, now so endemic to our political institutions that we may be tempted to define such institutions simply as legal structures rather than as social realities.[22]

But the state is by no means identical with its legal structure. The law is, rather, a specifically political invention made under particular historical conditions. The rule of ancient tribal leaders and prehistoric kings was, by contrast, personal in nature. To rule then was to make decisions as the moment arose, guided perhaps by tradition or the advice of elders or by divine auspices, but never by an appeal to abstract law spelled out and applied in some organized manner. From Aristotle's book on the Athenian Constitution, we can see that the early Athenian polis was as yet a pre-legal order.[23] The invention of law came about through a revolt against the older system of personal rule. This invention involved, first of all, a new capacity for understanding that various and often quite different situations can be treated the same. The resulting uniformity made ruling more regular, more predictable, more effective, and hence more "just." Citizens could now predict the actions of their rulers; they also now had a yardstick by which to measure their rulers' performance. This capacity for abstraction required a new use of language, the evolution of a new vocabulary, and more highly articulated propositions. Law and logic were thus from the start intertwined and still today we speak of both political and logical laws. There had to be in addition also a reliable method of recording, not mere dependence on human memory. The rise of literacy coincides naturally with the invention of both law and logic. This development brought, in turn, new professions into existence: the scribe, the clerk, the judge, and the rhetorician (we might say: the lawyer). As literacy became widespread, citizens themselves became able to read and dispute the law. Eventually, they began to demand a role in making and applying the law. The republican and the democratic state were products of this development.

The pervasiveness of the law in our political systems makes it pressing for political thought to ask how laws perform their distinctive function. Hans Kelsen, the eminent legal theorist, has argued that we should conceive of law as strictly determining its own applications. Wittgenstein's reflections on rule-following show us why this characterization is misleading. For what does it mean to say that a rule determines something or other? Kelsen's "pure theory of the law" has been rightly challenged on this point by Carl Schmitt, who maintained, in turn, that every application of the law involves a decision.[24] Schmitt's considerations resemble to some extent Wittgenstein's reflections on rule-following. But the latter also make clear why Schmitt, too, is incapable of explaining the unique function and purpose of the law. For if all rule is personal, as Schmitt insists, and if every application of a rule requires a brand-new decision, we cannot explain any more why law is needed at all. In opposition to such a "decisionism," Wittgenstein holds rightly that we are not deciding freely when we apply rules. It is, rather, that we *know* how to apply them. And this know-how is grounded in practices, habits, and customs. It is only our dissatisfaction with the claim that "logic" or "intuition" determines the application of the rule that makes us conclude "that a new decision was needed at every stage" (PI, 186). But this does not and cannot mean that each application of a rule actually involves a decision. Neither Kelsen's logical determinism nor Schmitt's decisionism can thus satisfactorily account for the reality of the law. A satisfactory account must rather see law as grounded in regularity, habit, and practice and cannot therefore avoid seeing political institutions as social realities.

Yet there is something more to be said on behalf of Schmitt's decisionism. In contrast to Wittgenstein, who focuses largely on the rules of mathematics and logic, Schmitt concerns himself specifically with the law and in this arena decisions play an indispensable role which they may not be doing in mathematics and logic. It is only through the decision of a lawgiver that a law is established. And laws are always interpretable. Their application is never fixed in the way in which that of the rules of mathematics and logic is. Schmitt understood, moreover, that decisions in the sphere of the law are always contestable both as to their validity and their content. The contestation of law is – for us moderns, at least – indeed, of the essence of politics. And such contestation calls always for new acts of decision making, whether in a court of law, by a lawgiver or by a sovereign (e.g., a parliament). An adequate philosophy of law and hence of politics will have to take this decisionist element into account. But it will also have to consider once more with Wittgenstein how interpretable and contestable rules can nevertheless come to have a binding force.

Schmitt takes his cue on this question from Hobbes, who writes that authority not truth makes the law.[25] Wittgenstein certainly recognizes the role of authority in the human form of life, as he makes evident in the *Philosophical Investigations* and even more so in *On Certainty*. "I learned an enormous amount and accepted it on authority," we read in the latter work (OC, 161). "As children we learn facts . . . and take them on trust . . . The child learns by believing the adult" (OC, 159–160). In order to judge at all, correctly or incorrectly, "a man must already judge in conformity with mankind" (OC, 156). And this suggests that "I must recognize certain authorities in order to make judgments at all" (OC, 493). For all that, he does no detailed work on the concept of authority and nothing to examine the distinction of social roles associated with it, nor does he explore the underlying notions of power and violence. This limits the insights we can derive from his work into the functioning of our society. More surprisingly, this lacuna also exposes limitation in Wittgenstein's philosophy of language. Our language is, after all, not the product of a free consensus among speakers; it is handed to us through the authority of parents, teachers, writers, academies, publishers, the media, and finally even government. Here, as in several other places, it becomes clear that confronting Wittgenstein's thought with questions of politics may also force us to reconsider aspects of Wittgenstein's philosophical thought.

The Unpredictability of Behavior

Our grammar is unsurveyable, and so are our various forms of life – and so is, finally, also the human form of life as a whole. We can certainly orient ourselves in our grammar, we can maneuver forms of life, we can live a human existence but this does not mean that we have or ever could have a comprehensive grasp of our grammar or of those forms of life. Our practical capacities systematically outrun, in other words, our ability to theorize about them.

Wittgenstein speaks in passing of the unpredictability of human behavior – though in somewhat different context (Z, 603). In the passage in question he considers this unpredictability to be one source of our inclination to say that "one can never know what is going on in anyone else." That leads in turn to the mistaken conclusion that what goes on in the human mind is "essentially" private and incommunicable. In the *Philosophical Investigations* Wittgenstein had battled at length against this conclusion. He had pointed out that while the other person does not feel my pain, he can still know that I am suffering. His so-called "private language argument" (PI, 246–315) offers us a series of subtle and complex considerations to show that inner states are in principle communicable. But to deny that there is an essential or absolute privacy to those states is not to deny that what goes on in the mind of another person is for the most part in fact unknown to us. And this factual privacy is surely one of the sources of the unpredictability of human behavior. For anyone interested in society and politics this unpredictability is of the greatest interest since it bears on how we must think about social and political action. We are familiar enough with the phenomenon of unpredictability, both in private and public life. We are used to being puzzled by the behavior of others (particularly of strangers) and make constant accommodations for this in advance. Even when we know people well, we may find ourselves surprised by sudden turns in their behavior ("I never expected X to be so . . . "). At the macro level we are regularly reminded of the failure of experts to predict developments in the economic and political sphere. This unpredictability has, of course, multiple sources. Conditions in the natural world are not fully predictable even though their course is in principle explicable in terms of natural laws, and this unpredictability introduces in turn unpredictability into human behavior. To this we must add the unsurveyability of human forms of life. This prevents us from formulating general explanatory and predictive laws of behavior. In social and political contexts we are, moreover, faced with the phenomenon of hyper-complexity. In order to have a systematic overview of a form of life, we would not only need that form of life itself to be surveyable but we would also need a surveyable grasp of the ways in which those engaged in that form of life in turn understand it. But at this point layers of unsurveyability pile on top of each other to prevent us from having a transparent view of the social and political reality.

These observations bear directly on the question of the possibility and nature of social and political science.[26] If Wittgenstein is right, these undertakings will never be able to achieve the status of explanatory and predictive sciences (like physics) with their precisely formulable laws. They will have to remain narrative and descriptive in nature, offering in essence the sort of informal explanations and predictions of human behavior with which we are familiar in everyday life. And this has, in turn, practical consequences. It forces us to admit that there will never be a scientific way of making social and economic choices. Libertarians like Friedrich von Hayek have concluded that such considerations about the complexity of social and political structures are sufficient to refute socialism with its social planning.[27] It is, of course, true that certain strong forms of "scientific" socialism will be incompatible with the view of society emerging from considerations of the sort we can extract from Wittgenstein. But the same must be said about certain other forms of capitalistic economic theorizing and policy making. It certainly does not follow that socialism in a broader sense is thereby refuted and that liberal, laissez-faire policies in economics are thereby justified.

The unsurveyability of our condition implies only that all of us operate under conditions of uncertainty. That is true for each individual, for each government, but also for each businessman and entrepreneur. There is no reason to think that any one of them has a decisive advantage in operating in the essentially complex and, indeed, hyper-complex system of our politics and economics. This does not mean that every agent is equally qualified or unqualified to act within the social and political arena. The information we have at hand will always be limited and fallible but it can also make us more or less qualified to act. But it does not follow that businessmen will generally be more knowledgeable and hence better equipped to act economically than governments. We might even say that under the conditions of hyper-complexity we should expect businessmen to act mostly from a very limited perspective while governments may be better equipped to work on behalf of their people. The unsurveyability of the human form of life is in no way a free ticket for economic liberalism; it calls rather for caution in whoever acts, for a readiness to anticipate the appearance of unforeseen consequences and events, and the ability to adjust to ever-shifting winds and unexpected disasters. We should not even think that the unsurveyability of human affairs provides an argument against large-scale planning. All economic and political action requires an overall conception of the social context in which it is to be executed. Both individual businessmen and government officials will have to resort to such overall conceptions. And both have to reckon with the uncertainty built into them. This brings me to a final point to extract from Wittgenstein's thinking for social and political theorizing.

Vision and Choice in Politics

From Plato to John Rawls political philosophy has always been a predominantly prescriptive enterprise. The political philosophers have never stopped telling us how we are to construct our state, what principles and laws we ought to adopt, and how we ought to act politically. A Wittgensteinian form of political philosophy will, presumably, have to follow a different path.

We can see this from the way Wittgenstein's reflections on ethics diverge from the standard model. Philosophical work in ethics tends also to be predominantly prescriptive in character. The moral philosophers commonly lay down their rules, their maxims, and imperatives and expect us to live up to them. But in Wittgenstein's discussion of ethics we find none of this. Nowhere in his "Lecture on Ethics" does he speak of normative principles. Instead, he describes what it means for us to see ourselves and the world in ethical terms. I have for that reason characterized Wittgenstein's ethical position as visionary rather than prescriptive or normative. It seems plausible to conclude that a political philosophy in Wittgenstein's sense would also adopt such a visionary stance. Wittgenstein himself, of course, never addressed this topic. In the "Lecture on Ethics" he is concerned only with highly personal forms of ethical awareness. What then would a visionary conception of politics look like? And why do we need one?

The second question is easier to answer than the first. Unless we have an overall vision of the meaning of political life, none of the political norms advanced by our philosophers will have a firm hold on us. Consider, for instance, John Rawls's theory of justice, which is currently attracting so much attention. Rawls advances a series of intricate reasons for adopting two specific principles of justice as guiding political norms. But he cannot explain to us why we should burden ourselves with political matters at all. Why should we not follow Wittgenstein's example and leave such matters aside? Why should they count as much as the wellbeing of our individual souls? And even if we engage ourselves politically, why should we be specifically concerned with the question of justice? Justice is an important political virtue, but is it the only one? Conceived by itself, it is the virtue of a cold, heartless world in which the only remaining issue is what I owe you and what you owe me. Is that how we want to understand our political lives? That we are inclined to see political in these terms today shows only too clearly how impoverished our vision of political life has become.

It is, of course, not easy to propose another, richer conception of the meaning of politics. It may not even be possible for a single individual by him- or herself to produce such a vision. It may take the efforts of many to give a new, positive significance to politics in the face of its current diminution. In recognition of this fact, and in an implicit critique also of the simple-mindedness of the normative tradition in philosophy, Wittgenstein wrote once that "the sickness of a time" can be cured only "by an alteration in the mode of life of human beings," and "the sickness of philosophical problems . . . only through a changed mode of thought and life, not through a medicine invented by an individual."[28]

notes

1 For a characterization of the so-called twentieth-century "world wars" as European civil wars see Geoffrey Barraclough, *An Introduction to Contemporary History* (Harmondsworth: Penguin, 1967).

2 This appears to be, at least, the most plausible explanation for the austerities of his life after 1918, his pessimism and anguish, and for his need to withdraw for long periods of time to the remote regions of Norway and Ireland.

3 In a letter quoted in Ray Monk, *Ludwig Wittgenstein: The Duty of Genius* (New York: The Free Press, 1990), p. 399.

4 Fania Pascal, "Wittgenstein: A Personal Memoir," in *Wittgenstein: Sources and Perspectives*, edited by C.G. Luckhardt (Ithaca, NY: Cornell University Press, 1979), p. 46.

5 See Rupert Read, "Wittgenstein's *Philosophical Investigations* as a war book," unpublished.

6 Norman Malcolm, *Ludwig Wittgenstein: A Memoir*, 2nd edition (Oxford: Oxford University Press, 1984), pp. 32 and 39.

what is the use of studying philosophy?

7 Especially in his conversations with Maurice Drury.
8 Hanna Pitkin, *Wittgenstein and Justice: On the Significance of Ludwig Wittgenstein for Social and Political Thought* (Berkeley: University of California Press, 1972), pp. 316 and 317.
9 Pitkin, *Wittgenstein and Justice*, p. 325.
10 Peter Winch, *The Idea of a Social Science and Its Relation to Philosophy* (London: Routledge, 1958).
11 James Tully, "Wittgenstein and Political Philosophy: Understanding Practices of Critical Reflection," *Political Theory*, 17 (1989), pp. 172–204.
12 For a representative sample of the literature see Cressida J. Heyes, ed., *The Grammar of Politics: Wittgenstein and Political Philosophy* (Ithaca, NY: Cornell University Press, 2003). The volume includes a useful bibliography.
13 Carl Schmitt, *The Concept of the Political*, translated by George Schwab, expanded edition (Chicago: University of Chicago Press, 2007), p. 20.
14 Schmitt, *Concept of the Political*, p. 22
15 Hannah Arendt, "Introduction into Politics," in *The Promise of Politics*, edited by Jerome Kohn (New York: Schocken Books, 2005) p. 93.
16 Michel Foucault, "The History of Sexuality," in *Power/Knowledge: Selected Interviews and Other Writings 1972–1977*, edited by Colin Gordon (Brighton: Harvester Press, 1980), p. 190.
17 Carl Schmitt, "The Age of Neutralizations and Depoliticizations," in *The Concept of the Political*, expanded edition (Chicago: University of Chicago Press, 2007), p. 85.
18 Carl Schmitt, *Der Begriff des Politischen*, 6th edition (Berlin: Huncker & Dublot, 1996), p. 26. The English translation unfortunately obscures this distinction.
19 Schmitt, *Concept of the Political*, p. 26.
20 Arendt, "Introduction into Politics," p. 108.
21 Arendt, "What Is Politics?" in *The Promise of Politics*.
22 Such a "juridical" definition of the state was put forward by Hans Kelsen in *Der soziologische und der juristische Staatsbegriff* (Tübingen: Mohr, 1922).
23 Aristotle, *The Athenian Constitution*, translated by P.J. Rhodes (London: Penguin Books, 1984).
24 Carl Schmitt, *Gesetz und Urteil: Eine Untersuchung zum Problem der Rechtspraxis*, 2nd edition (Munich: Beck, 1968), and *Political Theology*, translated by George Schwab (Cambridge, MA: MIT Press, 1988).
25 Carl Schmitt, *Political Theology: Four Chapters on the Concept of Sovereignty*, translated by George Schwab (Cambridge, MA: MIT Press, 1988), p. 33.
26 Winch, *The Idea of a Social Science*.
27 Von Hayek was, incidentally, related to Ludwig Wittgenstein and at some point attempted to write a biography of his philosophical cousin. This raises the question of his familiarity with Wittgenstein's work and whether his libertarianism is to some degree influenced by Wittgenstein's reflections on unsurveyability.
28 Ludwig Wittgenstein, *Remarks on the Foundations of Mathematics*, edited by G.H. von Wright, R. Rhee, and G.E.M. Anscombe, translated by G.E.M. Anscombe, revised edition (Cambridge, MA: MIT Press, 1983), part II, 23.

further reading

Heyes, Cressida, ed. *The Grammar of Politics: Wittgenstein and Political Philosophy*. Ithaca, NY: Cornell University Press, 2003.

Pitkin, Hanna. *Wittgenstein and Justice: On the Significance of Ludwig Wittgenstein for Social and Political Thought*. Berkeley: University of California Press, 1972.

what is the use of studying philosophy?

index

wittgenstein, First Edition. Hans Sluga.
© 2011 Hans Sluga. Published 2011 by Blackwell Publishing Ltd.